HOW MUTUAL FUNDS WORK

Albert J. Fredman
Russ Wiles

NEW YORK INSTITUTE OF FINANCE
New York London Toronto Sydney Tokyo Singapore

Library of Congress Cataloging-in-Publication Data

Fredman, Albert J.
   How mutual funds work / Albert J. Fredman and
   Russ Wiles.
       p. cm.
   Includes index
   ISBN 0-13-012501-6
   1. Mutual funds. 2. Investments.
I. Wiles, Russ. II. Title.
HG4530.F73   1993   93-1259
332.63'27—dc20   CIP

This publication is designed to provide accurate and authorative information in regard to the subject matter covered. It is sold with the understanding that the publisher is not engaged in rendering legal, accounting, or other professional service. If legal advice or other expert assistance is required, the services of a competent professional person should be sought.
From a Declaration of Principles Jointly Adopted by
a Committee of the American Bar Association
and a Committee of Publishers and Associations.

Printed in the United States of America

10 9 8 7 6 5 4 3

ISBN 0-13-012501-6

NEW YORK INSTITUTE OF FINANCE
Englewood Cliffs, NJ 07632

Simon & Schuster, A Paramount Communications Company

To our parents
A.J.F. and R.W.

Foreword

The popularity of mutual fund investing is undeniable. In little more than a decade, the total assets entrusted to the fund industry have exploded from less then $100 billion to more than $1.6 trillion. As America's baby-boom generation reluctantly begins to shift from a prolonged and free-spending youth toward the serious challenges of funding retirement and children's education, the number of investors turning to mutual funds is certain to increase.

Simply deciding to invest, however, doesn't guarantee that one's goals will be met. While the convenience, diversification, and professional management offered by mutual funds make them a logical choice for most investors, only those individuals who take the time to truly understand these investments are likely to attain their financial goals. That's where Albert Fredman and Russ Wiles' *How Mutual Funds Work* can help.

This text tackles the increasingly complex topic of fund investing from two perspectives: Professor Fredman's grounding in the academic community and Wiles' experience as a working journalist in daily contact with fund managers, investment advisers, and individual investors. Together, the authors have produced a book that can explain such esoteric terms as "R-squared" and the "Efficient Market Theory" in a manner that is not only understandable, but useful.

By bridging the theoretical concepts of beta and standard deviation and the practical aspects of developing a mutual fund action plan, *How Mutual Funds Work* both empowers investors and lends credence to the academicians. By bringing the best of academic theory to individuals, Fredman and Wiles allow investors to cut through many misguided assumptions; by testing theory in the real world, they separate what actually works from what doesn't. The result is one of the few texts to successfully integrate the burgeoning field of investment research with the practical interests of investors planning for real-life situations.

Ultimately, there is only one standard by which mutual funds should be judged: Do they help investors meet their goals? If this text were held to that same standard, I think the answer would have to be a resounding yes. *How Mutual Funds Work* offers no shortcuts to instant fortune, no action alerts on which high-risk fund to buy for the coming week. Instead, it lays out a thoughtful and intelligent approach that should greatly reward those investors who take the time to absorb its wisdom.

Don Phillips
Publisher
Morningstar Inc.
Chicago

Preface

The growth and maturation of the mutual fund industry is the greatest investment success story of the twentieth century. The first open-end funds date back to 1924, when Massachusetts Investors Trust and State Street Investment Trust were started. But the industry really didn't develop much until the 1970s, with the introduction of money-market funds and telephone switching.

The escalation in the number of funds, shareholder accounts, and total assets since the early 1980s has been nothing short of phenomenal. Fund families or groups have become more numerous and much larger. Today there are about 370 families.

These companies have brought out a huge assortment of investment products to meet the public's increasingly discriminating tastes. You name it, the industry probably has it—or soon will. Mutual funds invest in ARMs, junk bonds, zero-coupon bonds, convertibles, gold stocks, Japanese stocks, European equities, small companies, market indexes, utilities, Texas munis, and much more. Even portfolios within the same category often take a different orientation to investing.

Along with the proliferation of different portfolio types have come major changes in the way fees are charged. These days, it frequently isn't obvious whether or not a fund carries a "load" or sales charge. With 12b-1 plans, contingent-deferred sales charges, and different classes of shares, the subject of fund fees has grown complex. Although our biases are toward pure no-load funds, commission products have their place and might be best for certain people. But some load funds are much better deals than others.

As you might expect, growth in the mutual fund arena has not come without some resultant confusion and pain. Too many people don't understand what they're buying—or even what they're paying. With so many choices, you risk making the wrong ones. Besides investing in inappropriate and high-cost portfolios, people also buy laggards. There's no shortage of mediocre performers.

Thus, the growth and increased complexity of the mutual fund arena have led us to write *How Mutual Funds Work*. We feel a comprehensive, in-depth treatment of the subject is needed to help clear up the confusion. Considering our backgrounds as an investments professor and financial journalist, we have no axe to grind or products to pitch. We simply want to bring you a well-organized, readable guide that explains the intricacies of these very worthwhile investments.

We feel the book can be of use both to do-it-yourselfers as well as customers of brokers and financial planners. After all, better-informed clients will be able to tell if their investment professionals are doing the best possible job.

To invest profitably in mutual funds, it's crucial to have a firm grasp of how stock and bond markets work. You need to know what causes prices to move and how to tell when markets are cheap. That's why *How Mutual Funds Work* devotes so much attention to the different kinds of securities that funds invest in.

Other topics include: return and risk analysis, mutual fund analysis, the efficient-markets hypothesis, international diversification, currency fluctuations, the yield curve, bond characteristics, market timing, variable annuities, and investor services. The book also compares mutual funds to alternative vehicles, especially closed-end funds, unit investment trusts, and individual stocks and bonds.

We also will draw your attention to common investor pitfalls. An important element of success is knowing what mistakes to avoid. You'll learn about the risks of being in—and out—of the stock market. And we cover eleven different risk factors you should know about before investing in any fixed-income portfolio. Short cases and numerical examples illustrate important points. We conclude with a capstone chapter containing answers to dozens of commonly asked investment questions.

Unlike some other mutual fund books, our objective is not to profile individual funds and tell you what to buy. *No one knows which funds are going to perform best over the next one, five, or ten years.* The financial world is simply too unpredictable. Rather, we provide the background and tools to help you make better choices on an ongoing basis, which should lead to improved results.

Acknowledgments

It took more than a year of research to complete *How Mutual Funds Work*. Sheck Cho and Philip Ruppel, formerly with NYIF and now at John Wiley & Sons and McGraw-Hill, respectively, offered useful comments and encouragement during the project's early stages. Drew Dreeland at NYIF worked closely with us on the final manuscript and did an excellent job with the developmental editing, offering many good suggestions. Production editor Eve Mossman also did an outstanding job.

Much information for the book has been provided by Don Phillips, Amy Arnott, Jennifer Strickland, and others at Morningstar; Michael Lipper, Alling Woodruff, and Steve Schoepke at Lipper Analytical Services; Erick Kanter, Betty Hart, Frances Stadler, and others at the Investment Company Institute; Marc Zutty and Herbert Match at Smith New Court; and Avi Nachmany at Strategic Insight.

We also thank the countless individuals at many fund companies who answered our sometimes difficult questions. In particular, we acknowledge Steven Norwitz, Kenneth Waggoner, and others at T. Rowe Price Associates; Elizabeth Allan, Steven Aronoff, Cuyler Findlay, and Eleanor Mascheroni at Scudder, Stevens & Clark; Robert Rodriguez at First Pacific Advisors; Charles Dobson at Analytic Investment Management; Michael Kassen and Peter Sundman at Neuberger & Berman; Peter Langer at Capital Research and Management; Harold Sharon at Warburg, Pincus Counsellors; Gerald Perritt at Perritt Investments; and Louis Benzak at Spears, Benzak, Salomon & Farrell.

John Emery, chair of finance at California State University, Fullerton, offered support and encouragement. Kay Sullivan, a computer consultant also at CSUF, worked on the graphics.

Last, but not least, we thank our wives for their understanding and support.

Contents

CHAPTER 1

Building Wealth with Stock Funds

Making money is in vogue these days. Just ask the Russians, Hungarians, or Chinese. And investing is a big part of the money-making equation. Cash you don't need now can be put to work—to finance everything from a child's education or a new home purchase to your retirement.

Investors can put their money to work in various ways, but well-managed, diversified common stock portfolios are one of the best means to accumulate wealth over the years. It's a well-documented fact that stocks have far superior *long-run* returns relative to any bond investments, especially short-term debt instruments such as Treasury bills or money market funds.

And because the United States no longer dominates world markets—economically or financially—foreign stocks can help investors realize even better long-run performance. Pension-fund managers know this and, as a group, they are investing larger and larger amounts of money in companies based outside the United States. Mutual funds are an ideal vehicle for individuals wanting to buy into overseas markets.

Mutual funds have become extremely popular over the past decade or so. Today more than $1.6 trillion is invested in the "universe" of around 4,000 stock, bond, and money funds, according to the Investment Company Institute, a national trade group. One of every four households owns at least one fund. There are in excess of 72 million shareholder accounts.

This book aims to provide readers with enough background so they can learn to pick and choose the most appropriate and best funds from the thousands available. That requires an understanding of the securities held by the funds, as well as of the funds themselves. It also demands a knowledge of the many kinds of risks and pitfalls of different investments. With a little effort, anyone can develop the insight needed to build and monitor a portfolio of top-quality funds.

How Mutual Funds Work provides thorough coverage of the most interesting and promising galaxy of the mutual fund universe—the stock portfolios. Just look in Table 1–1 at the investment results for the past 30, 25, and 20 years, as calculated by Lipper Analytical Services Inc., a company that monitors fund performance. The three decades over which stocks returned an average of 11 percent a year contained major bull and bear markets as well as periods of economic and political trauma. It's clear that the average stock fund does better over long periods than do fixed-income portfolios, yet this relationship also holds true for much shorter intervals. Although stock market returns can be highly erratic over periods of a couple years or less, the results tend to smooth out over time.

Table 1–1
Long-Term Performance of Equity Versus Fixed-Income Funds

	30 Years	25 Years	20 Years
Equity Funds	11.0%	10.2%	11.6%
Fixed-Income Funds	7.8	8.1	8.7

Compound average annual total reinvested performance. Periods end 12/31/92.
Source: Adapted from data provided by Lipper Analytical Services Inc. Summit, NJ.

For most people, well-managed stock or "equity" funds offer the best chance for a successful, long-term experience in the stock market. Younger investors have a built-in edge because they have many more years to compound wealth. Unfortunately, some novices often make costly, rash mistakes by being overly aggressive, when all they need to do is take moderate risks and let time work for them.

Equity investing is also important for many older individuals. People today are living longer than ever before, and they need some protection to guard against inflation. A well-managed stock portfolio can provide a dependable long-term inflation hedge. For example, over the 30-year period when stock funds returned a generous 11 percent a year, the consumer price index rose at about a 5 percent annual rate. Less volatile, income-oriented stock funds often work well for retired people, especially when combined with some bond and cash holdings.

Though we're clearly biased in favor of stock funds, we offer complete coverage of bonds and bond funds—including their risks—in Chapters 8, 9, 10, and 11. Fixed-income investments play an essential role in a diversified portfolio. Tax-exempt bond funds are given special emphasis because of their growing popularity.

Market timing is an approach that can be applied to either stock or bond funds. Timers jump from one asset to the next—typically from a risky investment to "cash" and back again—as their outlook changes. Market timing is not as widely accepted as buy-and-hold investing, but proponents embrace it with steadfast loyalty. This controversial topic is covered in Chapters 12 and 13.

Though stock investments offer the best potential of the three main asset classes (stocks, bonds, and money market securities), they also come with many pitfalls, as everyone knows. In fact, people may end up doing far worse with poorly selected and poorly managed equity investments than they would by simply keeping their money under the mattress or in a passbook savings account. Stocks often have a habit of badly misbehaving, and they don't always do what their owners want.

Even stocks or stock funds that merely break even over time are really losers. That's because there is an "opportunity cost" to having an investment rise and fall and wind up, for example, where it started. For example, a $10,000 stake will double to $20,000 in a decade if it is placed in a low-risk vehicle returning just 7.2 percent. You have to move ahead in the investment world just to stay even.

But the first step to winning is simply not losing. Speculating big time on a few individual stocks is an easy way to get wiped out. Large losses can put you in a big hole and significantly cloud your financial future. Building wealth takes understanding, time, and patience. We feel that you should strive to do at least as well as major stock market indexes. Set your sights on some of the broader yardsticks, such as the Standard & Poor's 500, Russell 2000, Wilshire 5000, Value Line Composite, or the Morgan Stanley Europe, Australia, Far East (EAFE) index.

THE POWER OF COMPOUNDING

The key to investment success is earning a good return over a sufficiently long period. The first and most important lesson involves compound interest. *Time is extremely powerful* in the investment world. Wealth builds up steadily, bit by bit. Table 1–2 shows the effect of compounding $1 at various rates of return over differing time horizons. Note that a single dollar invested at 10 percent for 40 years produces $45.26. And remember, 10 percent is roughly what stock funds make over the long haul.

Table 1-2
The Power of Compounding a $1 *Initial* Investment

	Investment Time Horizon (Years)			
Rate of Return	5	10	20	40
4	$1.22	$1.48	$2.19	$4.80
6	1.34	1.79	3.21	10.29
8	1.47	2.16	4.66	21.72
10	1.61	2.59	6.73	45.26
12	1.76	3.11	9.65	93.05

It's fine to invest money in a lump sum, but you can do even better by following a regular savings program. Depositing modest amounts monthly, quarterly, or annually into a mutual fund can work much bigger wonders. Better yet, you won't miss the money as much when it's put away gradually. Table 1–3 shows the impact of investing $1 annually at the same rates and over the same periods as in Table 1–2.

Table 1–3
The Power of Compounding a $1 Annual Investment

Rate of Return	Investment Time Horizon (Years)			
	5	10	20	40
4%	$5.42	$12.01	$29.78	$95.03
6	5.64	13.18	36.79	154.76
8	5.87	14.49	45.76	259.06
10	6.11	15.94	57.27	442.59
12	6.35	17.55	72.05	767.09

Investing $1 a year for 40 years at 10 percent produces $442.59. Socking away $1,000 annually for 40 years at the same rate would produce $442,590.

The power of compound interest shouldn't be taken lightly, especially for people trying to save for retirement. According to several studies, retirement is the top investment goal for many mutual fund investors. By earning higher rates of return—and giving your money more years to work—you will build up larger amounts of cash.

EXAMPLE: Suppose Beth, a 25-year-old secretary, invests $2,000 at the start of each of the next 30 years. Further imagine she puts her money into a stock fund that earns 10 percent annually, the long-term historic average of the Standard & Poor's 500. Also assume that Beth uses a tax-sheltered retirement plan so her savings compound tax-deferred. Using a finance calculator, we find that she would have a $361,887 nest egg at the end of 30 years.

Consider the following facts about compound interest:

- A few extra years can make a huge difference in your final accumulation. Adding just seven extra years to Beth's 30-year investment period *doubles* her nest egg to $726,087.

- A seemingly small increase in yield can also work wonders. Raising Beth's return from 10 percent to 12 percent would boost her account from $361,887 to $540,585, or nearly a 50 percent gain.

- Taken together, the seven extra years and the 2 percentage-point increase in return result in a $1,217,661 nest egg for Beth, more than three times the $361,887 accumulated under our original assumptions.

MUTUAL FUND CHARACTERISTICS

There's no requirement that you must use mutual funds to build up wealth over time, but several unique features make them especially good choices.

A mutual fund is a diversified portfolio of stocks, bonds, or other securities run by a professional money manager or, in some cases, a management team. Funds must register with the Securities and Exchange Commission and must meet specific requirements such as those contained in the Investment Company Act of 1940. These regulations don't guarantee a fund will be profitable, but they do provide certain safeguards.

Mutual funds are also known as open-end funds because they stand ready to issue new shares to incoming investors at the current price or "net asset value" (NAV), plus any front-end "load" or sales charge. They must also stand ready to repurchase or redeem shares from investors exiting the fund at NAV, minus any back-end load or redemption charge. The NAV is calculated once a day based on closing market prices. It fluctuates based on changes in the values of the portfolio holdings. The computation of NAV for a hypothetical fund is illustrated in Figure 1–1. You can look up the prices or NAVs for individual funds by checking the daily mutual-fund table in newspapers. You can also obtain this information by calling the fund companies directly.

By calculating the daily percentage changes in NAV, you can get a good idea about how volatile the particular portfolio is relative to other funds and market indexes like the Standard & Poor's 500. But long-term changes in the NAV do not have the same significance as multiyear changes in a stock's price. In fact, long-term trends in NAV have significance only in a few isolated cases. For this reason, a fund's NAV isn't exactly like a stock's price, though there are similarities.

Think of it this way. If an equity fund never sold any of its stocks, changes in the NAV over the years would closely mirror the performance of the stocks held. However, funds sell stocks and realize gains and losses. Net capital gains must be distributed periodically to shareholders in accordance with IRS guidelines. When capital gains are paid, the NAV falls by the amount of the per-share distribution.

Figure 1.1. Computation of NAV

Cash and equivalent holdings	$200,000
Stocks held and market prices:	
10,000 shs A Co. @ $50 = $500,000	
20,000 shs B Co. @ $30 = $600,000	
50,000 shs C Co. @ $08 = $400,000	
Total market value of stock	1,500,000
Total assets	1,700,000
Less liabilities	100,000
Total net assets	1,600,000
Fund shares outstanding	100,000
Net asset value (NAV) per share	16.00

Explanation:

NAV is generally calculated daily, at the close of trading. First, the total market values of all the stocks held are computed. The total of the market values is added to the fund's cash and equivalent holdings. Liabilities (including accrued expenses) are subtracted. The result is total net assets. Dividing total net assets by the number of fund shares outstanding gives us the NAV per share.

Like total net assets, the number of fund shares outstanding changes daily. For example, if there is a net addition of new investor money, both cash and fund shares would increase. The opposite would be true if there were a net redemption.

Thus, because of the distributions, you can't meaningfully trace the changes of a fund's NAV over a period of years the way you might monitor the movement in a stock's price. To see how the fund did, you have to analyze it in terms of its compound annual total return, which is easy enough to do. We explain this process in Chapter 3.

There are about 370 different fund groups or "families." Most offer at least a few different types of funds, so as to give shareholders investment choices. The money market fund, which was popularized in the mid-1970s, served as the catalyst for the growth of families by providing a safe place for investors to park their cash during rough periods in the stock or bond markets. The smallest groups consist of a money fund and two additional choices—generally a stock along with a bond portfolio. Most families are larger, and some are huge. Families grow as they try to keep up with their rivals, introducing new types of products so as not to be left behind in the competition for more investor dollars.

Large fund complexes you probably have heard of include American Funds, Dreyfus, Fidelity, Franklin, Merrill Lynch, T. Rowe Price, Putnam, and Vanguard. Bigger families often offer a periodic newsletter or other educational material to shareholders. All the funds in some groups adhere to a particular investment philosophy. Examples include Neuberger & Berman, with its contrarian, value-oriented approach and Twentieth Century, with its focus on growth stocks showing earnings momentum.

Mutual Fund Organization

It's important to emphasize that each mutual fund—whether it stands by itself or belongs to a family—is a separate company. The basic mutual fund structure offers several inherent safeguards for investors. These are outlined below.

Shareholder Ownership. A mutual fund is a corporation or trust owned by its hundreds or thousands of individual shareholders. It's the shareholders, not the management company, who bear the fund's investment risk.

Board of Directors. Elected (or reelected) by shareholders, the board members are responsible for overall fund management and must keep a watchful eye on the management company or investment adviser. It's up to the board either to renew or reject the adviser's contract each year. The SEC requires that the board include a minimum number of independent, or outside, members.

Management Company. Daily administration is handled by the management company, which is usually the same firm that organized the fund. The management company also typically serves as the investment adviser, buying and selling stocks for the portfolio.

Adviser. This party runs the fund's portfolio in accordance with the objectives spelled out in the "prospectus" or shareholder contract. The adviser is compensated by a fee that it deducts directly from the portfolio in small amounts over the course of the year. This management fee, not the sales load, is what keeps the fund company in business. It typically runs between 0.5 percent and 1 percent a year. As discussed in Chapter 5, most of the sales load goes to the broker selling the fund and his or her firm.

Independent Custodian.   The fund's assets (stocks, bonds, and cash) are kept by an independent third party, typically a bank or trust company. This protects shareholders against theft by management. The custodian also handles payments and receipts for the fund's security transactions. The adviser merely buys and sells stocks or bonds on the fund's behalf.

Transfer Agent.   The transfer agent handles sales and redemptions of fund shares, maintains shareholder records, computes the NAV daily, and handles dividend and capital gains distributions. The transfer agent is usually a bank or trust company. Some fund families serve as their own transfer agents.

Principal Underwriter (or Fund Distributor).   Usually a management-company affiliate, the underwriter helps to distribute fund shares to the investing public. The underwriter may act as a wholesaler, selling shares to securities dealers, who then sell to investors, or it might deal directly with the public as a retailer.

Open-end funds must be distinguished from publicly traded investment companies, commonly known as closed-end funds. These are diversified, professionally managed portfolios that trade like regular stocks on an exchange or, less commonly, in the over-the-counter market.

The closed-end universe is much smaller than that of open-end funds. Also, in contrast to open-end funds, the closed-end relatives do not stand ready either to issue new shares or redeem shares. For this reason, the assets of a closed-end portfolio generally remain more stable. But they are riskier than open-end funds since their prices can fluctuate widely and don't necessarily correspond to NAV. In certain cases, the price may fall to a deep discount to NAV.

Sophisticated closed-end investors are bargain hunters. They search for portfolios selling at discounts, which they expect to narrow or even turn to premiums.[1]

THE ADVANTAGES OF MUTUAL FUNDS

People with the time and skill to analyze companies can do well by picking individual stocks, but for most investors mutual funds are probably a better way to go. Funds offer several important advantages over direct ownership.

1. *Diversification.* This is the idea of spreading your eggs around more than one basket. A well-diversified portfolio of at least 12 stocks contains very little company-specific, or random, risk. Funds have anywhere from a dozen or so stocks up to several hundred in the larger portfolios. A diversified portfolio generally holds up well even if a few of its stocks get wiped out. Other stocks will do much better than expected, offsetting losses on the dogs.

2. *Continuous Professional Management.* Mutual funds are managed by skilled, experienced professionals who are periodically judged by the total returns they generate. Those who don't produce are replaced. A number of managers, and management teams, have excellent track records. One of the key aspects of selecting good funds is picking the best managements, as discussed in Chapter 3.

3. *Low Operating Costs.* Because they are large professionally managed portfolios, mutual funds incur proportionately lower trading commissions than do individuals, even those who deal with the cheapest discount brokers. A mutual fund might pay only a few cents a share on a very large stock transaction, whereas an individual might pay 50 cents a share or more on that same stock. Lower transaction costs can translate into significantly better investment performance.

4. *Shareholder Services.* Mutual fund families offer many useful shareholder services. One of the most important is the automatic reinvestment of distributions for people who want it. When dividends and capital gains are used to buy additional fund shares, you compound your wealth more quickly. Owners of individual stocks often are more inclined to take their cash dividends and spend them. Many funds have systematic withdrawal plans, which are handy for retired individuals. Other important services include automatic investment plans, retirement plans, record keeping for tax purposes, and the ability to make telephone exchanges or switches between funds.

5. *Liquidity.* This refers partly to the speed and ease with which an asset—such as a stock, bond, mutual fund, or closed-end fund—

may be purchased or sold. A second requirement is that the transaction take place with no significant negative price impact. As an example of illiquidity, if you wanted to sell 5,000 shares in a small, thinly traded stock quickly, you may have to take a big hit on price.

In many cases, mutual funds offer more liquidity than individual stocks or closed-end portfolios do. Large amounts of money can be invested or redeemed at the fund's NAV for the day, plus any load charge or minus any redemption fee. Further, money can be efficiently switched between, say, a stock and a money-market fund at little or no cost.

On the other hand, mutual funds are not always liquid. For example, not all funds offer telephone switching, and not all investors sign up for it. In such cases, redemptions may take time and be somewhat inconvenient and confusing. We'll explain this in more detail in Chapter 16 and show how you can redeem shares efficiently.

6. *Safety from Loss Due to Unethical Practices.* You can certainly lose money if your fund's holdings decline in price. But the probability of loss stemming from fraud, scandal, or bankruptcy involving the fund's management company is very small. By transferring investment risk to shareholders, mutual-fund companies side-step the problems that have been especially painful for people dealing with certain thrifts, banks, and insurance companies, among others.

As noted, the legal structure and the stringent federal and even state regulation of mutual funds offer major safeguards. For example, self-dealing is prohibited. The management company and other affiliated parties can't engage in certain types of transactions, such as selling stock they want to get rid of to the fund. The bottom line is that the risks inherent in mutual funds generally arise from fluctuations in the stock or bond markets, not foul play.

Despite their many advantages, mutual funds aren't for everyone. Critics argue that funds are boring, since shareholders don't have any say as to which stocks are selected. You don't have the same opportunities, as you do with individual stocks, of finding Wall Street's future darlings.

That's a valid argument. Some people have been able to strike it rich with the right stock. But, there's also a danger of getting carried away and ending up with a big stake in a promising company that suddenly runs into deep trouble, plunges in value, and takes your life savings down with it. The chances of that happening with stock funds are much lower since they are diversified and professionally managed.

STOCKS: THE BUILDING BLOCKS OF EQUITY FUNDS

To understand equity funds you have to start at the beginning—with stocks themselves. Over the years, investors have come up with numerous ways to evaluate companies. Three of the most common and widely used yardsticks are the following:

1. *Price-Earnings Ratio.* This measures the stock's price divided by the company's earnings per share (or EPS) over the past 12 months. If a stock is trading at $25 and earned $1.25 a share over the past four quarters, its P/E is 20 ($25/$1.25). This, more precisely, is known as the "trailing" P/E. Stock analysts also use "forward" or expected earnings rather than past results, especially when dealing with growth stocks. (This makes the stock appear less pricey.) A forward P/E is simply the current price divided by the forecasted EPS for the next year.

   Value investors look for stocks trading at low P/Es, while growth investors don't mind paying high P/Es if they think the company's profits will be increasing rapidly.

   Average P/E ratios are also calculated for individual mutual funds. These tell you how the overall portfolio is valued. A growth fund would likely have a higher average P/E than an income-oriented portfolio. More on these numbers in Chapter 4.

2. *Dividend Payout Ratio.* This is the ratio of a company's indicated annual cash dividend per share to its EPS. It can range from zero to 100 percent. A utility that pays out $4 in dividends for each $5 of earnings would have a payout of 80 percent. The payout is above 50 percent for the average large industrial company and even higher for the typical utility. The higher the dividend payout, however, the less room there is for dividend increases, since less profit would be available to reinvest for future growth.

3. *Dividend Yield.* This measures the annual dividend divided by the stock price. For example, if a utility's dividend is $4 and its stock sells for $50 a share, the yield would be 8 percent. Like the P/E, the yield fluctuates with the level of stock prices. When P/Es in general are high, yields will be low.

Kinds of Stocks

Stocks can be lumped into any of several broad categories. These are general classifications, and a stock might simultaneously fit into two or more categories. For example, a "blue chip" may also be classified as "growth and income" and "defensive." And a "growth" company may be categorized as "speculative."

Blue-Chip Stocks. These high-quality companies are typically large, old, and well established, such as those represented in the Dow Jones industrial average. Examples include Coca-Cola, Merck, General Motors, and General Electric. Blue chips are often considered income stocks by virtue of their fairly high dividend payouts. Some, like General Motors, can be quite cyclical. Many of the companies included in the S&P 500 would also qualify as blue chips.

Income Stocks. These large, mature firms pay generous dividend yields. The 30 Dow industrial stocks have historically yielded between 3 percent and 6 percent, depending on the level of the Dow. Many utilities pay dividends nearly as high as some bond yields, although dividends aren't as secure as are bond interest payments. That's why the diversification and professional management of a mutual fund should be important for people interested in an income portfolio.

Growth Stocks. These companies feature above-average increases in assets and earnings. The stocks typically pay out little or no dividends since each company reinvests its earnings for expansion. The category covers firms of many different sizes, ages, and growth rates. Naturally, high expected growth and risk go hand in hand. The higher the expected growth rate, the riskier the company. The most exciting stocks sometimes have a tendency to become grossly overpriced—trading at P/E ratios of 40, 60, 80 or more. Needless to say, this makes them speculative.

Emerging-Growth Stocks. This category includes the stocks of smaller companies with favorable expansion potential. Many are firms with a brief track record, if any. Some have gone public only within the last few years. Emerging-growth stocks may offer the best growth potential of all, but they also typically carry the largest risks. The diversification and professional management available in a mutual fund are very important here.

Growth-and-Income Stocks. As the name implies, companies in this classification offer both dividend and capital-appreciation potential. The growth is typically lower than that of the average growth stock, and the dividend payout pales beside the yield offered by the average income stock.

Cyclical Stocks. The profits of these companies fluctuate in tandem with the business cycle. Examples are automakers, capital-goods manufacturers and home builders.

Defensive Stocks. Companies in defensive industries are more resistant to decline during periods of economic weakness, which makes their shares less volatile than the average stock. Typically, defensive firms provide some product or service that consumers regard as indispensable, such as food, beverages, electricity, telephone service, or medicine.

Speculative Stocks. This description could be associated with any type of company. Even the bluest of blue chips could be speculative if, for example, they were selling at outrageously high P/E ratios, as many did during the early 1970s. But most commonly, the speculative label applies to emerging-growth stocks. Many of these companies are volatile, with unpredictable revenues, earnings, and stock prices. Speculative companies may also be saddled with excessive debt.

COMMON INVESTOR MISTAKES

Even though mutual funds have grown astronomically popular over the past decade, there still are many individuals who prefer to invest directly in stocks. Unless they have been highly successful and gain considerable satisfaction from what they are doing, these people should reconsider mutual funds. After all, there's nothing boring about making money.

The reason most people don't excel at stock picking is that they succumb to certain common errors, many of which can be avoided or minimized with mutual funds.

Mistake 1: Unreasonable expectations of making money.

Overly aggressive investors are really speculating (or just gambling) if they exaggerate the profit potential or underestimate the risks. Many are ill-equipped to withstand the losses dealt them.

Mistake 2: Failing to do the necessary homework.

People who are not willing or able to put sufficient time into analyzing companies, industries, and the overall market risk making costly mistakes. No part-time investors can match the effort of even a mediocre professional money manager.

Mistake 2 would also apply to mutual fund investors who do not understand their fund's objectives, fail to study its track record, or ignore potential pitfalls such as excessive fees. Some mutual funds are lemons, too.

Mistake 3: Failure to diversify.

Many so-called investors put all their eggs in one or a few baskets. They face a serious risk that some if not most of those stocks might fall on hard times. Investors holding funds with several different objectives automatically sidestep Mistake 3.

Mistake 4: Becoming greedy or fearful at the wrong times.

Many investors panic when the market plunges on bad news and sell out at rock-bottom prices. Instead, this may be the time when they should be buying. Investors also tend to get greedy near the peak of a bull market—at the time they should be trimming back their holdings. A good mutual fund will almost always bounce back from a bear market—an important reassurance for skittish investors.

Mistake 5: Acting on the tip of a relative or friend.

Successful investors know how to think for themselves—they don't let well-meaning relatives or friends mislead them. Usually a "hot" stock tip is already old news to at least some of the analysts following a company.

Mistake 6: Failing to cut losses when things start to sour.

It seems easier for many stocks to fall rather than to rise. And in some cases, especially if the stock is a small, obscure one, the descent never seems to end. A stock that plunges 50 percent would have to rise 100 percent just to get back to even. Many people hate to admit they made a mistake and hang on tight, hoping things will improve. Things often get worse. People who average down with a particular stock face even bigger headaches if the company's problems compound.

Mistake 6 can also apply to those who invest in volatile funds, although, as noted, funds are more likely to rebound. More on this later.

Mistake 7: Failing to make a long-range commitment to the stock market.

People who got burned buying individual stocks sometimes resort to an ultra-conservative path. They think they will never lose any money again if they stick with passbook savings accounts, money market funds, Treasury bills, certificates of deposit, and the like. This is faulty logic. Being 100 percent in these "safe and secure" assets can lead to abysmal long-run investment performance, since inflation and taxes eat away at both income and principal. Stock funds, including those that invest in foreign markets, offer much better odds for long-term success.

Mistake 8: Lack of a sound investment plan.

If you sidestep this final mistake, you will be less apt to make any of the previous seven errors. Successful investing is serious business requiring a well-thought-out plan. It should address the following questions and concerns:

- Where are you in the life cycle?
- What are your financial goals?
- What is your risk tolerance?
- How have your investments performed in the past?
- How much can you save each month?
- Are you taking full advantage of tax-advantaged retirement plans?

- How should you allocate your investment portfolio among liquid assets, bonds, equities, real estate, and other categories?

A good financial plan requires you to include the impact of compound interest and to calculate future values under a variety of assumptions.

CONCLUSION

Diversified stock portfolios have offered superior long-term inflation protection. Equities are especially important today with people living longer and retiring earlier. To understand stock funds, you first need to be familiar with the characteristics of the different types of companies they hold.

"Winning" with stocks means performing at least as well as a major market index over the long haul. If you can sidestep the common investor mistakes, you've taken the first and biggest step in the right direction.

Note

1. For a thorough coverage of closed-end funds see Albert J. Fredman and George Cole Scott, *Investing in Closed-End Funds: Finding Value and Building Wealth*. New York: New York Institute of Finance, 1991.

CHAPTER 2

Equity Fund Categories

Mutual funds have become so popular that they now outnumber companies on the New York Stock Exchange. You can find stock portfolios that fit just about every investment style, approach, and focus. So where should you begin? People learn about funds and fund families in many different ways. You might see their ads or articles about them in metropolitan newspapers, national financial papers such as *The Wall Street Journal* or *Investor's Business Daily* or in various other publications such as *Barron's, BusinessWeek, Financial World, Forbes, Money, Smart Money, Worth,* or perhaps the American Association of Individual Investors *AAII Journal.* They could be mentioned, or their managers interviewed, on television programs such as *"Wall Street Week."* Or your friends could be talking about them. But how should you check out a mutual fund? And how can you find the best ones?

The first place to go would be your local library. Look in one or more of the mutual fund guidebooks for an overview. The major guidebooks are identified and briefly described in Appendix 1.

Two definitive sources of information on every mutual fund are the shareholder report and, especially, the prospectus. To get these documents, you'll need the fund's phone number or address. Most have toll-free 800 numbers, which you can obtain by calling 1-800-555-1212. The *Directory of Mutual Funds* published annually by the Investment Company Institute provides phone numbers, addresses, and a few other basic facts about the more than 3,000 funds covered. See Appendix 1 for more details on this low-cost publication.

The Securities and Exchange Commission requires funds to prepare and issue both an annual and a semi-annual shareholder report. The annual provides the most details and must contain a statement by independent auditors. Most funds also issue briefer quarterly reports. Among other things, the various shareholder reports list the fund's investments.

In general, however, it makes little sense for shareholders to spend time analyzing the stocks in a fund's portfolio for their investment potential. In fact, the most current report may already be somewhat out of date, especially if the manager trades a lot. However, by reviewing the major holdings you can at least determine whether management is sticking to its knitting. For example, if ABC Small-Cap Fund holds lots of medium-sized companies as well as some blue chips, it might not have the kind of portfolio it claims. The shareholder reports will also feature a summary of recent results, as well as some comments by management about the future.

THE PROSPECTUS

As a rule, the shareholder reports are more interesting to read than the prospectus, a legal document that discloses certain key information. But if you know what to look for, the prospectus can at least answer most of your questions about a fund. The federal Securities Act of 1933 requires mutual fund distributors and dealers to provide potential investors with a current prospectus. The document must be updated at least annually. The SEC has simplified prospectus requirements in recent years, but in many cases they can still be tedious to wade through. Anyone wanting more details than provided in the prospectus can request the fund's Statement of Additional Information, also known as Part B of the prospectus.

Here's what to look for in a prospectus:

1. A detailed explanation of the fund's investment objectives.

2. A description of the investment policies. Examples include the types of securities that may be purchased, how the fund's asset allocation may be changed, and the degree (if any) to which the manager might use options and futures.

3. Investment restrictions, or what the fund can't do. Included here would be a statement on maintaining portfolio diversification.

4. Shareholder transaction costs and ongoing expenses. The SEC requires these to be detailed in a standard *fee table*.

5. The fund's financial history based on data in the per-share income, capital changes, and ratios table.

6. A detailed discussion of the portfolio's investment risks.

7. An explanation of how to purchase and redeem shares, including initial and subsequent investment minimums.

8. Services offered such as the telephone exchange privilege, automatic share purchase plans, withdrawal plans, and tax-sheltered retirement programs.

9. Information on the fund's adviser and the advisory fees.

10. The names and addresses of the fund's custodian, transfer agent, and dividend-disbursing agent.

11. A list of dividend and capital-gains distributions and a discussion of tax consequences for the investor.

12. Information on the other portfolios available in the fund family.

Before anything else, you should seek out funds with the kinds of objectives you are looking for. The next step is to select the best portfolios within a given category. You will need to consider several criteria, the most important of which are performance and costs.

This chapter concentrates on the fund's objectives. Chapter 3 deals extensively with the per-share table of income and capital changes, fund performance, and management. Chapter 5 focuses on the fee table.

THE FUND'S BROAD OBJECTIVES

The *primary objectives* of any fund would fit into one of three broad categories:

1. *Income.* The emphasis is on producing a steady flow of dividend payments.

2. *Capital Gains.* The manager concentrates on increasing the value of your principal through appreciation of the stocks held.

3. *Income and Capital Gains.* Some combination of the first two approaches.

Many funds will also list *stability* or *capital preservation* as an ancillary goal.

Naturally, each objective has its drawbacks, and investors face certain tradeoffs. It would be virtually impossible to find a stock fund that simultaneously offers both generous income and exceptional capital gains. If you want maximum appreciation potential, you will have to forgo income.

As another example, the most stable portfolio would be one invested exclusively in Treasury bills. But it would offer no growth potential and less in the way of dividends compared to funds that hold riskier income-generating securities such as junk bonds.

There is, however, much more to a fund than merely its objectives. You must also decide how you want the manager to reach these goals. For example, a growth fund could invest in domestic or non-U.S. equities or some combination. It might or might not use options. It could be actively managed or follow a passive "indexing" strategy.

The prospectus describes both the objectives and policies. Many other research sources will also list this information. For example, you might find the following description for a typical aggressive-growth portfolio:

> Seeks capital appreciation through investment in common stocks. The fund is nondiversified. May concentrate investments in 12 issues or 4 industry groups; and may employ leverage and make short sales of securities it holds.

A brief statement of objectives such as this one is all you need to start with. If you become more seriously interested in a fund, you will require the prospectus.

STOCK-FUND CLASSIFICATIONS

The simplest way to categorize funds would be to group them as stock, bond, or money-market portfolios. Then you would want to fit them into the various subclassifications.

Equity funds can easily be divided into more than a dozen categories by objective. The distinction between different categories isn't always clear-cut. Many funds easily fit into two or three. To be really sure about how to classify a fund, you have to examine its underlying portfolio. For our purposes, stock funds are grouped into the categories highlighted in Figure 2–1. This chapter covers the general equity, hybrid, specialized, and sector portfolios. Index funds are discussed in Chapter 6, and international stock funds in Chapter 7.

GENERAL-EQUITY PORTFOLIOS

These funds typically diversify among different industries and mainly hold stocks of U.S. companies. Within this broad banner, the aggressive-growth funds would be the riskiest and the equity-income portfolios the least volatile. Of course, within any category there can be wide differences among funds, depending on the guidelines specified in the prospectus and the approach used by the portfolio manager.

Aggressive-Growth Funds

Aggressive-growth portfolios are also known as maximum capital gains, capital appreciation, performance, or go-go funds. Some are highly volatile and may use a variety of speculative strategies such as leveraging their portfolios or selling short stocks they feel might be due for a plunge. Many concentrate on a fairly narrow list of holdings, including smaller, unfamiliar companies. Aggressive-growth funds themselves tend to be smaller. With fewer assets, the portfolio manager can move around more nimbly.

Figure 2-1
Stock Fund Categories

GENERAL-EQUITY PORTFOLIOS

- *Aggressive-Growth*
Seek maximum capital appreciation. May employ speculative strategies.

- *Small-Company*
Invest in companies with relatively low market "caps."

- *Growth*
Invest in larger, established growth firms. Primary emphasis is on capital appreciation.

- *Growth-and-Income*
Invest in larger, established companies offering the potential for both growth and income.

- *Equity-Income*
Focus is on equities with high dividend yields.

OTHER EQUITY-ORIENTED PORTFOLIOS

- *Hybrid*
These are not pure equity funds. Some have a fairly heavy bond orientation.

- *Specialty*
Have a specific investment focus. For example, holdings might be confined to companies meeting certain ethical criteria or in a particular geographic region or industry.

- *Sector*
A kind of specialty fund focusing on a specific stock group. Typically limited to firms within a single industry like health care.

- *Stock Market Index*
Hold the same or similar stocks as would be found in a particular market index like the Standard & Poor's 500.

- *International*
Invest in foreign stocks, usually from several or more countries.

The more reckless of these portfolios can take shareholders on a roller-coaster ride, plunging far more than the overall market in a major sell-off and then outstripping the averages during rallies. They appeal primarily to risk-tolerant investors. They are not for the faint of heart.

The track record of management is of utmost importance with these funds because of the high-risk strategies they can pursue. A poorly managed aggressive-growth fund can be a long-term disaster. One such portfolio is 44 Wall Street. It was a great success from 1975 through 1980, but performed miserably for much of the 1980s. On the other hand, Twentieth Century Growth, Twentieth Century Ultra, and Twentieth Century Vista are aggressive-growth funds with commendable records.

Small-Company Funds

This is one of our favorite groups, especially for younger investors. They share similarities with the aggressive-growth funds and sometimes get lumped together. Some small-company funds are more conservatively managed, so there is a distinction.

Small companies can grow at a faster rate than large firms do because their expansion takes place on a smaller base of assets and revenues. For example, it's much easier for a firm with revenues of $10 million to double its sales than it is for a firm with $10 billion to do so. Small corporations usually have a much narrower business focus than do the big caps—they typically deal with one or a few closely interrelated products or services.

Most funds in this group have a growth orientation. They seek companies whose earnings are expected to increase at a high rate. These stocks generally have above-average P/E ratios. But some small-company portfolios, such as Pennsylvania Mutual Fund and T. Rowe Price Small-Cap Value, follow a value orientation. They look for stocks that are cheap in terms of their P/E ratios and other valuation yardsticks.

Small-stock funds are generally identified with the NASDAQ over-the-counter market. Many also invest in companies traded on the American Stock Exchange, along with some New York Stock Exchange firms. The increased interest in foreign markets has resulted in global and international funds with a small-cap orientation. There are even some small-stock index portfolios.

How small is "small"? Professor Rolf Banz, a pioneer in this sector, originally defined them as the bottom 20 percent of companies listed on the New York Stock Exchange, when ranked by market capitalization. (You arrive at a capitalization number by multiplying a company's current market price by the number of shares outstanding). The market cap defining the upper boundary of the bottom 20 percent, which was $110 million at this writing, changes as prices rise and fall. Most stocks on the Amex and NASDAQ are also considered small.

The cutoff point for small stocks is really not hard and fast, though. Small companies typically range from $10 million or less for "embryonic" firms (which most portfolio managers won't touch) to around $600 million. Some funds might include a stock with a capitalization as high as $1 billion. Certain managers mix in some medium or big caps as well.

One fund that focuses on smaller companies is Perritt Capital Growth. It targets stocks in the range of $3 million to $200 million. Another player is Babson Shadow Stock, which invests in companies of $20 million to $110 million. Vanguard Explorer emphasizes firms with under $300 million in market cap.

You can get a feel for the range of companies in a small-cap portfolio by examining the prospectus or contacting the fund. An easy way to judge the relative size orientation would simply be to examine the holdings. The fewer names you recognize, the smaller the stocks. In addition, *Morningstar Mutual Funds* (described in Appendix 1) supplies a median market cap for the funds it tracks. This single number tells you a lot about the size of companies held in any stock portfolio.

Funds with assets of about $100 million or less have an easier time investing in truly small stocks. There are two reasons for this. First, small companies tend to be illiquid. That means it's hard for a mutual fund to buy or sell a meaningful amount of shares without bumping up or undercutting the price in the process.

Second, "diversified" funds are essentially limited by SEC regulations to owning no more than 10 percent of the outstanding shares of a given company. This restriction applies to stocks making up 75 percent of the portfolio's assets. (Nondiversified funds generally must invest up to half their portfolios following the 10 percent ownership guideline, as explained later in this chapter.) The 10 percent limitation is designed to protect fund investors by minimizing the risks associated with holding a big chunk of a company's shares. Thus, a larger small-cap fund may end up owning several hundred stocks. Too much diversification can be unfavorable in the small-company arena, however, by diluting the impact of the most promising choices. It is best if the manager can focus on a shorter list of issues that appear most attractive.

Growth Funds

Funds in this category are generally less volatile than those in the previous two groups. As the name implies, growth portfolios hold stocks of firms whose earnings are expected to rise at an above-average rate. The companies tend to be larger, well-established firms such as Abbott Labs, Freddie Mac, General Electric, International Flavors and Fragrances, Merck, and Pfizer. The portfolio managers emphasize capital appreciation rather than dividend income.

Growth-and-Income Funds

Capital appreciation, dividend income, and even growth in future dividends are the features that appeal to growth-and-income managers. Typically, however, they concentrate most on the appreciation potential. These investments make sense for people who want somewhat more income and perhaps less volatility than provided by a growth fund. The portfolios consist of both growth companies and income stocks with good dividend-paying records.

Equity-Income Funds

The equity-income strategy is a special kind of value investing. These managers focus primarily on dividend yields. They seek yields *significantly higher* than that of an overall market yardstick such as the S&P 500. When a stock's price falls, its yield increases—assuming the company pays a dividend.

Equity-income holdings include high-grade industrial, utility, financial, and natural-resource companies. Some funds hold modest amounts of convertible securities, bonds, and preferred stock. Some of these companies may be temporarily out of favor. Whole industries can be depressed at times, offering higher than normal yields.

Equity-income funds should be less volatile than the overall market. They represent one of the lowest-risk approaches to investing in stocks. But by no means are they risk-free. High-yielding stocks tend to be especially sensitive to interest rates, as long-term bonds are. When rates rise, the prices of dividend stocks fall so that their yields can remain competitive with fixed-income securities.

Funds in the equity-income category tend to look more for dividends and less for appreciation. However, the distinction between these funds and growth-and-income portfolios is not that clear cut. Prospective investors should study the prospectuses and portfolios of funds in both groups to find the ones that emphasize what they are seeking.

Though equity-income portfolios are the least risky of the general stock funds, some have delivered outstanding performances over long stretches. This underscores the argument for investing in stock funds because it shows you can get good results and still sleep well.

HYBRID FUNDS

Funds in this group are simply those with a dual stock/bond focus. Three categories fall under the hybrid definition: balanced, convertible and asset-allocation.

Balanced Funds

Of the three, balanced funds have the longest history. Their conservative orientations appealed to the cautious, less-affluent investors of the 1930s, who sought preservation of capital. Industrial and Power Securities, started by Walter L. Morgan in 1929 and renamed the Wellington Fund in 1935, was one of the first. At last count, this popular Vanguard family member had over $6 billion in assets.

Balanced portfolios strive to achieve three goals: income, moderate capital appreciation, and preservation of capital. They do this by holding bonds, convertible securities, and perhaps some preferred stock, as well as common stock. The portfolios generally would range from 40 percent to 60 percent in bonds. They typically emphasize securities issued by high-quality companies. Balanced funds are especially appropriate for individuals who can afford only one fund, since they are diversified into both the bond and stock markets. They also make sense for investors who are just starting out and want something with a reasonably conservative orientation.

Convertible Funds

A convertible security is a bond or preferred stock that can be exchanged for a predetermined number of the company's common shares, at the holder's option. Convertibles have a split personality. At times they act like stocks and at other times, like bonds. They offer the downside protection of a fixed-income security and the upside potential of equity. Because of the hybrid nature of a convertible bond, a convertible fund would be somewhat similar to a balanced portfolio. It would have a greater emphasis on income and preservation of capital than the typical stock investment.

Asset-Allocation Funds

These funds diversify beyond equities into other asset categories, typically cash equivalents and bonds. Some, with a broader orientation, include foreign equities, gold stocks, real estate shares, and natural-resource companies. There are two types of funds in this category:

1. Stable-allocation portfolios, which hold relatively fixed proportions of the specific categories, and

2. Flexible-allocation portfolios, which vary their weightings depending on the manager's outlook.

The conservative Permanent Portfolio Fund, an example of the first type, holds fixed percentages in six categories: gold, silver bullion, Swiss francs, specific stock groups, long-term U.S. Treasuries, and short-term Treasuries. Some balanced funds might also fall into the first group. Most of the funds that investors think of as "asset-allocation" portfolios fit into the second group.

Like a balanced fund, an asset-allocation product could serve as a complete investment program for people who can afford to own only one fund. They provide diversification into stocks, bonds, and often other areas. There's not necessarily much of a difference between asset-allocation and "flexible" funds, except that managers of the latter group could make heavy bets on one asset class or another. Taken to the extreme, a three-asset flexible fund might move its holdings from 100 percent in bonds to 100 percent in stocks or 100 percent in money-market instruments.

There can be a couple of key problems with the most flexible funds. First, it is obviously easy for a manager who enjoys too much leeway to mess up. Second, these portfolios can have very high turnover, which leads to high transaction costs, adversely impacting performance. Restrict your flexible-fund investing to one run by a manager who enjoys an excellent reputation and track record.

SPECIALTY FUNDS

These funds have a specific narrow portfolio orientation. That focus may be on a certain industry (as in the case of a sector fund), on one geographic region of the United States, or on a special type of investment. Some follow well-defined social objectives and invest only in companies that satisfy their ethical criteria. For example, they may shun firms in the liquor, gambling, and tobacco industries. A few write covered calls on a portfolio of dividend-paying stocks. This strategy is described in the following section.

Option-Income Funds

While many funds use options in specific instances, the option-income products do so regularly. Lipper Analytical reserves this classification to those funds that write options on at least half their portfolio. For example, the list includes the Analytic Optioned Equity Fund, which considers itself a growth-and-income portfolio that specializes in option writing.

Many people equate options with high risk. But it really depends on how they're used, because options can help moderate volatility. The relatively conservative option-income funds invest in large, dividend-paying companies on which listed options are available. They then sell (or "write") options against their stock positions, collecting premium income in the process. These premiums, coupled with the stock dividends, result in a good income stream.

Option writing tends to cushion against losses in a moderately declining market, but it limits appreciation in a bull market. During sharp rallies, stocks could get called away from the fund at prices far below their current values. While some of these funds have been around since the 1970s, the group generally has not been successful, for various reasons.

SECTOR FUNDS

Certain portfolios target specific industries or stock market sectors. They're so focused that they give up broad diversification. Some can be nearly as volatile as individual companies.

The following are examples of sector-fund categories:

- Financial services
- Health care
- Housing
- Restaurants
- Telecommunications
- Environmental

Fidelity Investments, a pioneer in the sector-fund area, introduced its Select Portfolio family in 1981, with specialized portfolios in six areas. Today, Fidelity counts 36 sector funds, ranging from air transportation to utilities. The Select products are unique in that they are priced hourly so that people can move in and out of them quickly, getting trades executed at any of several possible prices during the day. The INVESCO Financial Funds and the Vanguard Group are among the other families that offer several specialized portfolios.

Narrowly focused sector funds—especially those investing in a single industry or in precious-metals stocks—have a tendency to be more volatile than broadly diversified portfolios. Their names often appear on lists of the quarter's best and worst performers. Also, their returns frequently do not move in sync with the market averages. However, sector portfolios make a lot more sense than investing in just one stock in an industry that you want to gain exposure to. The funds diversify within their chosen groups and thus carry no company-specific risk. But sector funds do not constitute a complete investment program and should be held along with other, more broadly diversified portfolios.

Timing purchases and sales is important with these funds. Value investors typically buy when a sector is depressed, while some growth players search for the hot industries. Making gradual purchases or "dollar-cost averaging" can work well with these volatile funds if you want to accumulate a position over time.

Utility Funds

Utility funds are generally far more stable than the typical sector product. In fact, they make a relatively low-risk play for people venturing into the stock market for the first time. They can offer higher income and greater safety than the more broadly diversified equity-income funds.

Like bonds, utility stocks typically generate high income. But unlike bond interest payments that remain fixed, utility dividends grow over the years—they compounded at about 5 percent a year over the past three decades. Utilities are defensive investments since their services are always needed, regardless of how the economy is doing. Many stocks in this industry fluctuate only about half as much as the market does.

Utilities have changed in character over the past several decades, however. Individual companies as well as the whole industry have confronted new difficulties and challenges. Nuclear power, acid rain, non-utility diversification, and other issues have made utilities more complex and riskier. A number of these stocks are definitely not for "widows and orphans." You can't just buy them, put them away, and plan on collecting a growing dividend stream for the next 30 years. Some run into severe difficulties and may be forced to cut dividends and see their shares plunge. Consolidated Edison, a big New York utility, had paid dividends every year since 1885. However, severe financial problems forced it to omit a dividend in 1974. Its stock, which descended to a low of $6 that year, had traded as high as $26 in 1973. There is a good case for using mutual funds to minimize the company risk associated with utility investing.

Utility portfolios differ from one another in composition and aggressiveness, although most emphasize income to varying degrees. Some make bets on the recovery of turnaround candidates, thus placing more emphasis on capital appreciation. The utility industry consists mainly of electric, natural gas, and telephone companies. The funds mix the groups in various ways. Some that are more specialized go with electrics, whereas others focus on the telephones. A couple even have a global orientation, investing in utilities domiciled in other countries.

Even though utility funds are ordinarily stable, they can be volatile at times. Like bonds they are interest-rate sensitive. As you'll see in Chapter 8, increasing rates depress high-yielding stocks as well as long-term bonds. The flip side is that utility funds can produce robust total returns during years when interest rates decline.

Utility funds, by definition, must invest at least 65 percent of their assets in the industry. That leaves up to 35 percent available for other areas. Be sure to check the portfolios of funds you're interested in to see where the money is invested.

Precious-Metals Funds

Gold has a rich history and a special allure. But owning the metal as an investment has its drawbacks. You must contend with broker fees, dealer markups, and storage and insurance costs. Besides, gold bullion or coins produce no income as you would get from a stock or a bond.

Gold funds offer a cost-effective way to participate in possible increases in the price of the metal. They focus primarily on the stocks of gold-mining companies. Some funds invest only in South African stocks, while others totally avoid these companies for political reasons. Still others own shares of mining firms based in all major gold-producing countries. Certain portfolios hold bullion as well as stocks, as the stocks tend to exhibit more price volatility than does the metal itself. Funds in this category may also buy shares in companies that mine other precious metals, especially silver and platinum.

Needless to say, gold funds by themselves do not offer a complete investment program. But you might want to allocate a small proportion of your assets, perhaps 5 percent, to a gold fund for diversification purposes. Gold sometimes moves inversely to the prices of stocks and bonds and occasionally performs very well during times of political turmoil or runaway inflation. Think of it as a kind of insurance policy.

The downside is that, like the metal, gold funds can be highly volatile. In addition, gold often does poorly relative to stock market investments. A group of industrials will likely fare better over the long run than will a group of gold-mining companies.

DIVERSIFIED OR NONDIVERSIFIED?

One additional classification reflects the degree to which a portfolio spreads its investments around. Most funds are categorized as "diversified," which means they adhere to the following guidelines:

1. They invest no more than 5 percent of their assets in any single company. If a stock position should appreciate to more than 5 percent of assets, however, the excess need not be sold.

2. They own no more than 10 percent of the voting stock of any company.

Funds that don't follow these two guidelines for 75 percent of their assets are "nondiversified" and tend to be more volatile. The statement of objectives in the prospectus will reveal this information.

Why would a fund not want to be diversified?

Some aggressive-growth portfolios find it easier to achieve their objectives by holding a smaller number of stocks, which lets them take bigger positions in a handful of companies. However, to qualify for the special tax treatment available to investment companies, all funds—nondiversified as well as diversified—must follow these two guidelines for at least 50 percent of their assets. This means that at the extreme, a nondiversified fund could concentrate the other 50 percent of its portfolio in just two issues. Only a small number of portfolios have chosen not to be diversified.

CHAPTER 3

Analyzing a Fund and Its Management

Much of the information you will need to analyze a fund can be found in its per-share table, one of the most useful parts of the prospectus. The per-share table contains data over the past 10 years or the fund's life, whichever is shorter. It is also included in the annual and semiannual shareholder reports. Three years of information for a hypothetical fund appear in Table 3–1. Mutual fund performance should be analyzed in two dimensions: total return and volatility. The former is discussed here, the latter in Chapter 4.

TOTAL RETURN

There are three components of total return on a stock fund:

Table 3–1
XYZ FUND
Per-Share Table (for a share outstanding throughout the year)

	Year ended December 31		
	1992	1991	1990
PER-SHARE INCOME AND EXPENSES:			
1. Investment income	$.20	$.18	$.14
2. Less expenses	.10	.10	.09
3. Net investment income	.10	.08	.05
4. Dividends from net investment income	(.10)	(.08)	(.05)
PER-SHARE CAPITAL CHANGES:			
5. Net realized and unrealized gain (loss) on investments	1.00	.10	1.50
6. Distributions from net realized gain	(.70)	(.40)	(1.00)
7. Net increase (decrease) in NAV	.30	(.30)	.50
8. NAV beginning of year	8.20	8.50	8.00
9. NAV end of year	$8.50	8.20	8.50
RATIOS AND SHARES OUTSTANDING:			
10. Ratio of expenses to average net assets	1.20%	1.20%	1.09%
11. Ratio of net investment income to average net assets	1.20%	0.96%	0.61%
12. Portfolio turnover rate	61%	70%	55%
13. Shares outstanding (in 000s) at end of year	39,500	34,000	32,000

1. *Dividends from Net Investment Income.* Investment income (line 1, Table 3–1) consists of dividends and interest earned on the fund's portfolio, less expenses (line 2). Mutual fund dividends are then declared (line 4). Tax law requires funds to distribute or pay out at least 98 percent of net-investment income. Because the amounts in line 4 are paid to shareholders they appear in parentheses.

2. *Distributions from Net Realized Gain.* Line 5 of the per-share table reports net realized and unrealized gain (loss) on investments. "Realized" refers to stock or bond positions that have been closed out at a profit or loss, whereas "unrealized" relates to positions still held. At least 98 percent of any net realized gain must be distributed to shareholders (line 6). Like the dividends in line 4, these amounts are in parentheses. As is evident in this illustration, there is no set percentage relationship between the numbers in lines 5 and 6.

3. *Net Increase (Decrease) in Net Asset Value.* The change in NAV (line 7) reflects appreciation or depreciation in fund holdings that are still "open" positions. In addition, it includes any undistributed net realized gains and/or net investment income.

Stock funds distribute income at least once a year, and many do so quarterly. The frequency depends in part on the extent to which the portfolio focuses on income or on growth. Current tax law requires capital gains dividends to be declared prior to December 31 and distributed by January 31 of the following year. Capital gains dividends are taxable to shareholders in the year declared. Either form of distribution can be taken in cash or in additional shares.

Computing Total Return

The most important way to tell how well a fund performed is to check its total-return, which includes the impact of appreciation and of dividends, if any. It's becoming increasingly common to find total-return numbers published in newspapers, magazines, or other sources. In addition, you can calculate them yourself, using the following formula:

$$TR = \frac{\text{Distributions} + \text{Change in NAV}}{\text{NAV at beginning of period}}$$

EXAMPLE: Each share of no-load XYZ Fund (Table 3–1), purchased on January 1, 1992, at an NAV of $8.20, had a capital gains distribution of $0.70 and an income distribution totaling $0.10. The NAV at year end was $8.50. The 1992 total return of 13.41 percent is calculated as follows:

$$\text{TR} = \frac{0.70 + 0.10 + 8.50 - 8.20}{8.20} = 13.41 \text{ percent}$$

By itself, the 13.41 percent says little. Total-return numbers need to be analyzed on a comparative basis, as explained later in this chapter.

The per-share table contains enough information to let you calculate the total return for a number of prior years. Note that this approach allows you to figure returns *without including the impact of reinvestment.* That is, it assumes all distributions are received at the end of the year in cash and not used to purchase more shares. But published total return numbers are customarily calculated *with reinvestment* by the organizations tracking them. Thus, the results will differ somewhat from those compiled using the preceding formula, as explained in Appendix 2. It's worth noting that reinvesting your dividends will help you to build up wealth faster. However, calculating total return without reinvestment is sufficiently accurate when you are doing it yourself using data from the prospectus.

The total return computations illustrated in this section track periods of one year or less. For longer time frames, you should use a geometric (or compound) average annual return based on results in the individual years. This procedure, which is a bit more complicated, is explained and illustrated in Appendix 3.

THE EXPENSE RATIO

This important statistic helps to shed light on a fund's efficiency and cost effectiveness. By definition, it is the ratio of total expenses to average net assets. Lower numbers are desirable. Past expense ratios can be found in the per-share table (line 10, Table 3–1).

Some investors erroneously believe that brokerage commissions on the fund's transactions are included in the expense ratio. Not so. But just about all other outlays are, as you'll see in Chapter 5, which focuses on costs.

We address the brokerage commission issue in the section on portfolio turnover later in this chapter.

Since the expense ratio can fluctuate, it's best to compute an average over the last three or five years. For XYZ Fund, the average expense ratio over the past three years is 1.16 percent (Table 3–1, the average of the three entries on line 10).

Depending on the portfolio, expense ratios vary from well under 0.5 percent to over 5 percent. The lowest ratios are found among the plain-vanilla stock market index funds, which follow a passive strategy of buying and holding the same stocks as in popular averages such as the S&P 500. Small, aggressive-growth funds that use leverage and incur high interest costs run up some of the highest expense numbers.

In general, any expense ratio below 1 percent is considered low. Sometimes you might have to accept a higher number if you want a particular type of portfolio. Here are four points to keep in mind:

1. Small funds tend to have higher expense ratios than do large ones, which benefit from economies of scale since their management fees and other costs are being spread over a bigger asset base.

2. The expense ratio tends to be higher for funds that have smaller average account sizes, other things being equal. These are often funds with lower minimum-investment thresholds. Smaller accounts lead to proportionately higher shareholder-servicing costs.

3. Funds that invest internationally tend to have significantly higher expense ratios than do domestic portfolios, due to the greater research and other costs associated with foreign investing.

4. Stock funds have higher expense ratios than do fixed-income portfolios.

When evaluating expense ratios, compare a given fund's current number with an average of its past values to spot the trend. You also want to compare the expense ratio with figures for other portfolios of about the same size. There is one thing to avoid for sure: a high 12b–1 fee, which can be a huge drag on results if the fund is held for a long period. The expense ratio includes the impact of 12b–1 fees, if any. The 12b–1 charge is used to pay a portion or all of the costs of distributing shares to investors. More on this in Chapter 5.

THE INCOME RATIO

Mutual funds also have an income ratio—technically, net investment income divided by average net assets. This statistic is akin to a dividend yield on a stock. It's not as significant as total return since total return is a complete measure of performance while this ratio focuses just on income. Using the data on our hypothetical fund (Table 3–1, line 11), the average ratio over the three years was 0.92 percent. For portfolios that concentrate solely on capital appreciation, this number would be very low—perhaps near zero. Conversely, for income-oriented equity funds and balanced portfolios, the ratio could be 4 percent or 5 percent or more.

PORTFOLIO TURNOVER RATE

This gauge measures the amount of buying and selling done by management. It is defined as the lesser of assets purchased or sold divided by the fund's net assets.

How do you interpret the numbers? A 100 percent turnover implies that management holds each stock or bond, on average, for one year. A 50 percent turnover says positions are held for about two years, 200 percent for six months, and so on. The turnover for the average equity fund ranges from 75 percent to 85 percent, but you might see portfolios with ratios above 500 percent or even as high as 1,000 percent. Others have low turnover, such as 10 percent for the Dodge & Cox Stock Fund over a recent five-year stretch.

The portfolio turnover for past years is found in the fund's per-share table. As with performance and expense numbers, you should compare turnover for similar types of funds and look at an average over several years. For example, XYZ Fund's average for the three years shown was 62 percent (line 12, Table 3–1).

Turnover varies by type of fund and the investment philosophy of the manager. Some managers seek quick profits and will tend to buy and sell aggressively. Others follow a long-term buy-and-hold strategy. Funds that rely on options, futures, and short-selling strategies could be expected to have higher turnovers and transaction costs. But unless this activity is accompanied by consistently good performance, look elsewhere. Other things being equal, you should lean to stock portfolios with turnover ratios below 60 percent. A high number can mean excessive transactioncosts.

Transaction Costs

You can locate the brokerage commissions paid by a fund in its prospectus. But there are other, more important cost components that are virtually impossible to document. They include dealer spreads and size effects, both of which can act to lower your return.

Dealer spreads. Every stock has both a bid and an asked (or offered) price. For example, ABC Corp. might be quoted at 20 bid, 20¼ asked. The fund manager would typically buy at the asked and sell at the bid. The ¼-point dealer's spread is a transaction cost component in addition to the commissions paid. Funds typically pay only 4 to 10 cents a share in brokerage commissions, but they can't so easily minimize the spread. Thus, the spread is generally a bigger cost component than are brokerage fees, especially if the manager deals in smaller, less liquid stocks.

Transaction size effects. If a stock is thinly traded and the manager wants to buy or sell a lot of it in a hurry, he or she will face adverse price impacts beyond the customary spread. Big orders send a signal that something unusual might be happening with the stock, and the puzzled dealer will quickly respond by adjusting the quote.

On a large purchase order, the original asked price of 20¼ could move up to 20⅜, 20½, or more. A large sell order could push down the 20 bid to 19⅞, 19¾, or lower. The degree to which the quote changes would depend on three factors: the liquidity of the stock, the quantity of shares the manager wants to buy or sell, and how quickly he or she wants to make the trade.

As noted, these factors do not show up in the prospectus but they can impair performance nevertheless. This is why investors are often better off with funds that do little trading. It's very costly.

SOURCES OF PUBLISHED PERFORMANCE NUMBERS

The most practical way to compare the performances of different funds is not to compute total returns from data in each one's per-share table.

Rather, it's most efficient to consult publications that regularly supply performance numbers. For example, *Barron's* quarterly report on mutual funds provides a comprehensive evaluation done by Lipper Analytical Services Inc. for the most recent quarter, year, and five-year period. The report includes tables listing the biggest winners and losers.

The Wall Street Journal greatly expanded its mutual fund table in 1993. Performance numbers and rankings for various periods are now available, based on Lipper Analytical data. Specifically, total returns (with reinvestment of distributions) for periods ranging from 4 weeks to 5 years appear on specified days; year to date returns appear daily. Fund performance is ranked each day based on the longest period listed. The details of the presentation are provided in the "explanatory notes" box in the fund table. Incidentally, other items of interest including fund objectives and expense ratios also appear in this comprehensive table.

Investor's Business Daily gives a letter grade reflecting three-year performance for more than 2,000 funds. The paper supplies the most recent four-week results for each fund in issues running Monday through Thursday. Also included are phone numbers and the total assets managed by the larger fund companies.

Comprehensive mutual fund performance analyses are also published annually or more frequently in *BusinessWeek, Forbes, Kiplinger's Personal Finance Magazine*, and *Money*. Several newspapers around the country, such as *The Arizona Republic*, also provide periodic performance listings, often on a more timely basis than the magazines.

Many investors are already familiar with Standard & Poor's monthly *Security Owner's Stock Guide*, available at brokerage offices and some libraries. Near the back of the guide, you'll find a wealth of information on many funds, including performance data.

For longer periods of 5, 10, or 15 years, you may see fund performance listed as "cumulative" total returns. Or you may see how $10,000 would have grown if it had been invested in the fund over various periods. For the sake of both consistency and clarity, you may wish to convert these bigger numbers to compound annual returns, if they aren't also reported. For example, a 1,000 percent cumulative return over 25 years converts into a 10 percent compound average annual return. A $10,000 initial investment in this portfolio would have grown to $110,000 over 25 years at the same rate. Appendix 4 explains how to make these conversions.

LOOK CLOSELY AT ESTABLISHED GOOD PERFORMERS

It is important to know how to study performance numbers once you've got them. Focus on results for the past 1, 3, 5, and 10 years. Longer-term periods might be misleading if there have been major changes in the fund or its management. But it doesn't hurt to look at the numbers anyway.

You always want to compare a particular fund's results with that of other portfolios having the same or similar objectives. For instance, small stocks greatly underperformed big-capitalization companies from the end of 1983 to the end of 1990. So it would be inaccurate to conclude that a small-cap fund has inferior management simply because it trailed some large-stock portfolios over that seven-year period.

What about funds with poor past performance? Generally, you should avoid those that have logged consistently subpar results over several years. Certainly, three or more years of inferior performance would be a red flag. Studies have shown a tendency for the long-term losers to continue doing poorly relative to others with the same objectives.

Also be skeptical of funds that have erratic records. Pay close attention to how a portfolio did in down years. Those that fare very badly in down markets should be avoided even by the most aggressive investors. *Morningstar Mutual Funds* reports quarterly as well as annual returns. It helps to study the quarterly numbers too, as yearly results can mask volatility. This will be illustrated in Chapter 4.

FUND SIZE CAN BE IMPORTANT

A fund's size or total assets is another factor to consider. Mutual funds range in size from under $1 million to more than $10 billion. The largest equity product, Fidelity Magellan, recently had assets in excess of $20 billion. Most of the largest funds are bond portfolios.

In general, you can classify stock funds into the following categories:

- *Tiny*: Under $10 million
- *Small*: $10 million to $100 million
- *Medium*: $100 million to $500 million
- *Large*: $500 million to $1 billion
- *Giant*: Over $1 billion

The main point to keep in mind is that size may affect performance for certain types of funds.

Advantages of Small Portfolios

Easier to maneuver. Small funds are more nimble than large ones, in that it's simpler for their managements to reshuffle holdings. A $5 billion fund will likely have some individual positions valued at $75 million or $80 million or more. It would be difficult and time-consuming for such a large fund to turn on a dime if it needed to eliminate certain big positions. To minimize the adverse price impacts of selling large holdings, the stock might have to be fed into the market gradually over a period of weeks or months.

Holdings can be limited. In addition to having smaller positions, small funds can also hold fewer stocks. Small-company and aggressive-growth funds can often accomplish their objectives more easily with less diverse portfolios. That's why the managers may close their doors to new investors and even limit additional purchases by existing shareholders if they feel the fund has gotten too large to reach its goals.

Superfluous diversification is avoided. This relates to the previous point. If a portfolio grows too large, it may wind up owning 200 or more securities. This is far more than necessary to achieve adequate diversification. Even if a dozen or more of the stocks turn out to be super performers, their gains will be diluted by the many others that post average results. Big funds simply cannot take meaningful positions in small companies. But if a small fund takes sizable stakes in several dozen stocks and a few do very well, it will have a measurable impact on performance. This is why it's much more common to see small funds recording abnormally big gains. Some families, including Janus, Twentieth Century, and Nicholas, have started clone funds when existing portfolios got too big.

It's hard for a large fund to beat the market. A giant portfolio will tend to perform like the market averages or an index fund, except that it has management and transaction costs. This cost disadvantage explains why managed funds often trail the popular market averages as well as index portfolios.

Advantages of Large Portfolios

Despite the many factors favoring small funds, large funds often post better performance. They benefit from the following characteristics:

Lower expense ratios. With more assets under management, large funds enjoy economies of scale. Other things being equal, lower expense ratios lead to improved results.

Large funds attract and retain better talent. The organizations that run large funds are generally prestigious and have the money to compensate the best portfolio managers and analysts. They also have more people watching different areas of the market and therefore get broader coverage.

Certain funds do best with large portfolios. Money-market and bond portfolios can fare better with more assets due to the nature of the fixed-income markets. Transaction sizes tend to be very large, and better deals can be had by those trading bigger blocks. Even funds investing in big blue-chip stocks often function well with a large portfolio.

CASH FLOW MAY AFFECT PERFORMANCE

Cash flow refers to *net new money invested* in a mutual fund—the excess of new purchases over redemptions. It should be expressed as a percentage of the portfolio's total assets to be meaningful.

EXAMPLE: Suppose an aggressive-growth fund's assets increased from $20 million to $40 million in a year. Assume further that $5 million of the advance was due to appreciation, and the other $15 million represented new shareholder money. The cash flow would therefore amount to 75 percent of the original $20 million.

During the late 1960s, mutual fund analyst Alan Pope popularized the link between cash flow and performance. Pope observed that certain funds delivered stellar results for a few years and then faded noticeably. Did these managers suddenly lose their Midas touch? Pope concluded that the funds did so well when substantial sums of new money were pouring in, then cooled off when the flow stopped.[1]

Why might a large net cash inflow favorably affect performance? Consider the following three reasons:

1. The fund manager can use the new money to add to positions in stocks he or she already holds. This additional demand will normally raise the price of the stock, more so if the fund invests in smaller firms with fewer shares outstanding.

2. The manager would not have to sell Stock A to buy Stock B. The new money would be invested in B, allowing A to remain in the portfolio with an additional chance to blossom.

3. A large cash flow occurring as the market peaks could be retained as a cushion against an ensuing decline. Thus, the manager would not be forced to sell existing holdings to build up cash and could use the money later to pick up some bargains. This assumes the manager does not adhere to a policy of staying fully invested in stocks.

Experts disagree as to how important cash flow really is. Despite the intuitive appeal of a large, steady inflow, it is probably only a minor factor in fund selection. Future cash flows are what is important, but they are hard to predict. Besides, a huge increase near a market peak could be a headache for a manager who tries to stay fully invested. The extra cash could force him or her on a shopping spree at a time of high prices.

Watch Out for Cash Flow in Reverse

Large, consistent net redemptions are a definite red flag. It means investors are bailing out because they are unhappy with the performance, the imposition of new fees, or some other negative development. This can force management to hold larger cash balances than it otherwise would and to liquidate positions—even promising ones—to be able to meet redemptions. The portfolio shrinks, management loses enthusiasm and self-confidence, and the expense ratio rises. Look at the per-share statement. A declining trend of shares outstanding at year end signals a pattern of net redemptions.

HOW LEVERAGE WORKS

Although relatively few open-end funds employ extensive borrowing or leverage, you may see some among the list of top performers in bull markets. This can entice unwary investors. Aggressive-growth stock funds sometimes use borrowed money to try to magnify gains when the outlook is bullish. So long as borrowing costs—as reflected by short-term interest rates—remain reasonable and portfolio performance stays good, leverage is favorable.

This, however, is a double-edged sword that can greatly magnify losses. Leveraged funds frequently rank among the worst performers in down markets. Shareholder redemptions exacerbate the usual problems as prices plummet. A fund using leverage extensively obviously carries greater risks. To the extent leverage is used, the NAV tends to rise and fall more rapidly.

The Investment Company Act of 1940 stipulates that open-end funds may borrow only from banks. Thus, leveraged portfolios draw on bank credit lines to meet short-term needs. Funds are also limited as to the amount they can borrow. Simply stated, a fund may borrow up to $1 for each $2 of net assets, or $5 million for a portfolio with assets of $10 million.

If the value of the portfolio grows, everything is fine and the ratio of assets to borrowings increases. But if the assets decline, the fund must also promptly reduce its bank debt. This could force management to sell stocks at depressed prices.

And, of course, the fund has to pay interest on its borrowings, which eats into returns. Interest costs are shown separately from operating expenses on an additional line in the per-share table. Leverage is especially painful with increasing interest rates and sideways or falling security prices, which often go together. Of course, it's unusual for any fund to borrow up to the limit. Many take out small loans to help management handle redemptions without liquidating stock holdings. If a fund you are considering does much borrowing, see its prospectus for details.

ANALYZING FUND MANAGEMENT

A portfolio is only as good as the people who run it. But how do you evaluate the managers? It's easy. Most of what has been covered in this chapter reflects the quality of management.

Specifically, you could expect funds that are well run to perform at least as well as the major stock market indexes—or index funds. Good managers are able to deliver consistent performance and to weather bear markets better than can rivals. In other words, they do a superior job of controlling portfolio risk. Minimizing losses in downdrafts is more important to long-run success than being an all-star in bull markets.

Good managers don't let transaction costs get out of control by doing a lot of trading. Rather, they take a longer-term viewpoint. Superior fund families also show an ability to keep expenses down—they don't get greedy with the advisory fee. On balance, a well-managed, well-performing fund attracts more investors, and its assets increase over the years. In addition to performance and expenses, other factors can help to identify top management companies. Consider the following questions:

- How long has the manager been running the fund? It is preferable—but not always essential—to have the same person at the helm for five years or longer.

- What is the background of the manager? If the person running the show has been at the fund for less than five years, look for related work experience and good education credentials. Morningstar's annual *Mutual Funds Sourcebook* supplies a basic biography for many managers.

- Is the fund run by one or two individuals or by a team?

Some funds that have delivered outstanding long-term results are managed by groups rather than by just one or two people. Examples include the Dodge & Cox Stock Fund and several products from the American Funds Group. Twentieth Century Investors has chalked up superior results with a management-by-committee approach.

Depending on how a team is organized, it may result in more stable performance. If the managers operate independently, as is the case at American Funds, a bad year for one person could be offset by better results from the others. The team approach also ensures continuity in the way the overall portfolio is run if only one of perhaps five or six managers leaves.

On the other hand, many observers feel that talented professionals work best by themselves. If they are forced to compromise their efforts to fit in with others in a group, they may not be as creative, or their results might be diluted. The vast majority of funds are managed by a single person rather than by committee.

ANALYZING INCOME RATIOS: A CASE

Frank, a 60-year-old attorney, will retire soon and is in the midst of planning how to restructure his mutual fund holdings. He also needs to decide where to invest a sizable lump-sum pension-plan distribution. He and his 58-year-old wife, Judy, understand the importance of equities and want to put as much as they can in several income-oriented equity or balanced portfolios—including, perhaps, a fund that specializes in utilities. They plan to use most of the income to meet retirement living expenses.

Frank wants stock or balanced funds with a relatively high and reasonably consistent income ratio. The first phase of his analysis is to determine the general make-up of the funds' portfolios and the yields they have been paying in recent years. He examines several prospectuses to determine the "ratio of net investment income to average net assets." Mutual-fund guidebooks generally provide this information too. Obviously, the yield wouldn't be as high for an equity fund as for a fixed-income portfolio, but with the latter Frank wouldn't get that all-important growth.

Although Frank plans to take his income dividends in cash, he will reinvest capital gains distributions to ensure growth of his principal. Some people may choose to receive both income and capital gains in cash, but there are two problems with this. First, the income is more predictable than the realized gains, which makes accurate planning difficult. The latter could be very low or nonexistent in poor markets. Second, and more important, reinvesting capital gains distributions will boost the value of your funds and, as a result, allow you to reap higher future dividends.

If a portfolio seems of interest, Frank will do the customary analysis of total return, volatility, expenses, turnover, and so on. It's important to keep things in perspective, remembering that the income ratio is only part of the story for any fund. Although Frank wants high income, he must recognize that each fund should also deliver good total return numbers relative to comparable portfolios. If it doesn't, he will be disappointed in his long-term results.

When he retires, Frank's total mutual fund assets will exceed $2 million, but he and Judy do not want to spend much of the money. They want to leave all they can to their two daughters and to several charitable organizations. A large investment spread among several conservative, income-oriented equity and balanced funds will best meet their needs.

Note

1. Alan Pope, *Successful Investing in No-Load Funds.* New York: John Wiley & Sons, Inc., 1983, pp. 97–8.

CHAPTER 4

A Careful Look at Risk

Most people would agree that high returns are good and risk is bad. The problem is that risk and return usually go hand in hand. To earn above-average gains over the years with your stock mutual funds, you must be willing to tolerate higher levels of volatility.

Risk is a difficult concept to deal with since there are various kinds. And sophisticated risk measures, like beta and standard deviation, can be tricky and have limitations. Risk, in a generic sense, is the possibility of loss, damage, or harm. For investments, a more precise definition would include variability, or period-by-period fluctuations in total return. This is the way security analysts and mutual fund managers view risk. Investors can also express it as a number, using a statistical measure such as standard deviation. The more variable an investment's returns, the greater the risk or standard deviation. More on this and other risk measures later.

What causes volatility? For mutual funds, four factors affect the variability of the investment performance.

1. *The kinds of stocks in the portfolio.* Small-growth companies would be more volatile than large blue chips.

2. *The degree to which a fund diversifies.* A portfolio of only a dozen stocks would tend to have greater volatility than one holding a hundred or more issues.

3. *The degree to which a manager uses leverage, or borrowing, in an effort to enhance performance.* Extensive use will increase volatility. Most funds do not leverage their holdings.

4. *The extent, if any, to which the manager tries to time the market or hedge.* A manager can smooth out volatility with options and futures or by raising the fund's cash position in anticipation of a market decline.

DIFFERENT KINDS OF RISK

The total risk of a stock portfolio can be separated into three categories:

1. Company Risk
2. Sector Risk
3. Market Risk

Company Risk. The most basic and potentially devastating danger, which most mutual fund investors happily avoid, is company-specific or random risk. This is the threat that a serious misfortune will afflict an individual company—leading perhaps to bankruptcy. Lawsuits, intense competition, loss of key personnel, serious mistakes made by management, changes in consumer tastes, and natural disasters all can send a corporation spiraling downward.

Academic research indicates that by holding at least 12 to 20 different stocks in a portfolio, we can eliminate most company-specific risk. The misfortunes that weigh heavily on some of the stocks will be offset by the good fortunes of others.

Most mutual funds hold at least a few dozen stocks; some hold several hundred. Of course, good selection and monitoring of investments also help to minimize the number of losers and to cut losses before they increase. This is where the manager's talent comes in.

Sector (or Industry) Risk. Diversification doesn't depend just on holding a large number of stocks. True, you can eliminate most company-specific risk if you own a dozen or so. But what if all of those firms are in the savings-and-loan industry? Or airlines? Or South African gold-mining companies?

Sector or industry risk threatens firms that provide similar products or services. Sectors can have extreme ups and downs. And so can mutual funds focusing on them. Individuals who invest in specialized equity portfolios must recognize their greater potential volatility. The prospectuses will warn that these types of funds are risky and do not constitute a complete investment program. Industry risk may also be present, albeit to a lesser degree, in diversified funds that take big positions in certain industries.

Market Risk. Market risk is really a double-edged sword. Most people regard it as the threat of facing a bear market. That's the most obvious danger. But it also involves the possibility of being on the sidelines during a bull market. Many investors do not recognize this drawback and always try to play it safe. But playing it too conservatively introduces a subtle danger: the purchasing power risk that investors face in an inflationary world.

Market risk is sometimes called "nondiversifiable" risk because you can't avoid it no matter how many stocks are held in a portfolio. All sorts of political and economic problems in a country, including uncontrollable inflation and skyrocketing interest rates, can send stock prices into a tailspin. Some fund managers try to hedge or offset market risk with options or futures. However, hedging has a cost, and these managers may be sacrificing return. Specifically, the manager may limit the fund's upside potential if the market goes higher, as often happens.

MARKET PHASE ANALYSIS

One can learn a lot about risk and return simply by studying the behavior of a stock market index, or an index of equity funds, over time. For instance, Lipper Analytical Services tracks the up and down phases of its Growth Fund Index over several market cycles as shown in Table 4–1. The first cycle begins August 21, 1975, with a Lipper Growth Fund Index value of 69.98. The phases in this table correspond generally with turning points in the overall market.

Table 4-1
Lipper Market Phase Analysis

Cycle	Up Phase			Down Phase		
1	10/11/90-	12/31/92				
	409.70	671.09	+63.8%			
2	12/03/87-	07/12/90		07/12/90-	10/11/90	
	295.65	519.62	+75.8%	519.62	409.70	-21.2%
3	07/26/84-	08/20/87		08/20/87-	12/03/87	
	190.43	427.28	+124.4%	427.28	295.65	-30.8%
4	08/12/82-	06/23/83		06/23/83-	07/26/84	
	125.95	231.94	+84.2%	231.94	190.43	-17.9%
5	03/27/80-	11/20/80		11/20/80-	08/12/82	
	106.21	169.40	+59.5%	169.40	125.95	-25.6%
6	11/16/78-	02/14/80		02/14/80-	03/27/80	
	88.72	129.14	+45.6%	129.14	106.21	-17.8%
7	08/21/75-	09/07/78		09/07/78-	11/16/78	
	69.98	104.41	+49.2%	104.41	88.72	-15.0%

This table contains approximate stock market turning point dates with Lipper Growth Fund Index values and percentage changes. For equity funds, up and down phases are defined as 10 percent or greater total return movements from the last turning point, as defined by the Lipper Growth Fund Index (a net asset value-weighted index of the 30 largest growth mutual funds), measured on Thursdays and/or at month-end.

Source: Adapted from data provided by Lipper Analytical Services Inc.

You can draw two conclusions from this information:

1. Up phases, on average, last longer than down phases.

2. The percentage changes are much greater in the up phases than in the down phases.

Keep in mind that these numbers encompass an unusually good period: the roaring bull market of the 1980s and early 1990s. Still, on average, stock funds tend to gain much more during uptrends than they surrender in down phases. Long term, the stock market has a distinctly bullish bias.

The lesson here is that you shouldn't panic and sell late in a down phase, just when the news typically appears the worst. Just as rallies eventually fizzle, bear markets always end. Obviously, it also pays to be cautious when you think the market is in the late stage of an up phase.

In short, it's much more significant to see how securities do over a cycle than over some arbitrary calendar period, although performance numbers for the latter usually are easier to come by.

TIME REDUCES MARKET RISK

To make money in the stock market, you have to go with the probabilities. That means hanging in there for the long term. One of the most important points to remember about risk is the following:

ANY STOCK FUND CAN BE VERY RISKY AS A SHORT-TERM INVESTMENT.

What do we mean by short term? Nobody can answer that precisely. It's possible, although not likely, for stocks to perform miserably for a whole decade. Certainly, you wouldn't want to put all your hard-earned savings into an equity portfolio if you think you will need to spend the cash in the next few years.

You can deal with market risk in several ways. First and foremost, you should be a long-term investor and accept the fact that stocks will fluctuate, sometimes violently. Stick with good equity funds through thick and thin because they will eventually bounce back. The worst you can do is yank your money out of a fund at the bottom of a bear market, just before the economy and stocks rebound. Consider this as the flip side of market risk—the danger of missing out on rallies.

As an example, let's look at Robert and Paula, who learned this lesson the hard way. A working couple with a young son, they were in their mid-twenties when they first invested in equities. They began with a volatile, no-load aggressive-growth stock portfolio in 1983. The fund was recommended by a wealthy acquaintance who appeared to know what he was talking about.

Robert and Paula planned to build up their position gradually and not redeem any shares until 1990 at the earliest. They managed to invest about $5,000 annually for the first few years. Then, in August 1987, the couple received an unexpected $25,000 gift from Paula's parents. They quickly added this to their fund account, paying no attention to the fact that the stock market showed obvious signs of overvaluation.

Their investment had done very well prior to that time, and they were bragging to all their friends and relatives. They put most of their extra savings into the one fund. Relatively little was held in liquid assets.

Then things took a turn for the worse. Robert lost his job in September 1987 and had to start looking for another. Although Paula was still employed, more bad news was just around the corner. Their aggressive-growth fund, which was fully invested and had used a fair amount of leverage, plunged 30 percent over a span of a few days, culminating in the stock market crash of Black Monday, October 19, 1987. Robert and Paula had never before experienced a bear market or any severe loss. They decided to cash out of their fund, though they really didn't need to take anything out at that time to meet living expenses since Paula's income was enough to get them by until Robert found another job. They simply feared losing everything. They switched their remaining stock-fund assets into CDs and money-market funds, and wound up missing the market's eventual recovery.

What went wrong?

Robert and Paula committed too much of their savings to the stock market and, especially, to an aggressive-growth fund.

Also, they should not have placed the entire $25,000 lump sum from Paula's parents into the equity fund all at once. They should have added the money gradually over time in smaller increments, thus not subjecting themselves to the risk of investing everything at a high point in the market cycle.

Then, they should not have panicked and yanked out their money after the October crash. The stock market is not a one-way street. The best buys often exist after a major plunge. Had Robert and Paula studied the fund's past returns, they would have noticed the portfolio's tendency to fall further than the overall market in down phases and appreciate faster during rallies.

In general, hanging on to good stock funds over time can lessen risk, since the market advances more years than it declines. On average, stock prices rise about 7 out of every 10 years. Just as risk can be reduced in an undiversified portfolio by adding more stocks, so can general market risk be lessened by adding more years to your holding period. "Time diversification" reduces the standard deviation of yearly returns.

Of course, time diversification won't help as much if you hang onto laggard funds. You must avoid long-term losers. And, as noted, it's important not to risk money that you might need in an emergency. Bear markets have a knack of arriving on the scene just when you may be forced to redeem shares. Cash held for liquidity or emergency purposes does not belong in a stock fund.

SIMPLE WAYS TO GAUGE RISK

You don't have to be a Ph.D. candidate to get a good handle on a mutual fund's risk. Several simple approaches can help you judge volatility and most don't involve much numbers-crunching.

The Prospectus. The first step is to read the prospectus, the closest thing to an owner's manual for a fund. The portfolio's objectives and risk factors are spelled out in detail. For example, an aggressive-growth fund may mention that it concentrates on a limited number of companies or uses leverage—two signs that it could be more volatile than normal. A sector fund investing in a specific industry or precious metals would also likely experience wider swings in NAV than a conservatively managed portfolio.

Annual Returns. Another simple way to eyeball a fund's risk is to examine its annual returns over a period of several up and down years. Compare the results with those of similar types of funds and a market index such as the S&P 500. How did the portfolio fare in weak market years such as 1981, 1984, 1987, and 1990? Annual returns can, however, conceal a lot of volatility along the way.

Quarterly Returns. For this reason, you may want to analyze quarterly or even monthly returns. Take a look at Table 4–2, which compares the quarterly and annual performance for a hypothetical volatile fund.

Table 4-2
Quarterly and Annual Returns for a Volatile Fund

Year	Quarterly Returns I	II	III	IV	Annual Returns
1	+10%	+18%	-5%	-10%	11.0%
2	-15	-10	+25	+20	14.8

The fund gained 11 percent and 14.8 percent in years 1 and 2, respectively. Considered by themselves, the annual numbers indicate relative stability. However, they hide a string of negative quarterly returns. Compounding the four negative quarters results in a loss of 34.6 percent. Anyone who had invested in the fund just before the tumble and sold right before its rebound would have suffered a staggering blow.

Past quarterly returns for funds are not as accessible as annual results are, especially if you want them for longer periods. *Morningstar Mutual Funds* provides quarterly performance over the past five years. You may also be able to get these numbers from the fund itself.

It is useful to know how a portfolio held up in particularly bad stretches such as the fourth quarter in 1987 and the third quarter of 1990. But for most purposes, a study of past annual returns will suffice.

Day-to-Day Fluctuations in NAV. You can gain a lot of insight by gauging your fund's short-term price swings. To do this, track its daily NAV against a relevant market index, such as the S&P 500, Wilshire 5000, NASDAQ Composite, or Russell 2000. Lipper publishes daily indexes for a number of different stock-fund categories that also can serve as useful benchmarks. For example, if you are tracking a small-cap fund, you could use the Lipper small-company growth index as well as the Russell 2000. If you're following one of the handful of U.S. funds targeting the Japanese market, you could use the Nikkei index.

You will need to convert all the fund's daily NAV changes into percentages, as shown in Table 4–3. For example, if the NAV on Monday was $10.00 and on Tuesday it's $10.40, the increase would be 4 percent [(10.40 - 10.00)/10.00].

Table 4–3
Gauging Day-to-Day Volatility of a Stock Fund

	Daily Percent Changes				
	Mon.	Tues.	Wed.	Thurs.	Fri.
Midas Touch Fund	+2.0%	+4.0%	+0.2%	-0.9%	-0.2%
Broad-Based Index	+1.0	+0.5	0.0	-0.4	-0.1

The Wall Street Journal tabulates daily percentage changes for more than two dozen different domestic market indexes. They appear in the

Journal's Stock Market Data Bank (part C). The Lipper indexes appear in the *Journal's* mutual funds table. Foreign indexes, such as the Nikkei and the Toronto 300 Composite, are found in the *Journal's* World Markets section (part C). On most days, the percentage changes on the various indexes run less than 1 percent or 2 percent. One of the most extreme moves in the U.S. market took place on Black Monday, October 19, 1987, when the Dow Jones industrial average plunged 22.61 percent.

To get a good feel for a fund's volatility, you should evaluate the percentage changes in NAV over several weeks since the movement on any one day may not be representative. The larger the market's rise or fall, the more meaningful your comparisons will be.

Gauging Risk in Pricey Markets

When stocks get overheated, risk ratchets higher, especially in the more aggressive portfolios.

Here are two useful yardsticks for determining the vulnerability of a particular fund.

The Fund's P/E. The price-earnings ratio, as explained in Chapter 1, can be a telling statistic of a manager's aggressiveness. The P/E for a portfolio is simply a weighted average of the P/Es of the stocks held.

Fund composite P/Es or "multiples" can range from below 10 to 30 or more, with higher numbers suggesting more vulnerability. *Morningstar Mutual Funds* includes P/Es in its stock-fund profiles. It also shows each fund's P/E relative to the S&P 500's multiple. For example, if a portfolio's P/E is 30 when the S&P 500's is 20, its relative value would be 1.5. P/Es calculated by Lipper Analytical Services appear in *Barron's* quarterly mutual funds report.

Be sure to compare fund P/Es with the multiples of similar portfolios and those of the market averages at roughly the same date. Keep in mind that P/Es for the funds may be several months old because of reporting lags. If the P/E for the market is high, near, or above 20, and the fund's multiple is even higher, the portfolio could fall sharply in a major sell-off. Excessive P/Es spell substantial risk.

In addition to the P/E, Morningstar also reports a price-book value ratio for each portfolio by itself and relative to the S&P 500. A widely used balance-sheet item, book value represents the common stockholders' equity in a company. This is another useful valuation gauge. Again, higher numbers reflect more risk.

The Fund's Cash Position. The cash (more precisely, cash equivalents) position sheds light on the overall percentage weighting of stocks in the portfolio. Some conservative managers increase their cash positions to perhaps 40 percent or more in anticipation of a market slide. Others tend to stay close to 100 percent in equities at all times. High cash positions result in much lower volatility. You can determine a fund's cash weighting by checking its shareholder reports or by telephoning the company.

PURCHASING-POWER RISK

We've talked a lot about volatility. But there's more to risk than ups and downs. Even an investment with a locked-in return and no danger of default, such as a Treasury bill, can be risky. Although there may be virtually no threat of price declines, such investments can be disappointing in another sense.

Along with taxes, inflation is a major enemy to anyone wanting to build wealth over the long haul. Ways to ease the tax bite, such as tax-deferred retirement plans and variable annuities, are covered in Chapters 14 and 15, respectively. The only way to reduce the impact of inflation is to compound your investments at higher rates of return.

Fixed-income securities—such as certificates of deposit, Treasury bills, money-market funds, and bonds—expose people to *purchasing-power* or *inflation risk*. They don't provide that much-needed inflation hedge. They're most appropriate as places to park idle cash for short periods or to keep money for possible emergencies.

These options can even appear attractive at times, such as in the early 1980s, when short-term rates touched levels as high as 17 percent or 18 percent. But 18 percent rates can become 3 percent rates, as money market investors have seen. In fact, over the long run Treasury bills have stayed only slightly ahead of the inflation rate.

As explained previously, equities offer the kind of long-term growth that you may need to provide for a secure retirement, to educate children, or to meet other major outlays. Along with good real estate, they provide a most effective inflation hedge. Unlike the fixed-interest payments on a bond, a stock's dividends tend to grow over the years.

And stock prices generally trend upward over time in tandem with the increasing level of dividends and profits.

STATISTICAL CALCULATIONS USED BY FUND ANALYSTS

You don't have to perform the complicated calculation of standard deviation, beta, and other risk measures, but you should be able to understand the degree of risk these figures signify. These statistics will not be mentioned in a fund's advertising or in its prospectus. Rather, you'll encounter them in some services and publications that monitor funds such as *CDA/Wiesenberger* and *Morningstar Mutual Funds*.

Standard Deviation

Standard deviation, as noted, is a way to quantify risk. It reflects the degree to which returns fluctuate around their average. The higher the standard deviation, the greater the risk. The measure is typically calculated using monthly results. A conservative equity fund might have a number below 3.5 percent per month, whereas an extremely aggressive one could have a value of 6 percent or more.

What do these numbers mean? About two thirds of the time a fund's actual monthly return will range within plus or minus one standard deviation of its monthly average. Its return will vary within two standard deviations about 95 percent of the time. Suppose an aggressive-stock portfolio has an average monthly return of 2 percent and a standard deviation of 6 percent. About two thirds of the time its monthly performance would fall within the -4 percent to +8 percent range. About 95 percent of the time returns should lie within the bounds of -10 percent and +14 percent. This gives you an idea of the magnitude of loss you might expect in an unusually bad month.

Standard deviation allows portfolios with similar objectives to be compared over a particular time frame. It can also be used to gauge how much more risk a fund in one category has versus a fund in another.

Table 4-4 presents a mini-illustration using hypothetical data. We include the returns on a market index, such as the Standard & Poor's 500, as a standard of comparison. ABC Growth Fund is an aggressive-stock portfolio that focuses on a small number of companies and uses leverage to try to enhance its returns. XYZ Income Fund is a conservative balanced portfolio holding both bonds and stocks.

Table 4-4
Monthly Total Returns Compared to Standard Deviation

| | Total Returns | | + |
Month	Market Index	ABC Growth	XYZ Income
Jan.	7%	12%	4%
Feb.	4	-6	2
Mar.	6	11	3
Apr.	-4	-11	-2
May	-1	5	1
June	5	7	2
July	-4	-8	-2
Aug.	4	8	3
Sept.	3	6	2
Oct.	2	5	1
Nov.	-1	-6	0
Dec.	-5	-8	-2
STD. DEV.	4.0%	8.0%	2.0 %

It's pretty clear from the negative monthly returns that ABC Growth has the greater risk. In fact, its standard deviation shows that it has about twice as much variability as the market index and four times as much as XYZ.

To be meaningful, standard deviations must be calculated over a sufficiently long period. Ideally, you would want 3 to 5 years of monthly return data, although many analysts commonly use 36 months. An individual could calculate standard deviations for older funds using annual return data. At least 15 years of information would be needed to obtain meaningful results.

Standard deviation can also be used to evaluate the riskiness of bond portfolios. The standard deviation of a bond fund's returns would reflect price fluctuations resulting from changing interest rates (interest rate risk) or changes in the quality of the bonds held (credit risk). As noted, standard deviations for individual funds can be found in *Morningstar Mutual Funds* and a few other publications. Morningstar uses total returns over the past 36 months in its calculation.

Morningstar also supplies its own risk measure, which reflects a fund's volatility relative to others in its general category. It's based on the idea that a person could always earn the Treasury-bill return as an alternative to investing in a more risky portfolio. Morningstar compares each of the fund's monthly results with the T-bill return. Only negative variations, or those that fall short of the T-bill rate, are considered in calculating the risk statistic. The more frequently a fund lags the T-bill return, and the greater the degree of underperformance, the higher its risk. This measure makes intuitive sense.

The Beta Measure

Market risk is commonly measured by what's known as the "beta coefficient." Beta relates the return on a stock or mutual fund to a market index, commonly the Standard & Poor's 500. This is often done by taking returns for, say, the past 36 months and correlating them with the index's monthly results.

Beta reflects the sensitivity of the fund's return to fluctuations in the market index. The beta for the average well-diversified portfolio equals 1.0. Betas greater than 1.0 indicate above-average volatility—the higher the beta, the greater the risk. For example, a fund with a beta of 1.5 would be expected to advance or decline 15 percent if the market rose or fell 10 percent.

Betas less than 1.0 reflect below-average volatility. These include defensive portfolios that invest primarily in slow-moving stocks such as utilities. Money-market funds have a beta of zero since their returns are independent of the stock market. Negative betas can exist but are rare.

Based on the data in Table 4–4, ABC Growth has a beta of 1.65, and XYZ Income has a beta of 0.48. (In statistical jargon, beta is the slope of a regression line relating the return on the fund, or the Y-axis variable, to the return on the market, the X- axis variable.) This confirms that the first fund carries significantly more risk than the second.

Beta Shortcomings

Beta isn't perfect. Academics have criticized it on several grounds. For instance, the measure isn't necessarily a reliable indicator of future performance, especially over shorter periods. A high-beta fund might not advance or may even decline if the market rallies.

Recently published research by University of Chicago Professors Eugene Fama and Kenneth French presents compelling evidence that beta is no longer a useful predictor of performance. That is, high-beta portfolios are not necessarily going to produce better returns than low-beta portfolios do.[1]

Also, beta's value depends on how an investor calculates it. For instance, a given mutual fund would have one beta based on data stretching back 36 months and another for 60 months. It would also vary depending on the market index that's being used as a benchmark—say, the S&P 500 versus the Russell 2000 or the much-broader Wilshire 5000.

Beta won't reveal much about funds with highly specialized portfolios, such as those investing in particular industries or in precious metals. These funds can be plenty volatile in the sense that their standard deviations are very high, but their betas might be well below 1.0, even close to 0. This is because the returns of specialized portfolios generally do not correlate closely with the overall market. Also, betas often don't work for foreign-stock portfolios, since international equities do not move in lock-step with the U.S. market.

Checking the "R-Squared"

A measure known as "R-squared" can help spot questionable betas. This statistic indicates how much of a fund's fluctuations are attributable to movements in the overall market.

R-squared ranges between 0 percent and 100 percent. The greater a fund's diversification, the higher the R-squared. The Vanguard Index Trust 500 Portfolio, which replicates the S&P 500, has an R-squared of 100 percent. Large, well-diversified funds have R-squared values of 90 percent or higher. But, funds classified as "nondiversified" could have an R-squared of 60 percent or less. A gold portfolio might have an R-squared of only 1 percent. *Morningstar Mutual Funds* reports these numbers, along with betas and standard deviations.

R-squared may be misleading for funds that retreat heavily into cash or into short-term fixed-income securities. If the fund has had a large cash position for some time, its R-squared could be relatively low. This is because the returns on cash equivalents do not fluctuate in sync with the stock market. When the portfolio gets back to a fully invested position, its R-squared number would tend to rise.

It's important to realize that the beta of a fund with a very low R-squared is generally not meaningful since that portfolio would have an extremely low correlation with the market index. For example, a gold fund may have a beta of only 0.1, yet have a very high standard deviation.

WHY STANDARD DEVIATION

Standard deviation, too, has its shortcomings since it's based on past data that might not be representative of the future. Nonetheless, it's the single best risk measure for stock funds. Here's why:

1. Standard deviation is a broader measure than beta, as it gauges total risk, not just market risk.

2. Standard deviation is a purer number. It doesn't depend on any relationship to another variable, such as an arbitrarily chosen market index.

3. It can measure the riskiness of specialized portfolios as well as of broadly diversified ones.

4. It can be used to gauge the variability of both bond and stock portfolios.

RISK BY CATEGORY

To determine the past riskiness of different fund groups, you could consult *Morningstar Mutual Funds*, which provides standard deviations and betas for various categories. Some sample statistics appear in Table 4–5. Aggressive-growth and a number of specialty portfolios carry some of the highest standard deviations—up to 6 percent or more.

Some of the lower numbers are found among utility, convertible, balanced, and asset-allocation funds. The fixed-income portfolios, with the exception of junk bonds, would generally have much lower volatility measures. Overall, the monthly standard deviation for bond funds averaged 1.4 percent during a recent three-year period.

Groups with higher standard deviations also tend to have higher-average betas, with some notable exceptions such as the precious metals funds. These portfolios often do not move in tandem with the U.S. stock market. When in doubt, use standard deviation, a generally better indicator of risk than beta.

RISK-ADJUSTED RETURNS

Since mutual funds are both popular and fairly easy to study, and because their performance results are readily accessible, they became the

Table 4-5
Category Risk Measures*

Fund Category	Standard Deviation	Beta	R-Squared
General Equity:			
Aggressive growth	6.3%	1.19	68%
Small company	5.9	1.16	69
Growth	4.7	1.01	83
Growth & income	4.0	0.87	87
Equity-income	3.4	0.76	87
Other Equity:			
Technology	6.9	1.31	66
Health care	6.4	1.17	62
Precious metals	6.3	-0.01	01
Finance	6.0	1.17	69
World stock	4.2	0.73	54
Natural resources	4.2	0.63	42
Convertible bond	3.1	1.29	26
Utility	3.0	0.51	51
Balanced	2.9	0.64	87
Asset allocation	2.7	0.53	75

*As of December 31, 1992

Source: Morningstar Inc.

subject of intense academic inquiry during the 1960s. This was at a time when scholars were seeking compelling evidence to show that stock markets were efficient, that past performance could not serve as a reliable guide to future results, and that the only way a fund manager or individual investor could achieve higher returns would be to take on greater risk.

When academics measure the performance of a portfolio, they look at risk and return together. When evaluating a mutual fund, you should consider not only the return but also how much risk was assumed to generate the results. Ideally, we would like to hold a fund that consistently earns generous returns while fluctuating less than other, comparable investments. Exceptional risk-adjusted performance would result from either superior stock selection, superior market timing, or both.

The Sharpe and Treynor Ratios

The Sharpe and Treynor ratios are two ways to gauge risk- adjusted performance. Both use what's known as a "risk premium," or the difference between a fund's average return and the average return on a riskless Treasury bill over the same period. The risk premium can be positive or negative depending on how the fund performed. The Sharpe ratio divides the risk premium by the fund's standard deviation; the Treynor ratio divides by beta. In either case higher values are favorable as they indicate more return per unit of risk.

EXAMPLE: Fund A had an average return of 2 percent monthly over a three-year period when the T-bill rate averaged 0.6 percent. Its standard deviation is 5 percent per month. Fund A's Sharpe ratio is 0.28 [(2 percent - 0.6 percent)/5 percent].
Fund B returned 1.4 percent monthly with a 2 percent standard deviation. Its Sharpe ratio is 0.4 [(1.4 percent - 0.6 percent)/2 percent]. So Fund B performed better than A on a risk-adjusted basis.

While logical and useful, the risk-adjusted measures are not perfect. The shortcomings of standard deviation, or beta especially, would affect them.

The Portfolio's Alpha

Another risk-adjusted gauge is the portfolio's *alpha*. Simply put, alpha compares the actual results of a portfolio with what would have been expected given the fund's beta and the market's behavior. If the fund fares better than predicted, it has a positive alpha. Below-par performance results in a negative alpha. Ideally, investors want managers who can consistently generate high positive alphas. Some services that monitor funds supply a risk-adjusted performance measure, such as alpha or the Sharpe or Treynor ratios.

CONCLUSION

The most basic and potentially debilitating investment danger is company risk. Stock fund investors automatically avoid this through the built-in diversification mutual funds offer. But market risk can't be avoided. In fact, it's really a double-edged sword: You risk losing in a bear market if you sell at the bottom, but you also face the danger of being on the sidelines when the bull stampedes. The best wealth-building strategy is to hang in for the long term.

Naturally, you have to assume greater risk or volatility to earn the higher long-run returns typical of equities. But if you allocate too much to Treasury bills, CDs, and the like, you could see your purchasing power eroded by inflation. There's more to risk than volatility.

Note

1. Eugene F. Fama and Kenneth R. French, "The Cross-Section of Expected Stock Returns," *The Journal of Finance*, June 1992, pp. 427–65.

CHAPTER **5**

Sorting Out Costs

The most important consideration in selecting a fund is its potential to perform well. If your manager has a superior knack for picking stocks, you will make money. Even so, you need to keep an eye on sales charges and expenses, which can seriously erode your returns, especially if the manager isn't faring well. A fund with higher costs than its peers is like a sailboat held back by excess weight.

Common sense tells us that lower expenses translate into a higher bottom line—in this case larger net returns for the shareholder. Higher costs will exert an even bigger drag when compounded over many years. A slight difference in the compounding rate (or the sum being compounded) can make a big difference in the amount accumulated over a long period. Lower-cost funds put more money to work for the investor. That's why it's important to study expenses carefully and to try to find the most efficient portfolios around, all else being equal.

KINDS OF COSTS

Four basic types of fees or expenses are generally associated with funds. They are:

1. Sales charges, which include front-end loads, back-end loads (the so-called "contingent deferred sales charges") and ongoing "asset-based sales charges," popularly known as 12b–1 fees.

2. Ongoing service fees that are paid by a fund company to brokers and other salespersons for personal assistance to clients, which consists mainly of investment advice. The service fee may be considered as an additional 12b–1 component.

3. Ongoing management and administrative costs. This category includes the manager's take as well as the various costs of running the fund, such as custodian and transfer-agent fees.

4. Costs associated with trading the securities in the portfolio, which were dealt with in Chapter 3. More frequent trading results in higher transaction expenses.

Portfolios with no charges in categories 1 and 2 above are known as "pure" no-load funds.

HOW FUNDS ARE DISTRIBUTED

To understand the purpose and impact of commissions, you need to know how funds are sold. Basically, there are two marketing avenues: through a sales force and directly by the fund complex.

The most common method of selling funds is through a sales force, in which case the fund's underwriter acts as a wholesaler or distributor to broker-dealers. These companies, in turn, sell shares to the public through their branch offices. A number of brokerages also offer their own private-label funds, including Dean Witter, Merrill Lynch, PaineWebber, Prudential Securities, and Smith Barney Shearson. These same firms also sell independent load funds, from companies such as American Funds, Colonial,

Franklin, MFS, Pioneer, and Putnam. Independent funds are not directly affiliated with a particular brokerage firm or with other financial services organizations. Insurance agents, financial planners, and bank representatives also market these products.

Almost anytime you buy through a sales force, you pay a commission, most of which compensates the salesperson and that individual's firm for guiding you through the fund-selection process.

Direct-marketed funds sell shares to investors without any middleman. They deal with prospective and existing shareholders through the mail, by phone, bank wire, or (in a few cases) at one of their local offices. These funds attract investors primarily through advertising and direct mail, as well as by word of mouth and favorable publicity. Buyers of no-load portfolios do their own research and make selections without the assistance of a salesperson.

Scudder, Stevens & Clark introduced the first no-load fund in 1928. Load portfolios dominated the industry until the 1970s, however, when a major movement toward lower costs was started to stimulate investor interest in a lackluster market environment

In earlier decades a clear distinction existed between load and no-load funds. The former frequently charged an 8.5 percent up-front commission on both initial and subsequent purchases. The latter charged nothing. But the introduction of 12b–1 fees by the Securities and Exchange Commission in 1980 changed things. The two types of products started to blur. Whereas you used to have just two flavors, chocolate and vanilla, you now find a rather confusing assortment of different flavors, or pricing structures, to choose from.

The main thing to remember about fees is that you don't get something for nothing. If you need help from a broker or other salesperson in selecting funds and managing your portfolio, you're going to have to pay for it—in one form or another. The prospectus discloses the details of the fund's pricing up-front, and should be studied carefully. Today there are more inclusive caps or limits on what funds can charge, which have been imposed by the SEC and the National Association of Securities Dealers (NASD).

Front-End Loads

As the name implies, the front-end load is applied up-front. The average front-end sales charge ranges from 4 percent to 5 percent. Suppose you invest $10,000 in a fund with a 5 percent up-front charge. The load would be $500, or 5.26 percent of the $9,500 actually invested.

You can easily spot funds with front-end loads in the daily newspaper listings. The offer price, also known as the "asked" price, would be greater than the fund's NAV, sometimes called the "bid." The former represents the NAV plus the applicable up-front sales charge.

Taking the offer price and NAV from the newspaper table, you can calculate the maximum front-end load. First, subtract the NAV from the offer price, then divide the difference by the offer price. A fund with an offer price of $20 and an NAV of $18.80, has a front-end load of 6 percent: ($20.00 - $18.80)/$20. Incidentally, once each week *The Wall Street Journal* provides the maximum initial charge for front-end load portfolios in its listings.

With larger purchases, this sales charge generally declines as specified quantity discounts or "breakpoints" are reached. Typically, you would pay a full load on investments up to some minimum threshold, which could range anywhere from $10,000 to $100,000. The breakpoints are listed in the fund's prospectus. Table 5-1 illustrates a commission schedule for a fund with a maximum 5 percent load. With some products, the charge disappears completely on very large purchases, usually $1 million or more.

Table 5-1
Commission Schedule for ABC Load Fund

Purchsae Amount	Public Offering Price	Net Amount Invested
Less than $50,000	5.00%	5.26%
$50,000 but less than $100,000	4.00	4.17
$100,000 but less than $250,000	3.00	3.09
$250,000 but less than $500,000	2.00	2.04
$500,000 but less than $1,000,000	1.00	1.01
$1,000,000 or more	0.00	0.00

Sales Commission as a Percentage of:

The commission table will also specify the dealer's cut as a percentage of the public offering price. Usually, the broker and his or her firm collect most, if not all, of the load. For example, the dealer commission on our hypothetical fund in Table 5-1 might be 4 percent for purchases of less than $50,000. So, if an individual makes a $10,000 investment, he or she would pay a $500 commission, $400 of which would go to the broker and his or her firm.

If a fund has no other sales charges, it could still have an 8.5 percent front-end load, but virtually none do. Some or all of the charge has been shifted from an up-front payment to an ongoing, annual 12b–1 fee, with a back-end load attached.

Ongoing Sales and Service Charges

SEC Rule 12b–1 allows funds to charge an annual levy for distribution costs, including advertising. The logic is that portfolios with the resources to promote themselves more actively will be able to attract more assets and thereby benefit more fully from economies of scale. A 12b–1 fee may also be charged for ongoing personal investor services rendered by a salesperson.

Some funds that formerly imposed 8.5 percent front-end loads reduced or eliminated those charges when they began to use the 12b–1 plan. The maximum permissible 12b–1 charge had been 1.25 percent annually up to mid-1993 but since then has dropped to 0.75 percent for the sales charge component (technically, the "asset-based sales charge"). In addition, there can be an ongoing "service" fee of up to 0.25 percent annually to compensate the registered representative or other salesperson for investment advice. For all practical purposes, lumping the 0.75 percent maximum sales charge and the 0.25 percent maximum service fee results in an annual limit of 1.0 percent that can be charged against assets for sales and service.

Incidentally, a fund with no front-end and deferred loads cannot be represented by a salesperson as "no-load" unless its combined asset-based and service fees do not exceed 0.25 percent of net assets yearly.

Well over half of all mutual funds today have the 12b–1 feature in one form or another. Sharp criticism has been voiced against 12b–1 plans. As one fund manager put it, the biggest negative is that the costs of gathering new money come out of the pockets of existing shareholders. Why should these investors be required to help pay for advertising? After all, it is management that really benefits most directly from new money, in the form of greater total fees. As a rule, you should avoid all funds with 12b–1 charges above 0.5 percent for sales and service combined; the longer you remain in a fund the more burdensome high 12b–1 fees become. You can be sure that most institutional investors won't have anything to do with funds that impose 12b–1 fees.

Contingent Deferred Sales Charges

The back-end load or contingent deferred sales charge (CDSC) is often used along with a 12b–1 plan for funds sold by middlemen. The idea here is to effectively guarantee some form of commission for the broker. If the investor remains in the fund for many years, the salesperson would be compensated through the ongoing service fee referred to above. But if the customer sells shortly after purchase, the broker gets paid through the CDSC.

The CDSC applies only if shares are redeemed during the first several years after purchase. If you hold the fund long term this exit fee—which decreases periodically in steps—usually disappears. For example, the CDSC might be 5 percent if shares are redeemed within the first year, 4 percent in year two, and so on until it phases out entirely after the fifth year. The CDSC is commonly levied against the value of the original investment. It may, however, apply to the redemption proceeds if the price of the shares has declined.

By looking carefully at individual fund listings in the newspaper, you can identify those with contingent deferred sales charges as well as 12b–1 fees. Watch for the following letters placed after the portfolio's name: **r** denotes a CDSC or a redemption fee may apply; **p** denotes a 12b–1 fee; and **t** indicates a redemption charge may apply and a 12b–1 fee exists. In other words, both the **r** and **p** footnotes apply.

Other Fees

You'll occasionally encounter funds with other charges. Here are three.

Redemption Fees. Unlike the CDSC, this is usually a relatively small percentage, such as 1 percent of the amount sold, and it typically remains at a fixed level. Sometimes the purpose is to discourage investors from selling soon after they buy. This charge is relatively uncommon. A handful of otherwise no-load portfolios impose a small redemption fee.

Fees on Reinvested Dividends. Most funds allow shareholders to reinvest both dividends and capital gains distributions into additional shares at NAV without paying any commissions. A few portfolios, however, do charge a fee on reinvested dividends.

Exchange Fees. There is usually no fee for moving your money between portfolios within a given fund family, although some companies charge $5 and a few $10 per telephone exchange. The exchange privilege is discussed in Chapter 16.

FLEXIBLE PRICING

The flexible pricing structure available today with an increasing number of broker-marketed funds gives investors a choice of how they can pay their sales charges. The earliest form of flexible pricing, called dual pricing, was introduced in 1988 by Merrill Lynch. You can choose between two different fee structures with Class A and B shares.

In general, the Class A shares charge a front-end load ranging from, say, 4 percent to 6 percent, while the Class B shares have no front-end commission but do impose a contingent deferred sales charge or redemption fee. Typically, a 12b–1 fee would also apply to the Class B shares. It may apply to the A shares as well. But if the A shares do carry one, it would be lower than on the B shares.

In most cases, funds structure their A and B shares so that it's not so easy to determine the best option. This requires a careful cost analysis. You would need to consider such factors as the size of your investment and how long you intend to keep your money in the portfolio. For example, a large investor may get a quantity discount on the A shares of a particular fund, but not on the B. In any event, avoid funds with high 12b–1 fees if you expect to stay in for some time.

Going beyond A and B shares, it's becoming more common to see other pricing options, like "level loads." In fact, you can find A, B, C, and D shares, all based on the same portfolio. At present there are no industry standard definitions for the C and D shares. Giving buyers different options make it easier for a company to sell its funds. Critics have called the proliferation of confusing choices "fee madness."[1] The bottom line is that you don't get something for nothing. Read the prospectus carefully. And if your salesperson can't answer your questions satisfactorily, it may be best to look for one who is more knowledgeable.

OPERATING COSTS

Ongoing management and administrative costs appear as a part of the expense ratio. The management company subtracts these operating costs bit by bit rather than in one lump sum. They stay in force for as long as you own a fund.

Management Fees

Management fees, common to virtually all portfolios, are charged by the advisory firm for the security analysis and portfolio management functions it performs. These fees generally range from 0.4 percent to 1 percent annually. At 1 percent, the expense would amount to $10 million each year on a $1 billion portfolio. A fund collecting relatively large management charges would make a statement such as the following in its prospectus: "Such fee is higher than that charged by most other investment management companies." Is the extra expense worth it? That depends on the size of the fee and the company's track record.

A detailed discussion of management expenses can be found in the fund's prospectus. In many cases, the adviser might state that it plans to reduce the fee percentage as the asset base swells. For example, the ABC Growth Fund may have a management fee of 0.7 percent for the first $100 million of assets, 0.6 percent for the next $400 million and 0.5 percent for amounts above $500 million. Watch out for companies that do not reduce their management charge as the portfolio grows. Make sure the fund is passing along to shareholders the economies of scale that it realizes.

Other Recurring Expenses

Mutual funds tack on several other ongoing expense items in addition to the management fees and any sales or service fees. Most apply to all funds. They include:

- Shareholder servicing costs
- Custodian and transfer-agent fees
- Shareholder report costs
- Legal fees
- Auditing fees
- Interest expense
- Directors' fees

Expense items such as these are detailed in the fund's statement of operations, which is discussed later in this chapter.

When you add the 12b–1 charges, management fees, and other costs, you get the total operating expense. Divide this by the fund's assets (technically, average monthly net assets) and you would get the all-important expense ratio.

Some companies limit their expense ratio, often for competitive purposes. For example, the adviser might reimburse the fund to the extent necessary to maintain the number at a maximum 1 percent. This would be accomplished by waiving a portion of the advisory fee. Details would be reported in the prospectus and the annual and semiannual reports. Expense ratio limitations are more common among newer, smaller funds and may be temporary.

THE STANDARD FEE TABLE

The SEC requires all fees charged by funds to be summarized in a prominently displayed table near the front of the prospectus. The fee table, which has been mandatory since 1988, is one of the most important parts of the prospectus and deserves careful consideration. It is divided into three sections:

1. A summary of shareholder transaction expenses.
2. A breakdown of the fund's operating expenses.
3. A standardized hypothetical example of the effect of fees over time.

The fee table for two hypothetical funds is illustrated in Table 5-2. The funds are similar in all respects except that ABC features a 6 percent front-end load and no 12b–1 fee, whereas XYZ has no up-front charge but a 0.75 percent 12b–1 fee. The 12b–1 fee raises the annual expenses of XYZ.

The 5 percent annual return and $1,000 investment used in the example are standardized numbers employed by all funds in their fee tables. This makes a meaningful comparison possible. Note that ABC has higher costs in the earlier years but lower later on. The 10-year expenses run $227 for XYZ versus $207 for ABC, proving that the 12b–1 charges can add up over the years. If you now assume XYZ is a pure no-load fund, without any 12b–1 fee, it would have a 1.2 percent expense ratio. Over 10 years, XYZ's total expenses would fall from $227 to $145.

Table 5-2
Sample Prospectus Fee Table Illustrations

Shareholder Transaction Expenses	ABC Fund	XYZ Fund
Max. sales load imposed on purchases (percent of offering price)	6.00%	0
Max. sales load on reinvested dividends	0	0
Contingent deferred sales charge	0	0
Redemption fee	0	0
Exchange fee	0	0

Annual Operating Costs (percent of average net assets)		
Investment advisory fees	0.70%	0.70%
12b-1 fees	0	0.75
Other expenses	0.50	0.50
Total Operating Expenses	1.30%	1.95%

Hypothetical Example

You would pay the following expenses on a $1,000 investment in each fund assuming (1) a 5% annual return and (2) redemption at the end of each period:

	Year			
	1	3	5	10
ABC Fund	$72	$99	$127	$207
XYZ Fund	20	61	105	227

This example assumes the percentage amounts listed under total operating expenses remain constant. It should not be considered representative of past or future expenses or performance.

LOWER COSTS TRANSLATE INTO HIGHER RETURNS

A less expensive fund will generate better results, other things being equal. Low fees are especially important to bond funds, since fixed-income investments normally don't produce the type of long-run performance available in the stock market. High sales commissions and management fees can turn an otherwise good bond portfolio into a laggard. In addition, there is more justification for paying a higher management fee to a talented stock picker with the ability to really add value. Bond fund managers enjoy less opportunity to move ahead of the pack, since bond results normally cluster within a narrower range. The annualized return on some funds may barely exceed the rate of inflation.

STATEMENT OF OPERATIONS

In addition to the fee table and expense ratio, you should examine a fund's statement of operations, which appears in its annual and semi-annual shareholder reports. It's wise to analyze this statement if the expense ratio appears excessive and you're not sure why. The statement of operations contains a detailed breakdown that allows you to see if the various expense items are in line with those of comparable funds. Also read all footnotes, as they give further information on items such as advisory fees and interest expense.

BEWARE OF LAYERED FEES

Some funds invest in other funds, but they are not common, and their record has not been that great. In theory, at least, their overly diversified portfolios tend to produce mediocre results, and a double layer of fees puts a drag on performance. Exceptions exist, of course, including a few fund families that offer economical access to related portfolios, usually charging just one layer of fees. Vanguard Star, for example, has no management fee of its own. This balanced portfolio invests in seven other Vanguard funds: four equity, two fixed-income, and one money market, and only the management expenses of these portfolios apply—on a pro-rata, not a cumulative basis. Two other multifunds that impose just one layer of fees are T. Rowe Price Spectrum Income and Spectrum Growth. Each invests in up to seven other T. Rowe Price funds, offering a means of getting widespread diversification in a single purchase.

WHY DO INDIVIDUALS PURCHASE COMMISSION-LADEN FUNDS?

It might seem odd that some people would willingly pay a sales charge, even though competitive no-load products are available. After all, it's apparent that the load hurts performance since it reduces the net amount of money invested. What you pay in commissions is gone. It cannot work for you. Yet roughly half of all fund purchases are made through a sales force. How can this be?

In truth investors buy commission funds for any of several reasons, some of which make a lot of sense and some of which don't:

- Many people learn about particular investment products through a knowledgeable salesperson. A casual investor might not understand the diversification merits of, say, an international stock fund, or may not be aware of low-risk CD substitutes, such as a short-term bond portfolio. It might require a broker, selling load products, to bring these investments to the person's attention.

- Some investors are gullible. They might fall for the old broker ruse that there's nothing free in life, so even no-loads have their hidden costs.

- Many individuals probably do not fully understand the impact of fees on performance. Instead, they think only about how much money they can make. Brokers often argue with some credibility that an up-front load won't make a big difference on a good-performing fund held many years.

- Many people simply do not have an interest in investments, so they need financial guidance. Perhaps they are too busy with their careers to educate themselves about financial matters.

- Some people just have a difficult time saying no to a charming salesperson with an exciting product.

We certainly won't go so far as to say, "Never invest in a load fund." In fact, purchasing a good one under the right circumstances can make a lot of sense. Some individuals definitely need the advice of a good broker or financial planner. Otherwise, they could be prone to making serious mistakes and losing lots of money. They might have trouble deciding not only what and when to buy, but when to sell.

Also, since load funds are actively marketed by a sales force, they sometimes attract more assets than equivalent no-load products, and may, therefore, have lower expense ratios.

And the load might not matter much to wealthier buyers, who can take advantage of quantity discounts. These discounts occur at specified breakpoints, as illustrated in Table 5-1. Individuals investing $50,000, $100,000, $500,000, or $1 million would pay successively smaller sales charges. In many cases, the commission might be quite reasonable.

On this latter point, the fund may grant you a nice discount if you execute a "statement of intent." This lets you receive a lower commission, even if you don't invest everything at once. Typically, you have up to 13 months to invest enough cash to meet the breakpoint. This way, all purchases over that period would benefit from the lower rate. By spreading out your purchases over a number of months, you also benefit from dollar-cost averaging, which means you avoid the risk of making your entire investment at what could be the fund's high price for the year.

Affluent investors should seriously consider the best front-end load funds, along with the best no-loads. Also, individuals participating in thrift programs offered by their employers, including 401(k) and 403(b) plans, can buy load products at little or no commission because of the quantity discounts the employer can pass along to the workers.

Many well-established load funds have excellent long-term records. You can see the names of some of them on *Forbes* annual honor roll. On the other hand, there's no reason for anyone to consider high-cost funds with mediocre performance. The sad fact is there are far too many of them.

EXPENSE RATIOS HAVE CREPT UPWARD

The mutual fund industry has grown astronomically in recent decades. Yet expense ratios over the same period have also risen, which suggests that investors aren't enjoying many economies of scale. The average expense ratio for equity funds has increased to about twice its level of the early 1950s.

Many funds have grown quite large, but their ratios haven't declined at all and sometimes have risen. This might seem illogical, since bigger portfolios should feature lower per-share fees due to economies of scale.

Several reasons explain why the trend of expense ratios has been upward in recent years:

- More funds have 12b–1 charges. In fact, none imposed these fees prior to 1980, when they were authorized by the Securities and

Exchange Commission. Any 12b–1 fees, as noted earlier, are included in the expense ratio.

- Management fees have also been increasing. This advisory charge accounts for a large chunk of fund expenses.

- Funds are offering more shareholder services, which cost money. Families produce newsletters and other educational materials, maintain toll-free 800 numbers and provide other benefits for a growing number of investors. Some families even operate walk-in investor centers in selected large cities.

- Perhaps most important, it can be complicated trying to analyze costs, as we've noted in this chapter. Thus, funds often can get away with increasing charges—or introducing new ones—because these changes may not be obvious to the average investor.

Note

1. Jason Zweig and Mary Beth Grover, "Fee Madness," *Forbes*, February 15, 1993, pp. 160-162 and 164.

CHAPTER 6

Efficient Markets and Index Funds

If you pick up a newspaper or magazine, you will likely encounter a story about a current hot fund. The press likes excitement and will often highlight the latest top-performing portfolio. But there's a lot to be said for avoiding these investments for something more predictable, such as an index fund.

Index funds are essentially unmanaged. They buy and hold the same stocks or bonds that are included in a popular benchmark, such as the Standard & Poor's 500. They appeal to investors seeking low costs and the assurance of very closely tracking the market's returns. Index portfolios make sense for anyone who wants to pursue a long-term, buy-and-hold strategy because of their low expenses and predictable returns.

In a pure, passive index fund, turnover and thus transaction costs are low. The management fee also tends to be minimal. The fund doesn't make bets on particular securities or industries. And it remains fully invested—no attempt is made to time the market. Of course, not every index mutual fund fits these descriptions precisely. Some quasi-index products follow different strategies.

THERE'S NO FREE LUNCH

Academic research in the 1960s and 1970s at the University of Chicago and elsewhere focused on the concept of market efficiency. Slowly, scholars began to accept the idea that stocks generally are correctly priced at any given moment and do not offer the potential for consistently exceptional returns. In other words, there was no free lunch awaiting investors.

The conclusion was that if you can't beat the market averages, you would be better off performing as close to the market as you could. This could be done by holding a large, well-diversified portfolio and trading as little as possible to minimize transaction costs. The simplest way to select stocks would be through a random process.

Professor Burton Malkiel of Princeton, in his highly acclaimed *A Random Walk Down Wall Street*, makes a compelling case for index funds. Malkiel holds that index funds should obtain better results than those produced by the typical portfolio manager. Why? Because substantial management fees and portfolio turnover eat into the bottom line. Index investors also enjoy the certainty of knowing they will always more or less match the market's return and never drastically underperform it.

THE BIRTH OF INDEX FUNDS

Indexing began to appeal to pension funds in the 1970s because of a growing acceptance of the stock market's "efficiency" and compelling evidence that two thirds to three quarters of all portfolio managers underperform the popular averages. The transaction costs associated with active management act as a big drain on performance, and expenses in general put managers at a disadvantage.

The first index mutual fund, the Vanguard Index Trust, was introduced in 1976 and has closely tracked the S&P 500 since then. At this writing, the Vanguard 500 portfolio had an average expense ratio of just 0.20 percent and an average turnover of 5 percent. It stands as one example of a fund that has seen its per-share costs decline in recent years because of the efficiencies of larger size. The fund crossed the $6 billion asset mark in 1992.

The 500 portfolio fared well during the 1980s because the big-cap stocks in the S&P 500 performed brilliantly over that period. This was partly due to the increased attention given to the S&P 500 stocks by professional money managers. A number of other index mutual funds have been introduced in recent years, both by Vanguard and by other families. All told, there are some five dozen portfolios offering a variety of indexing strategies.

DON'T LOOK TO YOUR INVESTMENTS FOR THRILLS

In a sense, index funds can be viewed as boring, since they will never beat the market. But the investment arena isn't the place most people should look for fun and excitement. Sometimes, the best portfolios are dull, in that money compounds slowly but steadily over time. Needless to say, many other activities in life offer more stimulation than playing the stock market. Remember how difficult it is even for professionals to consistently beat the popular averages. The danger of underperforming is very real. This produces the kind of excitement that leads to sleepless nights of tossing and turning.

STUDIES OF STOCK MARKET EFFICIENCY

The question of stock market efficiency is of great importance to every investor. Why? Because the only way you or your portfolio manager can beat the market is by buying and selling inefficiently priced securities at the appropriate times.

The earliest research on market efficiency focused on studies of past prices. The overall conclusion of the studies was that prices generally take a "random walk" across time. In other words, studying a stock's past movements will not provide the information needed to beat the market since prices generally do not follow repetitive patterns. These findings became known as *weak* evidence in support of market efficiency.

In quest of stronger evidence, researchers subsequently studied the effect of other kinds of publicly available information on prices. This includes the "announcement effects" of changes in the Federal Reserve's discount rate, stock splits, dividends, and corporate earnings. Generally, the studies concluded that it would be difficult to beat the market by trading on this publicly available information after transaction costs were factored in.

In addition, the researchers examined the performances of mutual fund managers to see if they could produce superior risk-adjusted returns. Here again, the evidence suggested that markets are generally efficient and that the only way a portfolio manager could earn a higher return is by taking on higher risk.

PRICE = VALUE WITH 100 PERCENT EFFICIENCY

Security analysts determine the investment or intrinsic value of a stock by calculating its estimated future benefits, usually its forecasted dividends. They then "discount" these at a rate that reflects the general level of interest rates and the stock's riskiness.

In an efficient (or random walk) market, stocks virtually always sell for what they're worth. There are no underpriced or overpriced issues. Each stock hovers very closely around its investment value. New information can and does cause the value of a company to change from time to time. Prices respond instantaneously to *unanticipated* news, moving up or down rapidly. News itself appears randomly over time. The faster the stock's response to the news, the more efficient the market.

Figure 6–1 illustrates both efficient and relatively inefficient pricing. With perfect efficiency, prices would always exactly equal the corresponding value per share, and the price and value lines would coincide. But markets have not become totally, 100 percent efficient, and they never will.

In the figure, you can see that unanticipated favorable news boosts the stock on trading day t. With the efficient pricing line, there's an immediate upward shift to the new, higher value. The inefficient pricing line, however, appears to fluctuate in a relatively independent manner and deviates widely from the stock's value much of the time.

Fluctuations above and below the intrinsic value are due to both "noise" and "liquidity" traders. Noise traders buy and sell in response to unsound information or emotional impulses. They could be reacting to rumors, tips, or their own superficial research. Liquidity traders are passive investors who may sell a stock simply because they need the money, or they may invest in one simply because they now have the money. In fact, index-fund managers are liquidity traders. When they get a large inflow of cash, they need to invest it in the stocks comprising

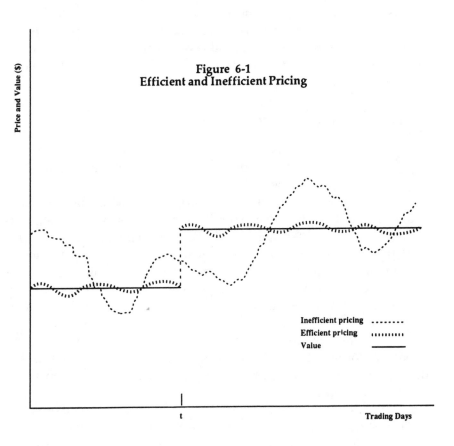

Figure 6-1
Efficient and Inefficient Pricing

their target index. Liquidity trades are generally made without considering the link between price and value.

With inefficient pricing, there are opportunities to outperform the market by making bets. A manager would buy when he or she thinks the price is significantly below value and sell when it equals or exceeds this value. This is also known as value investing. If the market were completely efficient—which it isn't—price and value would never diverge far enough for anyone to earn an extraordinary profit, especially after factoring in the high costs of frequent trading.

WHAT MAKES MARKETS EFFICIENT?

An efficient market depends on the watchful eyes of a large number of intelligent, highly trained security analysts who respond instantly to any significant news item. The stock market is far more efficient today than it was in the 1930s, when security analysis was in its infancy and there were fewer skilled competitors. Benjamin Graham, the father of modern security analysis, recognized that changes occurring gradually over the decades since then have produced a more efficient market. Extensive use of stock-evaluation techniques, which worked well in the old days, generally have become less rewarding, as he explained at a seminar in 1976.[1]

These days, according to efficient-market advocates, it's practically impossible for investors or fund managers to do better than average by quickly reacting to news. There are simply too many skilled competitors able to move quickly.

Yet market efficiency, as noted, isn't perfect. The important question is: How efficient is it? Evidence indicates that while the market may be highly efficient for large, heavily researched, actively traded companies, pockets of inefficiency exist. Examples include many small, obscure, thinly traded companies. In addition, investors tend to overreact to both good and bad news. And there is a considerable amount of noise trading going on.

As you might expect, the efficient-markets school has been a target of some strong criticism. In the 1980s, academics searched intensively for anomalies to the efficient-market hypothesis and they found some. Now the pendulum has swung back somewhat from the view of pure efficiency to a position of compromise.

STOCK MARKET ANOMALIES

Stocks apparently do not always sell exactly for what they are worth. As noted, investors tend to overreact to both good and bad news. We may see a sudden, severe sell-off when there is strong likelihood of a major war or other catastrophe. If the situation is unexpectedly resolved, prices often bounce back just as quickly. The same kind of overreaction occurs in response to favorable and unfavorable news on individual companies. But price usually fluctuates more widely than value. So times of investor panic, when stocks trade at depressed P/Es, often provide bargain hunters with some great opportunities. And when investors become wildly optimistic and companies sell at outrageously high P/Es, good money managers often cut back on their equity positions. Periods of overvaluation and undervaluation can persist for some time, on individual stocks or in the market as a whole.

In the 1980s, research turned up a number of different anomalies, like the low-P/E, small-firm and neglected-firm effects. Certain calendar anomalies have also been documented, including the January effect and the Super Bowl phenomenon.

These exceptions indicate that there are a number of strategies that may allow you to beat the market, at least to a limited extent. For instance, portfolios of low-P/E stocks have been shown to produce better performance than have portfolios of high or average-P/E stocks. In addition, purchasing the shares of good closed-end funds trading at abnormally wide discounts can prove quite profitable.

Mutual fund investors should pay some attention to market efficiency because they will want to know whether a highly skilled manager can continue to outperform. Efficient-market mavens would argue that the handful of managers who have consistently delivered superior gains have simply had a run of good luck and can offer no assurance their winning streak will continue. This is debatable. Some fund managers are very talented and capable of generating above-normal returns. The real issue is: Can you identify today those managers who will significantly outperform the market over the next decade or so? If you don't think you can, then an index fund could be appropriate.

THE MARKET INDEXES

Of course, your investment success depends in part on the index you choose. Each one reflects a different sector of the market, such as big blue chips, small stocks, and European stocks. Others track industries such as utilities. Further, these various indexes are sometimes calculated in different ways. For instance, the venerable Dow Jones industrial average is *price weighted*, which means only the share prices of its 30 component stocks are used to derive its value. The Dow is really just a crude indicator that contains a small number of big blue-chip companies.

With the far more common market-value (or capitalization) weighted indexes such as the S&P 500, each component stock is calculated in proportion to its size. This is reflected by a company's capitalization, or price per share multiplied by the number of shares outstanding. For example, a $40 stock with 10 million shares would have a $400 million market cap.

Suppose four companies make up a hypothetical F&W 4 Index, as shown in Table 6–1.

Table 6-1
The F&W 4 Cap Weighted Index

Stock	Share Price	Shares Outstanding (millions)	Total Capitalization (billions)	Weight in Index
A	$80	25	$2	16.7%
B	60	100	6	50.0
C	50	60	3	25.0
D	100	10	1	8.3

Stock B, with the highest market cap, $6 billion, has the largest weight in the index at 50 percent, while Stock D has the lowest, 8.3 percent. The weights are found by dividing each stock's market cap by the $12 billion total for all the companies in the F&W 4. Conversely, if the F&W were price-weighted, each stock's weight would simply be its price divided by the sum of all prices, $290. Stock D, with the highest price, $100, would make up a leading 34.5 percent of the index, despite its low market cap. The more sophisticated cap-weighted indexes are generally thought to be more reliable than their simpler price-weighted counterparts.

Giant companies such as Exxon, General Electric, and WalMart exert the largest influence on a cap-weighted index such as the S&P 500. For example, Exxon accounts for about 3 percent of the value of the S&P 500. If the index were equally weighted, Exxon, like any other stock, would account for only 0.2 percent, or 1/500th. In fact, the largest 50 companies in the S&P 500 represent around 50 percent of the weighting, even though they comprise only 10 percent of the group numerically. The performance of the 50 largest stocks is, therefore, much more important than that of any randomly selected 50 companies in the index.

THE INDEX FUND MENU

Index mutual funds offer a broad array of investment choices. Garden-variety portfolios can be found that track well-known indexes pegged to small stocks (such as the Russell 2000), larger companies (the S&P 500) or a sampling of the entire domestic equities market (the Wilshire 5000).

A few new quasi-index funds have introduced a special twist by emphasizing growth (high earnings gains) or value (potentially under-priced) companies. The stocks in a broad index are simply split into growth and value categories and packaged separately for investors. It's a low-cost way to have either of two distinct portfolios.

Several international index funds invest in European, Pacific Basin, or even Japanese companies. You can make a good argument for holding bond index portfolios; they tend to outperform well over half of their actively managed rivals. If you want both bonds and stocks in one product, a balanced index fund might be the answer. You can even find a few highly specialized funds targeting gold stocks or the natural-gas industry.

An efficient market buff could easily assemble a widely diversified mix of domestic and foreign securities based entirely on index mutual funds. In addition to Vanguard, which offers an extensive menu of index products, various other companies have at least one such fund. The list includes Benham, Bull & Bear, Colonial, Dimensional, Dreyfus, Federated, Fidelity, Gateway, IDS, SEI, Portico, Rushmore, Charles Schwab, SEI, and United Services.

One caveat about index funds is that some passively replicate an index while others try to outperform the benchmark through active management. If a portfolio uses options or futures heavily and has a high expense ratio or a relatively high turnover, it can't be a pure index fund. In addition, not all index products are truly no-load. Be sure to read the prospectuses carefully. There can be huge differences among funds based on the same index.

Funds that do not follow a traditional, passive indexing strategy are not necessarily bad investments. But you need to compare the costs with the expected benefits. And don't buy anything you don't understand. It's our opinion that index funds make most sense when they are truly passive and consist of big blue-chip stocks that tend to be efficiently priced.

THE INDEX COMPROMISE

With index funds, you forgo the opportunity to beat the market, but you are assured of not being a laggard, either. The pure, passive ones have a lot going for them. On the other hand, many actively managed mutual funds have performed as well as, or better than, the popular averages over fairly long periods, even with their higher costs. You can see some of these all-stars each year in the *Forbes* honor roll. Managed portfolios also make sense for less-efficient segments, such as small stocks and turnaround or other "special situations." And they are a good choice for foreign markets, many of which are relatively inefficient.

Since even the domestic equity market is not totally efficient, it still makes sense to look for value. As a drawback, index funds do not set limits on what they will pay for individual stocks. By definition, traditional index funds are not concerned with finding bargains. They simply want to replicate a benchmark as closely as possible. As a compromise, you could invest some of your assets in active funds, or even in individual stocks, and the balance in index portfolios.

HOW INDEXING FITS IN: A CASE STUDY

The case of Maria, an affluent 40-year-old New York advertising executive, shows how index funds can be used as the keystone of a broader portfolio. Maria is fascinated with the stock market and has been investing since her late teens, but she was not particularly successful during her early years. In fact, she once took a five-figure loss on the shares of a small computer company that ultimately went bankrupt.

But Maria has learned a lot from her mistakes and has developed a plan for building and protecting her wealth, most of which she received as an inheritance. She plans to retire at age 50, by which time she hopes her daughter, currently age 10, will have enrolled in college.

Maria has an adequate reserve of liquid assets to meet unexpected emergencies and about $1 million invested in a Long Island home, which she leases. She also has $200,000 in highgrade municipal bonds. But she considers index funds her most important asset, providing her with a low-anxiety investment foundation.

One lesson Maria has learned over the years is that it's exceedingly difficult for an individual to perform better than or even on par with the market averages over the long run. For that reason, she has built a broadly diversified index portfolio, totaling about $1.5 million spread over five funds. Her choices include large and small domestic stocks, European, Asian, and Pacific Rim stocks, and bonds. About 35 percent of her total index holdings are in the international stock sphere, and 40 percent in domestic equities, with roughly half of that in small stocks. Bonds account for the remaining 25 percent. She adds fixed amounts to each portfolio monthly through an automatic investment plan.

Maria still likes to dabble in the stock market, however. At the top of her investment pyramid, she has $200,000 spread among a dozen or so emerging-growth companies that she follows closely. She attends shareholder meetings and keeps up on each one's progress. By staying close to timely information on the companies, she feels she enjoys an edge.

But the $200,000 invested in individual companies represents only a fraction of her $1.9 million financial portfolio. Since most is in the index funds and high-grade munis, she feels comfortable holding the aggressive stocks. Even if she lost all of that money, which is unlikely, it would not materially alter her standard of living or her retirement plans. In any event, she feels that she has escaped the boredom of having everything in index funds and likes the challenge of managing her own stock portfolio.

Note

1. John Train, *The Money Masters*. New York: Harper & Row, Publishers, 1980, p. 103.

CHAPTER 7

Internationally-Oriented Portfolios

Diversification reduces risk. That's the major advantage of investing in mutual funds. But you still face the danger that the overall stock market will perform poorly. That risk is greater for United States investors who confine themselves to funds holding domestic equities.

By spreading your assets over different stock markets, you can reduce your volatility without sacrificing returns. In fact, over long periods you will tend to post higher gains. That's what international diversification is all about.

THE MUTUAL FUND ADVANTAGE

For individual stock buyers, investing in foreign markets is more complex and costly than staying within the United States. It is harder to obtain meaningful, timely information on foreign companies and to analyze financial reports and other data. Overseas markets, especially those in developing countries, are more volatile and less liquid than our own. Transaction costs can be very high. In addition, many markets are subject to far less regulation.

Mutual funds offer an ideal way to invest in foreign stocks because they're run by experienced portfolio managers. Fund managers often "kick the tires" by visiting companies and meeting top executives, as well as suppliers, customers, bankers, and accountants. Field research is essential where published information is inadequate. It's easy to see why management fees can be higher for international funds.

MORE OPPORTUNITIES BEYOND OUR BORDERS

With today's sophisticated communications, the world has become much smaller. Just about every hour of the day, trading is going on somewhere. The United States remains the world's biggest financial market, but its impact has gradually lessened in the global equities arena. At the beginning of the 1970s, about 30 percent of the world's stock market value existed outside the United States. By 1980, the proportion had risen to just over half, and by 1992 it was about 60 percent. In addition, the proportion of global gross national product generated in foreign nations has registered a corresponding increase.

Excellent growth opportunities can be found in many of the more than four dozen stock markets around the globe, especially in those of emerging nations.

Furthermore, some of the world's biggest and best companies are based outside the United States. A purely domestic portfolio would ignore: 7 of the world's 10 largest insurers; 8 of the 10 biggest chemical companies; 8 of the 10 top electronics firms; 8 of the 10 largest automakers; 9 of the 10 biggest machinery manufacturers; 9 of the top 10 utilities; and the 24 largest banks.[1]

Globalization

The deregulation of financial markets that began in the United States in the 1970s has spread to a number of other countries, including the United Kingdom, Germany and Japan. Deregulation makes foreign securities more accessible to global investors.

During the 1980s, international investing caught on in a big way with institutions, especially pension funds, and with a growing number of individuals. The mutual fund industry responded with dozens of new foreign portfolios. At this writing, Lipper Analytical Services tracked 56 global, 9 global small company, 107 international, 27 European-region, 23 Pacific-region, 3 Latin American, 6 Japanese, and 3 Canadian funds. In addition, there are more than 40 closed-end single-country portfolios.

Enhanced Diversification

As noted earlier, global investors can earn greater returns for a given level of risk. In addition, at any moment some markets offer better values than do others, giving overseas buyers more places to search for bargains and pricing inefficiencies. And since the United States economy is more mature than most, it can be expected to grow at a slower rate. Mature industries here, such as the cement business, may be expanding wildly in developing economies.

The reason for the risk reduction is that different stock markets do not always move in tandem with our market or with each other. One might zig while another zags. The degree of association of price movements between markets—measured by the correlation coefficient—can be quite low, especially with emerging nations such as Chile, Greece, Indonesia, Mexico, the Philippines, Thailand, and Turkey.

What is the correlation coefficient and how is it derived? It is a statistical measure computed from two "time series" of numbers, such as stock prices in the United States and those in Mexico. It gauges how closely the two series move together. A +1.0 correlation indicates a perfect positive association; a value of 0.0 reflects complete independence—in our case a zero correlation means that the price variations in the two countries are totally unrelated. The closer the correlation to zero, the weaker the stock price relationship and the greater the diversification benefits.

Time series of stock prices in different countries are generally positively correlated, but the coefficient is typically well below 1.0. Researchers have found the relationship between the United States market and some foreign bourses to be 0.5 or less. This is good news for international investors.

Table 7–1 shows some examples. They range from a low of 0.12 (United States vs. Austria) to a high of 0.74 (United States vs. Canada).

Sixteen of the 22 correlation coefficients are less than 0.5. The link between the United States and Japan, for instance, is only 0.27. This information makes a compelling case for the risk-reducing benefit of international diversification.

Table 7-1
Correlations of Price Returns to U.S. Stock Market*

Australia	0.38	Malaysia	0.50
Austria	0.12	Mexico	0.15
Belgium	0.41	Netherlands	0.57
Canada	0.74	New Zealand	0.26
Denmark	0.32	Norway	0.46
France	0.47	Singapore	0.53
West Germany	0.33	South Africa	0.22
Hong Kong	0.31	Spain	0.37
Ireland	0.45	Sweden	0.39
Italy	0.26	Switzerland	0.52
Japan	0.27	United Kingdom	0.57

*In U.S. dollars, December 1981 to December 1992

Source: Goldman, Sachs & Co., based on the *FT-Actuaries World Indices* [TM/SM] jointly compiled by The Financial Times Limited, Goldman, Sachs & Co., and Country NatWest/Wood Mackenzie in conjunction with the Institute of Actuaries and the Faculty of Actuaries.

Of course, with the growing trend toward globalization dominated by multinational businesses, the economies of the world are becoming more closely linked and interdependent. This means that different markets will tend to exhibit higher correlations. But it might be a long time before the major markets move in sync with one another.

SPECIAL RISK CONSIDERATIONS

Even though international diversification can reduce volatility, investors still face certain dangers. These risks can be grouped into three broad categories:

1. *Country Risk.* This covers a variety of economic difficulties and political problems, including war and natural disasters such as

earthquakes. Country risk is relatively small in the United States but is very high in nations such as South Africa, with its racial tensions. Investors who concentrate in just one or a few markets heighten their exposure to country risk.

2. *Stock Market Risk.* Foreign markets generally are not as developed or as efficient as ours. Also, they are less well regulated and, of course, do not enjoy the protections of the United States Securities and Exchange Commission. Many overseas stocks are thinly traded and volatile. They often sell at excessively high price-earnings ratios, making them vulnerable if investor sentiment turns sour. Country and stock market risk often go hand in hand, especially in developing or emerging nations.

3. *Currency Risk.* If the United States dollar appreciates against the currency in which a foreign investment is denominated, your returns will be adversely affected. Conversely, a declining dollar will boost the value of foreign holdings, including international mutual funds.

The country and stock market risks can be considerable. To gain the benefits possible from international diversification, you should invest in at least a half dozen countries—which the typical foreign mutual fund does. But this same approach won't necessarily reduce your currency risk. As a result, international funds generally can't sidestep the danger of a strengthening dollar.

CURRENCY RISK

Yen, pound, franc, mark, peseta, peso, lira, and krona. Foreign-fund managers deal daily with these currencies and more. Stocks trading on overseas markets are usually purchased with the local money. Thus, a foreign security combines both an investment in a particular stock or bond and a currency speculation.

Simply put, currency risk can work for or against a United States investor in the following ways:

- If the dollar strengthens (the foreign currency weakens), the American incurs a loss.

- If the dollar weakens (the foreign currency strengthens), the American realizes a gain.

EXAMPLE: Suppose the exchange rate of French francs is 5 to the dollar, or 20 cents per franc, when you invest in a French security. Over the next year, the franc gains value to where it now trades at 4 to the dollar, or 25 cents each. Thus, the franc has appreciated 25 percent relative to the dollar. If the French stock rose, say, 20 percent during the year, the total return for a United States investor would be 50 percent.[2]

Table 7–2 illustrates the impact of currency risk for an American investing in a French security. As noted, currency fluctuations pose an additional danger. They can boost the return, as in cases 1 and 2; reduce it as in cases 4 and 5; or have little or no impact as in case 3.

Table 7-2
Impact of Currency on Total Returns

Case	Return on French Security	Return on French Franc	Total Return to U.S. Investor
(1) Gain on security and franc	+20%	+10%	+32%
(2) Breakeven on security; gain on franc	0	+10	+10
(3) Gain on security; breakeven on franc	+10	0	+10%
(4) Gain on security; loss on franc	+20	-10	+08
(5) Loss on security and franc	-20	-10	-28

Obviously, you can make a lot of money with foreign equities when the dollar depreciates. This happened in a pronounced manner in the mid- to late 1980s and was highly beneficial for United States investors holding overseas stock or bond funds. On the other hand, if the dollar rises, your foreign returns will be adversely affected.

It is difficult to predict short-term fluctuations in exchange rates. The long-term behavior reflects both political conditions and growth of a nation's economy. Strong, prosperous countries with a continuing balance of payments surplus and low inflation, coupled with fairly high interest rates, tend to have strong currencies.

Currency risk generally does not pose a significant problem for long-term investors using a well-diversified international mutual fund. That's because the favorable and unfavorable fluctuations should more or less balance out over time. Thus, currency changes are not the major component of long-run total return.

Hedging Currency Risk

Still, funds holding foreign stocks have the ability to reduce the threat posed by adverse currency fluctuations. They can hedge, or control an unwanted risk by initiating an offsetting position. To hedge, fund managers use currency options, futures, or so-called "forward contracts."

Of course, a hedge can also lower your return if the manager incorrectly anticipates the currency's move. Plus, there are expenses involved. That's why managers usually hedge their portfolios only to a limited extent, if at all. You can find out about a fund's hedging activities by studying its prospectus, asking your broker or calling the fund's customer representative.

FOREIGN-FUND CHOICES

The selection of non-United States portfolios has exploded in recent years. Whereas international investing was a rarity in the early 1980s, today all but the smallest fund companies offer something in this arena. The international sphere includes ample numbers of both open- and closed-end funds. These products fall into the following categories:

1. *Single-country funds:* Invest in companies domiciled in one nation, such as Germany, Japan, or Mexico. Most funds within this category are closed-end.

2. *Regional funds:* Invest within a major region, especially in Europe, Asia, and the Pacific Rim, or Latin America.

3. *International funds:* Typically can invest anywhere outside the United States. Most hold positions in a wide assortment of countries.

4. *Global funds:* Invest both stateside and abroad. The typical global portfolio commits more than half its assets to non-United States markets. But the flexibility to move into American stocks gives these funds an edge.

Some foreign portfolios offer a further degree of specialization. For example, they might focus on small international stocks or those in a specific sector, such as health care. Further, some foreign products are structured as index funds. In general, the fewer countries or sectors, the less diversification available.

Single-Country Funds

More then 40 closed-end portfolios confine themselves to a single market. The countries targeted appear in Table 7–3. By contrast, only a handful of funds in the open-end group narrow their focus in this manner. These few exceptions mainly target Japanese or Canadian stocks.

Table 7-3
Countries Targeted by Single-Country Funds

Argentina	India	Philippines
Austria	Indonesia	Portugal
Australia	Ireland	Singapore
Brazil	Israel	Spain
Canada	Italy	Switzerland
Chile	Japan	Taiwan
China	Korea	Thailand
France	Malaysia	Turkey
Germany	Mexico	United Kingdom

Why this difference? The closed-end format is essential for single-country funds that invest in emerging markets because of their high volatility and illiquidity. As noted previously, closed-end funds don't have to redeem shares, so they can retain assets even when their prices are gyrating strongly. By contrast, massive shareholder redemptions in an open-end portfolio could prove disastrous to the fund and might even hurt the stock market if it's a small one.

Single-country investments can be extremely risky. The volatility of a particular foreign market is amplified by the closed-end structure, which allows for large premiums and discounts. Because these portfolios trade like stocks, their share prices can—and invariably do—fluctuate much more widely than do their NAVs.

It's not uncommon to see one portfolio priced at, say, an 80 percent premium to NAV, while another trades at a 20 percent discount. The discounts and premiums on individual closed-end funds are listed every Monday in the Publicly Traded Funds box in *The Wall Street Journal*. They also appear weekly in *Barron's* and a few other newspapers.

To do well with single-country funds targeting smaller markets, you need to hold at least five or six of them to ensure adequate diversification. You also need to know when to buy and when to sell. High discounts may offer exceptional values, while large premiums invariably entail above-average risk.

The Japanese Stock Market

Japan provides a good case illustration of the benefits and risks of investing in a single country.

This nation was one of the first to attract U.S. investors. During much of the post-World War II period, it experienced remarkable economic development and vigorous growth. Japanese companies now represent nearly one quarter of the world's stock market value, ranking second behind the United States. Japan boasts more than 2,500 publicly traded companies and eight stock exchanges. Open-end funds investing in Japan are offered by Capstone, Fidelity, GT Capital, T. Rowe Price, and Scudder. Many other foreign stock portfolios—particularly Pacific Rim funds—focus heavily on Japan.

Investors who bought shares of the closed-end Japan Fund after it went public in 1962 and held on were richly rewarded. From that point through 1989, the compound annual return of the Japanese market was 22.4 percent, compared with 9.3 percent for United States stocks, according to data provided by Morgan Stanley Capital International.

The Japanese market can be highly volatile, though. The Nikkei Index of 225 stocks, which represent the cream of the Tokyo Stock Exchange, gained 29 percent in 1989. The Nikkei hit an all-time high of 38,916 on the last trading day of that year. But then, the index headed straight south. By the summer of 1992, the Nikkei had fallen more than 50 percent below its record high reached fewer than three years earlier. Even at this low level, global traders remained nervous about further declines. They felt the market was still overvalued in terms of its high P/E ratios, skimpy dividend yields, and dismal earnings outlook, coupled with rising business failures in Japan.

In August 1992, after the Nikkei had hit a six-year low of 14,309 (63 percent below its December 1989 peak), the market reacted favorably when the Japanese government announced plans to bolster the sagging economy and stock market. Within several weeks the Nikkei had rebounded more than 25 percent on this news. However, the economic problems were still there, and investors remained skittish.

The wide, unpredictable fluctuations of different markets, even a major one such as Japan's, underscore why you shouldn't concentrate your stock portfolio in a single country. The lesson here is to diversify your holdings across many nations to reduce risk.

Regional Funds

Most regional funds focus either on Europe or Asia and the Pacific Basin, although a few concentrate on Latin America. Investors buy these portfolios when they have an especially positive outlook on a certain area of the globe. For example, the "Europe 1992" integration theme has attracted considerable investor interest, as have the recent emergence of Latin American stocks and perennially high growth in Southeast Asia.

Because of their narrower regional focus, these portfolios can be expected to be more volatile than broadly diversified global or international funds. But the advantage of investing in a regional product over a group of single-country funds is that you have a professional manager making the allocation decisions for you. Assets can be shifted from a falling market to a rising one.

International Funds

These portfolios invest virtually all their assets in non-United States markets. The oldest such funds include Kleinwort Benson International Equity, Scudder International, and T. Rowe Price International. Because of their wider investment parameters, these products generally make a much better choice for the average person than does a single-country or even a regional fund.

One caveat, however: International portfolios often have a large share of assets allocated to Japan since Japan accounts for such a big slice of total world market capitalization. In comparing different international funds, pay special attention to the weighting given to Japan and make sure it suits your own preferences.

A fund's positioning in various countries such as Japan might reflect the manager's ability to think independently, as opposed to merely going along with the rest of the professional investment crowd. Independence is a trait often seen in the most successful managers. It is especially important in the international realm, which offers many more opportunities to be creative and add value.[3]

Global Funds

Global funds differ from international portfolios in that they also hold United States stocks or bonds. The details about where a fund invests can be determined by studying both its prospectus, which provides general guidelines, and a recent shareholder report, which will give a percentage breakdown of the portfolio, by country.

Global products differ widely in their exposure to U.S. investments. Some face restrictions on the proportion they can place in (or outside) the United States; others simply go after the best opportunities wherever they find them. Within the general guidelines specified in the prospectus, managers can typically shift assets between the United States and foreign nations depending on their outlook for the different markets, companies within these markets, and the dollar. Because of their broader approach, global funds might be best suited for someone just getting acquainted with international diversification.

But if you choose a global portfolio, recognize that you could be getting a large exposure to United States equities. Always check the percentage breakdowns, by country. It's important to know where the money is going.

Small Cap Funds

Because of illiquidity, the unavailability of information, and other problems, most foreign stock funds stick with the larger overseas corporations—ones that are easier to find, research, and follow. Yet smaller companies, whether in this country or elsewhere, often have above-average growth potential. Only a few foreign small-company funds have been around for more than a few years, but if their brief track records are any indication, you can expect some roller-coaster rides in the future. Still, the funds do invest in stocks and in markets with good potential—in many cases, better prospects than are available here. And because they do not move in sync with small United States stocks, they provide an added layer of diversification. Of course, a small-company global or international portfolio does not offer a complete investment program. Lean toward these products only if you have a multiyear outlook and a fairly aggressive appetite for risk.

CONCLUSION

About 60 percent of the market value of equities worldwide exists outside the United States. This creates many interesting investment opportunities across our borders. For various reasons, mutual funds are an excellent vehicle for smaller investors to gain exposure to foreign stock markets.

According to some common rules of thumb, between 10 percent and 40 percent of your holdings could be allocated to international equities for diversification purposes—but don't earmark more than you're comfortable with. Like stateside investments, foreign investments should be viewed as a long-term commitment. You can expect ample returns over time, but also plenty of volatility.

Be careful about single-country portfolios and regional funds that take big positions in a small number of countries. And, be aware that fluctuating premiums and discounts make closed-end portfolios riskier than open-end funds. The more limited a fund's diversification and the greater its risk, the more you need to analyze the investment. The movements of Japanese stocks over the past three decades illustrate the inherent risks and returns in the international arena.

Notes

1. Marc A. Zutty, controller, Smith New Court.

2. To calculate the United States investor's total return, express the percentage changes as decimals, add 1.0 to each, and multiply: $(1.25)(1.20) = 1.50$. Then subtract 1.0 from the product to get 0.50 or 50 percent.

3. Ken Gregory, "Traveling Overseas Via No-Load Mutual Funds," *AAII Journal*, October 1991, p. 25.

CHAPTER 8

How Fixed-Income Securities Work

Bond and money-market portfolios together make up the largest proportion of the mutual fund business, accounting for nearly three quarters of industry assets. These two groups have grown rapidly since 1980, paralleling the expansion of the fixed-income market. Innovative types of securities have been unveiled in recent years, especially in the mortgage-backed category. These introductions have resulted in the wide assortment of fixed-income portfolios that are available today. Lipper Analytical Services tracks about 70 major categories of bond and money-market funds.

When measured by total value, the domestic fixed-income market dwarfs the stock market by a wide margin. Much of the buying and selling activity involves blocks of $1 million or more traded by professionals, including fund managers. Generally speaking, a $500,000 transaction is considered the minimum "round lot" in the institutional bond market.

Money-market securities refer to short-term debt instruments including Treasury bills, commercial paper, repurchase agreements, certificates of deposit, and Eurodollars. Money-market instruments mature in one year or less. Repurchase agreements often come due the next business day.

The fixed-income capital market, popularly known as the bond market, is the place for longer-term securities. It can be separated into six general segments:

1. Corporate debt

2. U.S. Treasury securities

3. Federal agency debt

4. Mortgage-backed securities

5. Tax-exempt bonds

6. Foreign debt

Our major focus will be on the capital markets and the many categories of bond funds. The simpler, more homogeneous money-market portfolios, which function mainly as a parking place for cash, do not require nearly as much attention.

WHY INVEST IN FIXED-INCOME SECURITIES?

Common stocks provide much better long-run returns than fixed-income investments. So why bother with them? Three primary reasons are *liquidity*, *capital preservation*, and *income*. These attributes of bonds and bond funds give them certain advantages over stock investments.

1. *Liquidity*. Few people would want a portfolio made up exclusively of stocks. It wouldn't make sense to buy and sell equities all the time to meet short-term cash requirements. Money-market funds can meet these liquidity needs. They provide a cash reserve to handle emergencies or take advantage of attractive investment opportunities. Bond funds with shorter portfolio maturities also offer liquidity. Money required within the reasonably near future

could be invested in a short-term bond portfolio to minimize risk yet provide higher yields than available on money markets.

2. *Capital Preservation.* Bond funds generally fluctuate less than stock investments. The shorter the average term to maturity, the more stable the price. Capital preservation goes hand in hand with liquidity. Of course, some fixed-income products can be pretty volatile, as individuals who held junk-bond funds during 1989 or 1990 well know.

3. *Income.* Debt securities generally offer higher, more dependable income than stock portfolios. Municipal-bond funds pay yields that are partly or wholly tax-exempt. They have grown considerably in importance in recent years as a means to shelter income from Uncle Sam.

Bond fund investors must choose between liquidity and capital preservation, on the one hand, and income on the other. The highest-yielding bonds are usually the riskiest and thus should not be relied on for safety or ready money.

To put the role of bond funds into perspective, it helps to think in terms of the familiar investment pyramid. The lowest-risk investments form the pyramid's base or foundation, indicating that this is where you place the majority of your money. Liquidity and capital preservation are essential prerequisites for these foundation holdings.

But despite their relative price consistency (compared to stocks), both bonds and bond funds can be confusing. To understand how these investments work, you need a general knowledge of the fixed-income market and the factors that cause prices and yields to fluctuate.

BOND CHARACTERISTICS

Bonds have different features from stocks—at least a dozen unshared attributes. Their major characteristics can be summarized as follows:

1. A bond is a contractual commitment between issuer and investor. The *bond indenture,* a disclosure document, spells out the terms of the contract.

2. Corporate and municipal bonds (but not federal government securities) have credit risks of varying degrees. The creditworthiness of an issue is judged by independent rating agencies.

3. Bonds have a par value (also known as the face or maturity amount). It is commonly $1,000 for corporates and $5,000 for municipals. Bonds that trade below par are said to be selling at a *discount*; those priced above par trade at a *premium*.

4. Most bonds pay periodic interest, which is generally fixed and expressed as a "coupon" rate. Payments are typically made semi-annually. An 8 percent coupon bond with a $1,000 face value would pay $40 in interest every six months. In contrast, *zero coupon bonds* do not pay interest until redemption; instead, they're sold at a discount to their maturity value.

5. Bonds mature on a specific date. At redemption, the bond-holder receives a principal payment equal to the security's face value.

6. Mortgage-backed securities, such as Ginnie Maes, differ from other types of bonds. They pay both principal and interest monthly, as they are self-liquidating. They do not have a specific maturity date. That's because prepayments by mortgage holders, which cannot be forecast precisely, will shorten an issue's life.

7. Bonds are generally "callable" prior to maturity. This means the issuer may choose to redeem some outstanding securities if interest rates have fallen sufficiently. In essence, this allows the issuer to replace expensive debt with bonds bearing lower interest. But investors would have to reinvest the proceeds at lower, currently prevailing rates.

8. Bond yields move in the opposite direction of prices. This can best be illustrated in terms of *current yield,* which is defined as the annual interest payment divided by the bond's price. If an 8 percent coupon bond sells for $1,000, its current yield would be 8 percent. But assuming the price falls to $920, the yield rises to 8.7 percent (80/920). An increase to $1,080 would lower the yield to about 7.4 percent (80/1,080).

9. Bond prices vary inversely with market interest rates. Rising rates depress prices, while lower rates spark rallies. This is the flip side

of the inverse relationship of yield to price. If interest rates increase, for example, yields on outstanding bond issues must move up (and their prices fall) to be competitive with rates paid by new issues of comparable bonds.

10. The longer the time to maturity, other things being equal, the greater the percentage change in a bond's price for a given move in interest rates. More on this later.

11. Bonds with longer maturities and/or lower ratings carry bigger risks. Riskier debt securities *promise* higher returns but may not *deliver* them.

12. Short-term yields fluctuate more than yields on long-term debt. For example, rates paid by money funds have historically ranged from under 3 percent to over 18 percent. This is evident when one studies the behavior of the yield curve over the years.

THE YIELD CURVE

This analytical tool shows graphically how yields vary for different maturities of bonds. You can gauge the level and shape of the curve daily by looking at the Treasury bills, notes, and bonds column in *The Wall Street Journal* (part C) or by examining a chart in *Investor's Business Daily* newspaper. The yield curve can assume one of three general forms.

1. *Upward Sloping.* This is the usual pattern, indicating longer-term bonds are paying higher rates. For example, if Treasury bills yield on average 6 percent; notes, 8 percent; and bonds, 10 percent; the curve is positively sloped. This is illustrated in Figure 8-1, Panel A. If the curve slopes sharply upward, investors in general expect rates to rise.

2. *Flat.* If bills, notes, and bonds all were paying about the same rate on average, the yield curve would be flat or horizontal.

3. *Inverted.* Occasionally, the curve is inverted or negatively sloped (Panel C). This means payments on bills exceed those on notes which, in turn, exceed those on bonds.

The flat and inverted patterns exist when rates are relatively high and investors expect them to come down. Usually the yield curve slopes up-

Figure 8-1
Yield Curve Patterns

A upward sloping
B flat
C downward sloping

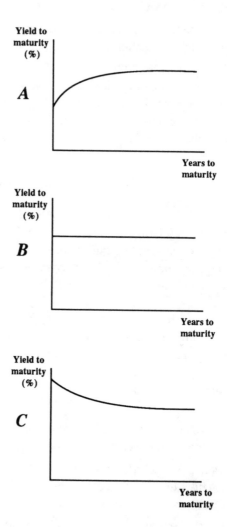

ward, which shows that longer-term bonds generally yield more than shorter-term instruments. Longer-term bonds normally should yield more since they have a greater exposure to adverse price fluctuations. In addition, the risk of default is somewhat higher with corporates and municipals since there is more time for the issuer to get into trouble.

The level and shape of the curve also may reveal where "yield-sensitive" investors are likely to be moving their money. As short-term rates fall and the curve slopes upward, you can expect investors to go "further out" into longer-term bonds. Usually, there will be a place where the curve is particularly steep, which might offer a good opportunity to pick up some extra income without incurring much additional risk. When short rates rise to where the yield curve becomes inverted, investors move out of bonds and into money-market funds.

A BRIEF INTEREST-RATE HISTORY

When investing in bonds or bond funds, it pays to know something about the past. Yields on different kinds of bonds have tended to follow the same trends over long periods. The following themes have characterized roughly the last six decades of market activity:

- Long-term bonds had low yields from the mid-1930s to the mid-1950s. For a good portion of this period, they paid less than 3 percent. This was an era of very low inflation, sometimes approaching 0 percent.

- Starting in the mid-1950s, interest rates began a long, gradual climb that accompanied an upward drift in inflation. In the early 1970s, inflation began to accelerate, but bondholders didn't anticipate the increasingly bad news that was in store. Interest rates finally surged in the late 1970s and early 1980s in tandem with what seemed like "runaway" inflation. The rising rates caused havoc with bond and stock prices. Long-term yields on quality bonds peaked at over 15 percent in 1982.

- Interest rates began to fall substantially in 1982, accompanying similar declines in the rate of inflation. Long-term yields fell below 10 percent in 1985 and have remained at or below that threshold in recent years. This trend greatly benefited both the bond and the stock markets.

BONDHOLDER RISKS

Bonds are generally less volatile than stocks, although they can still get hit hard during periods of higher inflation. They also carry a variety of other dangers, including some subtle ones that might catch the uninitiated off guard.

The following 11 risk factors can affect bond-fund investors as well as people holding individual bonds. Portfolio managers can minimize some, but not all, of these dangers.

1. *Interest Rate (or Market) Risk.* When rates rise, bond prices fall. The longer the maturity and the lower the coupon rate, the greater the vulnerability.

2. *Credit Risk.* This reflects the possibility that the issuer will not make promised interest and principal payments on time or in full. Treasury securities are perceived to have no credit risk. The risk with corporate and municipal bonds varies inversely with their quality ratings.

3. *Purchasing-Power Risk.* Inflation erodes the value of fixed returns. People who stash a large portion of their long-term wealth in debt securities face substantial purchasing-power risk, though they might not realize it.

4. *Reinvestment Risk.* When interest rates fall, so do the rates at which bond interest payments can be reinvested. This reduces bondholders' realized yields, since they will be earning less "interest on their interest." Zero-coupon bonds don't make periodic interest payments and thus don't have any reinvestment risk.

5. *Rollover Risk.* When interest rates decline, cash received from maturing fixed-income securities must be reinvested by the fund manager at lower yields. This is a major threat with money-market funds, which hold short-term debt that must be rolled over frequently.

6. *Call Risk.* This reflects the danger that a bond might be called or forcibly redeemed during a period of declining interest rates. Those who see their high-yielding investments called will likely have to reinvest the proceeds in obligations that pay less. Fund managers can reduce this risk by holding issues with longer periods of call protection.

7. *Prepayment Risk.* If mortgage rates fall sufficiently, homeowners will refinance. This affects mortgage-backed securities, such as Ginnie Maes, because refinancings will shorten the lives of these securities and consequently reduce the total interest paid by them. Ginnie Mae investors would also have to reinvest their money at lower rates.

8. *Currency Risk.* This affects anyone who invests in global or international bond funds. When the dollar strengthens relative to the foreign currencies in which the bonds are denominated, the values of the funds decline.

9. *Liquidity Risk.* Thinly traded securities, including many municipal bonds, carry this danger of not being easily salable. It means the fund manager may have to take a big hit in price if he or she must quickly unload an illiquid bond. This can also be a problem for junk-bond funds.

10. *Event Risk.* This reflects the chance that a leveraged buyout, takeover, or other recapitalization would materially weaken the claims of existing bondholders, sometimes to the benefit of stockholders. A classic example was the buyout of RJR Nabisco. The company's bond prices declined after its creditworthiness was downgraded to reflect a higher debt load.

11. *Tax Law Risk.* Congressional changes in tax laws can affect the prices of municipal bonds, either in a favorable or an unfavorable way. If personal income-tax rates drop significantly, muni bonds become less valuable. Their prices will fall to the point at which their yields are in line with the new tax structure. The reverse happens when tax rates rise.

Different kinds of fixed-income funds are subject to the range of risks in varying degrees. Here are a few illustrations:

- A money-market portfolio holding U.S. Treasury bills would have no interest rate or credit risk, but it would subject shareholders to rollover risk during a period of declining rates. It would also expose them to purchasing-power erosion over the long term.

- A junk-bond fund would subject investors to both credit and liquidity risk, especially during recessions, when some marginal issuers might fail. Interest-rate risk, on the other hand, would generally be less of a problem since high-yield bonds aren't very sensitive to rate changes.

- A long-term U.S. government fund with a big position in 30-year Treasuries would be vulnerable to a high degree of interest-rate risk. But there would be no credit risk and virtually no call dangers. Depending on the issue, Treasuries are either not callable or callable only during the last five years of their lives.

MORE ON INTEREST-RATE RISK

When rates rise, prices of longer-term bonds fall more dramatically. Table 8-1 displays the percentage change in price of an 8 percent coupon bond when interest rates rise and fall by one percentage point. For instance, when rates increase by one point, the 30-year bond falls 10.32 percent. This decline more than offsets the 8 percent interest income earned by the bondholder, resulting in a negative total return. If rates fall, on the other hand, the investor benefits from appreciation. The longer the maturity, the greater the potential for capital gains as well.

Table 8-1
Price Volatility Varies Directly with Maturity

	Bond Price Changes*	
Maturity in Years	Rates *Increase* 1 Percentage Pt.	Rates *Decrease* 1 Percentage Pt.
1	-0.94%	+0.95%
3	-2.58	+2.66
5	-3.96	+4.16
10	-6.50	+7.11
20	-9.20	+10.68
30	-10.32	+12.47

*Assumes an 8% coupon bond initially priced at par.

Portfolio Duration

Time to maturity is not the only determinant of a bond's interest-rate risk. The size of its coupon also plays a role. For any given maturity, the lower the coupon payment, the greater the volatility. Thus, zero-coupon bonds (and funds) are highly interest-rate sensitive.

Fund managers measure volatility by the bond's *duration*, a term you may come across. The idea behind duration is that bondholders recoup their investments little by little through the periodic receipt of interest payments and from the eventual repayment of principal. The longer this takes, the longer the duration and the more price-sensitive the bond or portfolio is to rate changes.

Here's a somewhat more technical definition:

Duration: A measure of the average lifetime of a bond, where the period of each coupon or principal payment is weighted by a number that reflects the "importance" of that period's payment relative to the total value of the bond. Thus, duration increases with time to maturity. In addition, for a given maturity, the *lower* the coupon payments the *higher* the bond's average lifetime or duration.

Duration is calculated with a formula incorporating the bond's coupon, its time to maturity, and its current price. The duration for a coupon-bearing security is less than its time to maturity. For example, the duration of an 8 percent bond maturing in 30 years and selling at par is a little more than 12 years. In contrast, the duration for a 30-year zero-coupon bond is 30, its time to maturity. Duration numbers ranging from about 8 to 12 are considered high; those above 12 are very high. At the other extreme, money-market funds, which have virtually no interest-rate risk, have durations near zero.

Bond funds sometimes report an average portfolio duration, but they're not as widely available as average portfolio maturities. Services that track mutual funds generally don't provide duration information. If the shareholder report does not list this number, you should be able to get it by contacting the fund company. For most purposes, the average maturity of a bond portfolio is an adequate risk indicator.

Interest-Rate Risk Also Affects Stocks

Like bonds, stocks rise and fall according to interest-rate swings. Both types of securities compete for investor dollars, so when rates rise, people move from equities into the fixed-income arena to capture the higher, more secure yields. Stock prices decline as investors sell out.

The impact can be readily seen on utility stocks, which pay relatively high dividend yields. During a period of rising rates, utility prices will tend to fall as investors sell. The lower prices would result in higher dividend yields, bringing the shares in line with the prevailing financial conditions.

EXAMPLE: A utility stock pays a dividend of $4 a year and sells at $50, for a yield of 8 percent (4/50). But suppose interest rates rise to the point where the stock has to yield 10 percent to attract investors. The price would have to fall to $40.

In addition, rising interest rates mean higher corporate borrowing costs, which erode profit margins, further depressing stock prices.

CREDIT RISK

Default danger affects corporate and municipal bonds. Since a bond is basically an IOU, investors must assess the likelihood that the issuer will live up to its promises. The credit risk of an obligation can be gauged by examining its rating. Bond funds discuss credit risk in detail in their prospectuses. They also indicate the amount of credit risk of all bonds held by listing their ratings in the annual and semiannual reports to shareholders.

Moody's Investors Service and Standard & Poor's Corp. are the two best known of the various independent rating agencies. A grade represents the agency's assessment of the issuer's ability to pay principal and interest on time and in full. The agencies consider factors such as the issuer's general financial health and ability to generate enough profits to make bond payments. They also examine provisions in the bond's indenture that might affect the security offered.

In a broad sense, bonds fall into two general quality categories: investment grade and speculative. And within each main group there are a number of gradations.

Investment-grade securities carry any of the top four ratings of Moody's and S&P's. For example, the S&P ratings are AAA, AA, A, and BBB. Nonrated bonds might also fall within this category provided they are judged to be of investment-grade caliber based on an analysis performed by the fund manager. Rating agencies may modify a letter grade to indicate finer quality distinctions. For instance, S&P alters its ratings with a plus or minus sign, so a bond rated A+ would outrank a simple A.

Within the investment-grade category, the triple-A and double-A designations represent *high grade* issues. So-called "gilt edge" corporate or municipal bonds, rated triple-A, offer the most creditworthiness, although they would still carry a slight amount of default risk compared to Treasuries, which have none. Single-A and triple-B bonds are designated *medium grade* issues. There is always the chance that a bond's rating could be lowered if the issuer's financial condition deteriorates; this would result in a lower price for the security. On the other hand, a bond might also see its rating upgraded.

Speculative issues are those below triple-B, again, with various gradations. The lower the rating, the greater the risk. Debt securities rated double-B or lower are known pejoratively as junk bonds. Convertible bonds generally carry ratings below investment grade, too. The ratings assigned by Moody's range as low as single-C; those of S&P drop to single-D. Issues with the lowest grades are probably in default. As explained previously, the most important advantage of a mutual fund is the built-in diversification it offers. An individual who buys a single bond would need to be very concerned about credit risk. But this is not nearly as big a problem for a portfolio of bonds. By holding 50, 100, or more issues, the fund manager can reduce the overall default danger.

It's worth noting that managers won't always accept agency ratings at face value. They will often dig into the company's financial statements and make their own assessment. The manager's expertise is especially important with a junk-bond portfolio, or when dealing with a significant number of smaller, nonrated issues. Some of these securities can represent good values for the astute professional.

In analyzing the credit risk of a bond portfolio, you should consider its proportionate breakdown in the different letter-grade categories and the fund's average rating. For high-yield funds, this analysis is especially important. Be sure to check what percentage of the bonds carry ratings below triple-B. A percentage breakdown by credit quality can be found in the fund's prospectus or in the profiles compiled by *Morningstar Mutual Funds*.

PURCHASING-POWER RISK

Consider the following facts:

- At 4 percent inflation, $1 would lose nearly one third of its value in 10 years.

- At 4 percent inflation, that same dollar would lose over half its purchasing power in 20 years.

- At 5 percent inflation, you would need $105,600 in 40 years to buy a Toyota now costing $15,000.

The numbers in Table 8-2 show the purchasing-power erosion of $1 at different inflation rates for several periods. For example, at inflation of 4 percent annually $1 today will depreciate to 21 cents 40 years from now. If inflation runs at 6 percent, the 21 cents becomes 10 cents. The higher the inflation and the longer the period, the greater the bite.

Table 8-2
Future Purchasing Power of $1

Inflation Rate	Years in Future			
	5	10	20	40
4%	$.82	$.68	$.46	$.21
5	.78	.61	.38	.14
6	.75	.56	.31	.10
8	.68	.46	.21	.05
10	.62	.39	.15	.02

The Real Return Is What Counts

What you earn on a fixed-income security or portfolio after inflation has been stripped away is called the *real rate* of return. This simply reflects the growth in your wealth in the absence of any inflation.

Nominal (or observed) fixed-income yields normally contain a built-in *inflation premium*, which varies with the bond market's consensus expectation for inflation at the time. The higher the consensus forecast, the higher the level of interest rates in general. Changes in the inflation outlook lead to fluctuations in nominal or observed yields.

Suppose the one-year T-bill yield is 6 percent. If the consensus anticipates inflation of 4 percent for the next 12 months, one could expect to earn a real rate of about 2 percent. If inflation estimates increase, T-bill rates should rise correspondingly. The same holds for other fixed-income securities.

Suppose, however, that an investor purchased the one-year T-bill yielding 6 percent, but, to the surprise of many, inflation turned out to be 6 percent for the year. The real return would be zero. You can see from this illustration that a major risk faced by bondholders is that inflation-adjusted rates may be too low because *investors can underestimate future inflation.* This could lead to extremely low or even negative real returns.

The discussion on nominal and real returns can be summarized as follows:

- The higher the real return, the better the actual performance, regardless of the level of nominal yields.

- Bondholders get hurt when they underestimate future inflation and yields turn out to have been insufficient.

- Bond funds become more attractive when their probable real rates appear generous. This would be a good time to increase your stake in these investments.

THE BONDHOLDER'S TOTAL RETURN

The total return earned on an investment during a year equals its income plus any price gains (or minus any losses). For multiyear periods, the interest earned on the reinvested interest exerts a big influence on the total return. Bondholders who don't understand this may be doing worse than they think. The following illustration demonstrates why this compounding effect is so important.

EXAMPLE: You buy a 10 percent coupon bond at par, or $1,000. The bond pays annual interest and matures in 25 years. You hold it to maturity. Would you realize a 10 percent *yield to maturity*? (This is the true compound rate of return that professionals focus on.) The answer depends on what you do with the interest payments, which total $2,500 over the 25 years ($100 per year × 25).

If you spent your interest checks when received, your yield to maturity would not even be close to 10 percent. It would be a paltry 5.14 percent.

Instead, suppose you reinvested in a passbook account at 4 percent. You would accumulate $4,164.59 in interest, but your realized yield to maturity would still be only 6.79 percent.

To get the full 10 percent yield to maturity, you would have to reinvest each payment at 10 percent. The accumulated interest would amount to $9,834.71.

Thus, even when you buy an individual bond, you can't always tell what you will be earning. The important point to remember is that interest on interest—compounding—is a powerful concept. The longer you hold onto a bond or bond fund, the more significant it becomes. By reinvesting interest payments (or mutual fund distributions), you will realize a better return.

It's easier for most individuals to reinvest income at favorable rates through bond funds. Why? Because the funds will credit you with fractional-share purchases, even on small dividends, usually without charging any loads or commissions. Try making a $20 or $100 or even $700 investment in an individual bond.

INTEREST-RATE FORECASTS

You could generate a fortune in the bond market by making accurate interest-rate predictions even most of the time. What's the track record of professional rate forecasters? Mediocre at best. Rate movements depend on changes in economic conditions, especially inflation. It's very difficult to make such predictions consistently, since there are too many unknowable factors.

The best strategy for most investors is simply to use bond funds to meet liquidity, preservation of capital, and income needs. Don't expect to build a fortune in the bond market by forecasting interest rates. For amassing wealth, stock portfolios provide much better opportunities.

Nevertheless, astute investors can generate slightly better than market results by reading the economic tea leaves and adjusting their portfolios accordingly. The manager of a bond fund may lengthen the maturity a bit when he or she expects rates to fall and shorten when rates appear likely to rise. But the fund will maintain a multiyear focus throughout—it's just that at times it will have a longer average maturity than normal. Some bond funds—the so-called "flexible" portfolios—enjoy considerably more leeway to alter maturities than others.

YIELD SPREADS

We've already talked about inefficiencies in the stock market. Such opportunities also exist in the bond arena, and it's the goal of good managers to take advantage of them.

One way they do this is by monitoring *yield spreads*. These are yield differences between individual bonds or bond portfolios. (Don't confuse this with the difference between the bid and asked in a bond's quotation—also called the "spread.")

For example, suppose a portfolio of triple-A corporates yields 8 percent, while double-B corporates yield 10 percent. The spread is two percentage points or 200 basis points. (Each basis point equals 1/100 of a percentage point.)

There are several categories of yield differentials:

Maturity Spreads: As noted earlier, the yield curve normally slopes upward, which means longer-term bonds typically pay more than shorter-term issues. The maturity spread reflects the fact that longer-term issues are exposed to greater interest-rate risk.

Quality Spreads: These refer to differences in yield among bonds with varying degrees of creditworthiness. For example, during a deepening recession investors get nervous and you see a "flight to quality." The spread between, say, triple-A and double-B corporates widens as people shift their money from the latter to the former. When the economy is healthy, you would expect to see a much narrower differential.

Segment Spreads: These help to compare issues in the bond-market segments—Treasuries, agencies, corporates, and municipals. They tend to expand and contract as sectors go in and out of favor. For example, you could expect to see the spread between Treasuries and corporates narrow during good times and widen during bad.

Spreads Between Newly Issued and Seasoned Bonds: Here the comparison would be between yields on the same type of bonds, with the only difference that some are new and others old. The new bonds might have higher or lower coupons than the outstanding securities, depending on how interest rates have behaved in the interim.

Many other illustrations could be provided. The point is that yield spreads change over time, and perceptive portfolio managers can profit from these changes. Abnormally wide or narrow differentials spell opportunity. For instance, during the worst of the 1989–1990 bear market in junk bonds, the gap between junk and high-grade corporates exceeded 10 percentage points. This was followed by a strong rally in the junk market in

1991 and 1992. A profit results when an abnormal spread returns to normal. Astute fund managers can exploit these opportunities.

BOND FUNDS VERSUS INDIVIDUAL BONDS

The fact that bond-fund assets have surged so much in recent years underscores their popularity. But many fund investors probably don't realize that what they own doesn't behave exactly like an individual bond. A mutual fund is, after all, a managed portfolio. It has certain important differences from an individual debt security.

1. Unlike a bond, the typical fund has no maturity. The manager buys and sells on an ongoing basis, generating trading profits and losses and changes in the portfolio's yield.

2. It can be argued that the rate of return on a fund is considerably more difficult to predict than that of an individual issue bought and held to maturity.

3. The fund's dividends are not fixed like the interest on a bond. The income could rise or fall with changing interest rates, or with different cash flows as investors enter or exit the portfolio.

This third point deserves elaboration. During a period of falling rates, your bond-fund dividend could be cut. This may be disturbing to some investors but it's generally nothing to worry about because you will also be benefiting from appreciation. Income dividends are only part of the total-return equation.

Disadvantages of Bond Funds

From this brief discussion, it should be apparent that individual bonds enjoy an edge over managed portfolios in certain respects. Bond-fund disadvantages include the following:

1. *Expenses Reduce Returns*: The management fees and other costs to operate a fund can significantly lower your results.

2. *Extensive Diversification May Be Unnecessary*: You don't really need that many different bonds to be well-diversified, assuming

you stick with top-quality issues such as Treasury notes and bonds, agency securities, or high-grade munis or corporates.

3. *More Predictable Results*: As noted, you can anticipate more reliable returns with the right individual bonds compared to the typical, changing fixed-income portfolio.

Advantages of Bond Funds

Still, for many people, the fund route is the way to go. Smaller investors, in particular, will enjoy several advantages with a packaged portfolio compared to individual holdings. These benefits include the following:

1. *Easy Access*: It is often difficult and expensive for smaller investors to deal directly in the bond markets, which are oriented toward professionals. Transaction costs are higher and liquidity is lower for people buying and selling in relatively modest amounts. To be successful at bond investing, you need to shop around among different dealers for the best prices.

2. *Liquidity*: It is easier to take your money out of a fund without adverse price consequences than to sell thinly traded bonds prior to maturity. This especially applies to less-liquid high-yield corporate debt and many municipal issues. The dealer's spread may be quite wide when it comes time to sell.

3. *Monthly Income*: Bond funds generally declare dividends monthly. Conversely, individual bonds usually pay interest semiannually. Retirees looking to their investments for supplemental income especially might appreciate the monthly distributions.

4. *Ease of Reinvestment*: Bond funds offer convenient reinvestment of dividends and capital-gains distributions, even for small dollar amounts. This allows for more efficient compounding, which can lead to higher returns over time.

5. *Professional Management*: Fluctuating interest rates and other factors make a buy-and-hold bond strategy perilous. Better returns often result from an actively managed portfolio. Good managers can react to opportunities in the fixed-income market and enhance performance. They can also unload lower-quality issues

when their risks increase to unacceptable levels. For these reasons, bond funds often make more sense than individual holdings.

6. *Diversification:* Since a mutual fund holds dozens if not hundreds of bonds, it exposes shareholders to far less credit risk than would be assumed by taking positions in one or a few issues. This aspect can be especially important to investors of limited means.

CHAPTER 9

Taxable Bond Funds

It's not enough to simply classify bond funds into the two basic groups of taxable and non-taxable. Within this huge universe, individual portfolios differ greatly in terms of the kind of securities they hold, their risks, and potential returns.

The individual fund groupings generally relate to the manner bonds themselves are categorized. Fixed-income securities can be classified in four ways.

1. *By term to maturity.* Short-term bonds come due in 1 to 3 years, intermediate term in 3 to 10 years, and long-term issues in more than 10 years.

2. *By type.* Major classifications here include coupon bonds, zero-coupons, mortgage-backed issues, and foreign bonds.

3. *By quality.* Default-free Treasuries top the list, followed by gilt-edge corporates and insured munis, then medium-grade corporates and munis, and finally speculative corporates and munis.

4. *By taxability.* Interest on municipals is tax-exempt at the federal level and may also be at the state level. Interest paid on Treasuries generally avoids taxation by state and local governments.

Of the four groupings, bonds (and bond funds) are most generally distinguished by their taxability. This chapter focuses on taxable bond funds, and Chapter 10 examines the tax-exempt portfolios. There are, however, significant differences among funds within each of these two basic classifications. This is evident in Figure 9–1, which provides a brief description of the 12 bond-fund categories used in this book.

Figure 9–1 Fixed-Income Fund Categories

TAXABLE PORTFOLIOS

U.S. Government Bond Funds:
Invest primarily in U.S. Treasury and agency securities. May emphasize short-, intermediate-, or long-term issues.

Target-Maturity Funds:
Invest mainly in zero-coupon obligations maturing in a specific year. Like bonds, they promise a specific maturity value.

Mortgage-Backed Securities Funds:
Invest primarily in the various mortgage-backed bonds such as Ginnie Maes. Some, called ARM funds, focus on adjustable-rate mortgages.

High-Quality Corporate-Bond Funds:
Generally restrict holdings to issues rated single-A or better. May also own Treasury securities.

Corporate-Bond Funds:
Hold investment-grade corporate debt, which is rated triple-B or higher. Treasury securities may also be held. May emphasize short-, intermediate-, or long-term bonds.

High-Yield Corporate-Bond Funds:
Invest primarily in lower-rated, higher-yielding corporates known as "junk bonds."

Global-Bond Funds:
Invest in government and corporate debt denominated in foreign currencies, perhaps with U.S. securities included. Some emphasize short maturities, others focus on longer-term bonds.

Flexible-Bond Funds:
Can invest in a variety of bonds and can alter the mix. The manager does not face restrictions on quality or maturity. These funds are also known as "mixed" portfolios.

TAX-EXEMPT PORTFOLIOS

National Municipal-Bond Funds:
Invest in bonds from a number of different states, perhaps with a focus by type of issuer, quality or maturity. May emphasize short-, intermediate-, or long-term obligations.

Single-State Municipal-Bond Funds:
Hold the bonds of one state so as to provide its residents with income exempt from both state and federal taxes.

Insured Municipal-Bond Funds:
Hold bonds guaranteed by an independent insurance consortium. Available in both national and single-state versions.

High-Yield Municipal-Bond Funds:
Invest in munis with lower ratings and higher yields.

U.S. GOVERNMENT BOND FUNDS

The market in federal government debt is far and away the largest securities market in the world. U.S. Treasuries (which are issued by Washington to raise huge sums of money) are the staple of government portfolios. In fact, the Securities and Exchange Commission requires that these funds *normally* invest at least 65 percent of their assets in bonds issued or backed by the federal government. (The 65 percent threshold also applies to other bond and stock categories where a fund's name implies that it focuses on a particular type of security. Municipal-bond and money-market funds are subject to an even higher percentage.)

Treasuries come in three forms: as bills (maturing in 1 year or less), notes (1 to 10 years) and bonds (10 to 30 years). Both the notes and bonds are coupon-bearing. Treasury bonds, as noted previously, are either non-callable or callable only during the last five years of their lives.

There are also zero-coupon Treasuries known as "strips." The acronym stands for Separate Trading of Registered Interest and Principal of Securities. Strips are derived from Treasury notes and bonds by separating them into interest and principal components. Each individual payment effectively becomes a zero-coupon issue. For example, a 30-year Treasury would have 60 semiannual coupon payments and one principal payment.

Besides Treasuries, the U.S. government funds include agency and mortgage-backed securities. As the name implies, agency securities are issued by various federal organizations, such as the Government National Mortgage Association and the Tennessee Valley Authority, to finance their activities.

When evaluating a government-bond fund, examine the average maturity and how the portfolio is structured. Find out how the manager tends to invest any money that's not held in U.S. governments. As noted, SEC regulations allow managers to invest up to 35 percent of the portfolio in other securities.

Government bond funds offer investors a break since state and local governments generally do not tax income earned on Treasuries. This exemption is not trivial if your state has a high tax rate.

Option Writing Doesn't Always Pay

Some of the longer-term government funds sell options against the bonds they hold to derive additional income. This yield-enhancement strategy works fine during periods of stable interest rates. But it cuts off appreciation when rates fall (and prices rise) since holders of the options would exercise their right to buy the bonds from the fund at below-market prices.

TARGET-MATURITY FUNDS

If you are looking for a fund that will make a fixed principal payment on a specific date, like an individual bond, target-maturity portfolios may be the answer. The funds in this small group pay no income until maturity because they hold zero coupons coming due in the same year, say 2015. As the zeros mature in the appropriate year, the proceeds go into short-term U.S. Treasuries that are held until the investors are paid off toward year-end.

To produce a competitive return, long-term zeros have to sell at prices substantially lower than their maturity values. That is, they trade at deep discounts. Suppose a zero comes due in 30 years for $1,000. If it yields 8 percent to maturity (reflecting comparable bond-market rates) it would now trade just under $100. The price will gradually appreciate over the years as the maturity date gets closer.

Because they pay no periodic interest, zeros are highly volatile, as explained in Chapter 8 in the section on portfolio duration. The longer the time to maturity (or duration), the greater the fluctuations. This makes zeros highly sensitive to changes in interest rates. Suppose long-term rates rise by one percentage point. The 30-year zero referred to would tumble about 24 percent in price. Conversely, if rates fall by one percentage point, that bond would appreciate 32 percent.

Despite this volatility, if zeros are held to maturity, you can earn a predictable return. Zero holders face no reinvestment risk, since there are no periodic payments to be reinvested.

Like the price of a zero-coupon bond, the NAV of a target fund will gradually increase over time—although it might experience extreme ups and downs along the way. One fund's prospectus encourages investors to hold their shares until the portfolio's target-maturity year to reduce the interest-rate risk. As noted, these investments will liquidate when the zeros mature. Benham and Scudder, among a handful of other families, offer target-maturity portfolios.

Why Invest in a Target Fund?

Since strips are Treasury securities, they have no default risk. And the absence of reinvestment risk offers another major advantage, especially during times of falling interest rates.

Even though zero-coupon bonds pay no interest, the IRS still requires investors to pay taxes based on an "imputed" interest each year. The same applies to people investing in target-maturity funds, which make no cash distributions. You can avoid this problem if you hold a zero or target-maturity portfolio within a tax-deferred retirement plan, such as an IRA.

What kind of people use target-maturity funds? On the one hand, they make sense for conservative long-term investors who expect they will need the money for a specific purpose at a certain time, such as to help finance retirement or a child's college education. On the other hand, zeros appeal to aggressive individuals who like to trade actively based on interest-rate forecasts.

Before you purchase shares of a target fund, determine its expected growth rate. This number should be available from the fund. It is the compound annual return you could expect to earn if you hold the shares to maturity. In periods of low interest rates, these portfolios can make poor investments since their NAVs will be higher, their discounts smaller and their expected growth rates lower. The reverse holds true when rates are abnormally high.

MORTGAGE-BACKED BONDS

This fund category traces its roots to 1970, when mortgage-backed obligations were introduced by the Government National Mortgage Association (Ginnie Mae). The concept proved very popular, and these debt instruments have experienced explosive growth. Referred to as "pass-through" securities, mortgage-backed bonds produce relatively high cash flow since the principal is paid back gradually, along with interest, rather than at maturity, as with an ordinary bond.

Besides Ginnie Maes, mortgage-backed securities include obligations of the Federal National Mortgage Association (Fannie Maes), the Federal Home Loan Mortgage Corporation (Freddie Macs), and others. These various pass-through investments have little or no credit risk since the government either specifically guarantees payment of interest and principal—in the case of Ginnie Maes—or implies such backing.

The "Pass-Through" Concept

Basically, a mortgage-backed security has characteristics of both a bond and a mortgage. Figure 9–2 explains how the process works with Ginnie Maes.

Homeowner prepayments accelerate during times of falling interest rates. Mortgage-backed securities yield more than Treasuries because of this prepayment risk. If rates drop significantly and prepayments surge, investors will be disappointed. They won't receive a capital gain, as they would from a conventional bond, and their principal will have to be reinvested at lower yields.

If rates rise, the principal value declines. Like a conventional bond, a mortgage-backed security has interest-rate risk. Thus, a period of stable rates works best for mortgage- backed investors. These securities aren't as sensitive as long Treasuries to rising rates, however, because of their shorter durations.

Figure 9–2
How Ginnie Maes Work

Pools of single-family mortgages with similar characteristics are assembled by a mortgage lender, such as a savings and loan. Every $1 million worth of home loans is carved up into 40 Ginnie Maes, each with a $25,000 face value. The lender delivers the pools to a securities dealer, which sells them to investors, including mutual funds.

The lender collects monthly interest and principal payments made by homeowners on the underlying loans and forwards the money to the Government National Mortgage Association, which passes along the income to investors. The agency makes payments regardless of whether homeowners have fulfilled their obligations—that's the federal guarantee.

Because of unpredictable principal prepayments by homeowners, there's no way to tell exactly when a Ginnie Mae will mature. Most come due within 12 years, even though they're based on a pool of 30-year mortgages.

Adjustable-Rate Mortgages

From the original pass-through concept, many innovative investment products have since been created. These include bondlike instruments based on automobile and credit-card loans.

Another new category is the adjustable-rate mortgage, or ARM. ARMs have become an increasingly popular way to finance home ownership in recent years. Like fixed-rate mortgages, ARMs have a specified maturity date, by which time the principal must be paid back. But unlike their fixed-rate cousins, the interest rates on ARMs fluctuate at regular intervals according to movements in some base index.

ARMs provide greater price stability than fixed-rate mortgage securities and higher yields than money-market funds. Because the rate paid by the homeowner is adjusted (or reset) periodically, usually once a year, ARM yields tend to track short-term interest rates. ARM yields usually run 1.5 to 2 percentage points above a benchmark index such as the one-year T-bill rate. Since most ARMs limit the amount that mortgage payments can rise in a year or over the life of the loan, their yields might not keep pace if rates should jump sharply.

HIGH-QUALITY CORPORATE-BOND FUNDS

These funds invest in debt issued by the nation's strongest, most secure companies. Most of the portfolios stick with bonds graded single-A or better, including some governments. But important differences exist between the high-quality corporate-bond funds and pure Treasury portfolios. First, the former have some credit risks. Second, as noted previously, the interest on Treasury securities is generally not taxable at the state and local levels. For both these reasons, the high-quality corporate funds tend to yield slightly more than government portfolios.

CORPORATE-BOND FUNDS

Funds in this broad category mainly hold investment-grade corporate debt—ratings of triple-B or better. Thus, in general they have somewhat more credit risk than the high-quality corporate portfolios. An individual fund might be substantially more speculative if it concentrates on the lower end of the investment-grade range or emphasizes the longest-term bonds available.

HIGH-YIELD BOND FUNDS

These portfolios invest in bonds with less than a triple-B rating, also known as junk securities. Some issues may even be near, or in, default. These bonds exhibit considerable price volatility. Issuers include some well-known firms such as Caesar's World, Kroger Co., R. H. Macy, RJR Nabisco, and Turner Broadcasting, as well as many small firms you probably haven't heard of.

In a sense, junk obligations behave more like stock than bonds since so much depends on the issuer's financial condition. Junk prices are less sensitive to interest rate changes but more vulnerable to developments at the company or in the economy. A high-yield bond could perform very well if the issuer's condition improves. But its price would plunge if the company defaulted and declared bankruptcy.

There are two general categories of high-yield bonds: fallen angels and original-issue junk. The former include bonds that originally carried an investment-grade rating but were downgraded as the company got in trouble. The latter were created by Michael Milken at Drexel Burnham Lambert starting in the early 1970s. They include the bonds of small, emerging companies in relatively weak financial condition. In the 1980s, many of these issues were used to finance mergers and takeovers.

Credit Risk

This is the major danger faced by high-yield bond investors. Because of it, the yield spread between junk and high-quality debt can be several percentage points.

It is dangerous to hold just one or a few junk bonds. The same firm-specific risk that affects stocks also applies here.

But credit risk can be reduced dramatically in portfolios that combine many different issues hailing from a good mix of industries.

Still, poor credit quality can be a problem even for a diversified portfolio during periods of economic downturn. Prices could decline since a recession would lessen the ability of many highly leveraged companies to pay interest and principal. If some of these firms defaulted, the fund would be hurt.

Liquidity Risk

Another danger characteristic of high-yield funds is illiquidity. Many high-yield bonds are thinly traded, and their prices could plunge in the event a significant number of investors decided to sell.

This poses problems for the fund. If the manager needs to dispose of a particular issue in a hurry, he or she may have to accept a low price. It's often difficult just to value illiquid high-yield bonds due to an absence of meaningful price quotes.

Liquidity risk was especially evident in 1990, when the high-yield market nearly collapsed on the heels of the excesses of the 1980s. Drexel Burnham, the principal market maker at the time, failed. The yield spread between junk and quality bonds widened to about 10 percentage points.

Despite paying double-digit rates, junk-bond funds suffered an average return of -11.1 percent in 1990, according to Lipper Analytical Services. The price declines, in other words, more than offset the interest income. Many individual funds performed much worse.

But unusually high yields and low prices inevitably attract bargain hunters, and the junk market rebounded nicely in 1991. In fact, these funds were the best-performing bond category that year with a 36.4 percent total return, according to Lipper.

Good Managers Add Value

Thus, mutual funds serve an especially important purpose in the junk arena. In addition to diversification, they offer the talent and analytical resources of a professional. Good managers can scrutinize financial reports and cherry-pick the best issues. And they can decide the best times to buy and sell. High-yield bonds cannot simply be purchased and held like Treasuries. They need constant monitoring. A good high-yield fund manager can add a lot of value, just as a superior stock buyer can.

Junk funds increase in popularity during times of falling interest rates, when investors are in search of more generous returns. Unfortunately, many people probably don't understand the risks they're assuming with these products.

Before you invest in a high-yield fund, ask yourself the following questions:

- Is this a good time to buy in the high-yield sector, given the direction of the economy?
- Is the interest spread between junk and high-quality bonds sufficiently wide?
- Am I able to tolerate the greater volatility of a high-yield portfolio?
- How would I react if the junk-bond market starts to falter?

Clearly, these funds are not for everyone. They can take unsuspecting investors for a roller-coaster ride. The losses could run in the double digits if you had to sell out at the bottom, as many did in 1990. A high-yield fund should not be used for more than a modest fraction of your assets. And it should not be used to play short-term swings in the bond market.

Junk Bonds Offer Diversification

So why invest in low-quality bonds at all? For fairly aggressive investors, one compelling reason is that they can add diversification to a portfolio since high-yield bond returns have such a low degree of correlation with other debt categories.

As noted, junk bonds are not as vulnerable to interest-rate risk as are longer-term Treasuries and high-grade corporates. An important explanation for this is that the former tend to have higher coupons and shorter maturities—that is, shorter durations. High-yield bonds can't totally avoid interest-rate risk, of course, but the negative price impact during a period of economic recovery would be more than offset by rising investor confidence in the economy and in that particular companies.

Capital Loss Carry-Forwards

On occasion, junk-bond funds offer another attraction. Capital loss carry-forwards are special tax advantages available on portfolios that have sustained massive losses, as high-yield funds did in the 1989–1990 debacle. Junk funds were forced to dump illiquid bonds at fire-sale prices to meet strong shareholder demand for redemptions.

The funds use these trading losses to offset capital gains in future years until the carry-forwards are all used up. The result: capital-gains distributions that are partially or completely tax-free. For example, suppose a high-yield fund had a 30 percent total return in 1991, 12 percent from income and 18 percent from realized capital gains. A large loss carry-forward could offset the entire 18 percent gain, requiring shareholders to pay taxes on only the 12 percent distributed from income.

GLOBAL-BOND FUNDS

There are 13 major bond markets in the world. About half of the approximately $10 trillion worth of total world debt trades outside the United States.

Global-bond funds invest in foreign as well as in U.S. bonds. The ratio varies but most place the bulk of their assets in non- U.S. markets. Portfolios that invest virtually all of their money in overseas obligations are more properly called *international-bond funds*.

Government and high-grade foreign corporates dominate the holdings of the global-bond group—some such funds invest only in governments. All foreign portfolios are subject to currency risk. They lose money when the U.S. dollar appreciates and gain when the greenback weakens. Chapter 7 includes calculations showing the impact of exchange-rate fluctuations on global investments.

Current income is the major objective of most domestic-bond funds, but the global portfolios also try to obtain some capital appreciation, based on currency gains. Global managers look for the best interest-rate plays and a chance to gain on a currency movement. Global-bond funds can make good investments when it appears likely that the dollar will weaken. They also provide added diversification for a person whose assets are dominated by U.S. securities. But if you invest in a fund holding foreign bonds, make sure you understand its policy with respect to hedging against currency risk.

FLEXIBLE-BOND FUNDS

Chapter 2 discussed the hybrid flexible funds that can invest in stocks as well as in bonds, varying proportions depending on the manager's outlook. This section looks at flexible funds that focus on different areas of the bond market. They can also be thought of as mixed-bond portfolios since their managers are not restricted to securities of a particular quality, maturity, or type of issuer.

These funds may appeal to investors who know they want a bond product but are not sure what kind. This way, a shareholder gets a variety of debt instruments in a single portfolio. A fund might include corporate bonds of various grades, mortgage-backed securities, plus an assortment of Treasuries and even some foreign issues. Thus, the portfolio is mixed in terms of credit risk, type of security, maturity, and possibly currency risk.

Well-managed flexible funds can take advantage of (or protect against) changing interest-rate and bond-market conditions. With flexible portfolios, the experience and track record of the manager count heavily since the wrong moves can hurt performance badly. That's the obvious pitfall of having too much flexibility.

STRATEGIES USED BY MANAGERS

Access to good professional management is an important reason for choosing a fund over individual bonds or a unit investment trust. An astute bond expert can quickly adapt a portfolio to changing market conditions using any of several strategies. Here are some of the approaches used.

The Maturity-Concentrated Portfolio

Aiming At Falling Rates. Fund managers often adjust portfolios based on their outlook for interest rates. As noted, some enjoy more flexibility and thus can make bigger moves than can others.

When rates appear likely to fall, an aggressive manager could simply lengthen portfolio duration. At the extreme, this might be done by moving into 30-year Treasury bonds, perhaps mixing in some long-term Treasury strips for an even higher duration. This is known as a *maturity-concentrated* portfolio.

Admittedly, this is a highly risky stance since the fund could get clobbered if rates head up rather than down. The manager may adopt a less aggressive posture by concentrating on, say, 10-year Treasuries instead.

Aiming at Rising Rates. A manager who thinks rates will increase might shift into shorter maturities, such as Treasury bills, to minimize possible losses. By shortening maturity too much, however, interest income would be sacrificed if rates don't move up significantly. The outcome would be worse if rates fell.

Fund managers who don't want to bet heavily on an interest-rate move can design a compromise portfolio using a barbell approach. Here are some simple illustrations.

The Barbell Portfolio

This strategy gets its colorful name from the fact that the fund concentrates at the two maturity extremes (T-bills and long-term bonds), with little or nothing in between.

A Structure for Rising Rates. A manager feels interest rates will increase and wishes to reduce to 9 years the present 24-year maturity of a Treasury portfolio. A barbell could be created by investing in a mix of T-bills and bonds averaging 9 years in maturity. An appropriate allocation would be 70 percent in 90-day bills and 30 percent in 30-year bonds.

The barbell would produce better results if rates rise than would a maturity-concentrated portfolio composed exclusively of Treasury notes with a nine-year maturity. That's because the 70 percent in bills could be rolled over into successively higher-yielding bills if rates ratchet up. But if they don't rise, or don't increase much, the portfolio would earn higher income than one completely in T-bills since 30 percent is in 30-year Treasuries. And if rates fell, the T-bond portion would appreciate, offsetting the lower income from the T-bills.

A Structure for Falling Rates. The barbell could also be tilted toward declining rates. More would be invested in the long-term Treasuries and less in bills. The bonds would appreciate if rates did drop.

Hedging with Derivatives

Some managers use options and futures to guard against rate movements. For example, to hedge against an expected rate increase, the manager could employ T-bond options or futures as an alternative to restructuring the fund's holdings. Hedging reduces risk, but it can also limit returns if the timing is off. Plus, hedging adds transaction costs. In general, we prefer funds that do little or no hedging with derivatives.

A Credit-Quality Barbell

Another approach is to set up a barbell that concentrates assets in the quality extremes. For example, a manager might hold 75 percent in high-grade corporates and U.S. government securities, 5 percent in cash equivalents, and the remaining 20 percent in junk bonds and convertibles. The latter are not so prone to interest-rate risk, but are sensitive to unfavorable economic conditions. A primary objective would be to smooth out volatility by diversifying in both the high-quality and the speculative categories. Another goal might be to find value among the lower-rated issues and thereby boost returns.

DO-IT-YOURSELF STRATEGIES

Bond-fund investors sometimes develop innovative portfolio combinations on their own. Here are just a couple of examples.

The "Homemade" Barbell: An individual holding several fixed-income funds within a family could create the following barbell: Invest some of the assets in a short-term government bond or money-market fund and put the remainder in a long-term government or target-maturity portfolio. The more money allocated to the long-term product, the greater the interest-rate risk. But the investor could shuttle cash between the two funds to change the proportions as market conditions warrant. The most extreme barbell would split the assets between a money-market and a target-maturity fund.

The Laddered Portfolio. Suppose you like government bonds and want to follow a long-term buy-and-hold strategy. Yet you may also need to liquidate some holdings during the next few years and don't want to risk doing so at a loss.

A laddered portfolio of government funds is one possibility. Under this scenario, you would invest equal amounts in bonds with evenly spaced maturities staggered across a wide range—say, from one to 30 years in increments of 5 years.

A laddered portfolio is a compromise. But it's a strategy for people who feel that they can't predict interest rates. It provides more principal stability than long bonds and greater income than a money fund. In the case of bond funds, you might approximate a laddered approach by investing one third each in short-, intermediate-, and long-term governments.

The Multisector Portfolio. This involves diversifying into the different types of bond funds, especially high-yield corporate, government, and international. A simple strategy would be to invest equal amounts in each.

Dollar-Cost Averaging

This sensible approach, which is popular among equity-fund investors, is also catching on with bond shareholders. Suppose you want to invest in a fairly volatile fund. With dollar-cost averaging, you protect yourself from risking a large sum at or near a market peak. By putting away equal amounts of money at periodic intervals, say a few hundred dollars monthly, you will tend to buy more shares when prices are low and fewer when they're high, thereby reducing your average cost per share. This strategy takes the guesswork out of timing.

If you don't need the income now, consider holding your funds in an IRA or other tax-deferred retirement plan and reinvesting the dividends. More aggressive bond investors with a longer time horizon should consider the more volatile portfolios.

CHAPTER 10

Tax-Exempt Bond Funds

Few financial terms have such a nice ring as the words "tax free." With investors facing burdensome obligations to federal, state, and local governments, some people will do whatever they can to retain as much income as possible. Since the Tax Reform Act of 1986, which crippled limited partnerships, individuals have not had many alternatives for sheltering their earnings. That's why demand has increased for municipal securities and the funds investing in them.

Commonly called "munis," tax-exempt notes and bonds are coupon-bearing securities issued by state and local governments and government agencies, including those in Puerto Rico and other United States territories. Proceeds from the sale of municipal debt are used to finance public services and projects. Municipal notes come due in a year or less, while the bonds have maturities extending beyond one year.

Munis are generally regarded as having fairly little credit risk, al-though they obviously rank below default-free U.S. governments in this regard. But because this is such a large and heterogeneous group, there will always be some munis carrying high credit risk. In fact, there have been a number of defaults in the muni arena in recent years.

The appeal of these bonds depends largely on your personal tax bracket. Individuals in higher brackets are the predominant buyers of municipal debt today. These people can either purchase the bonds directly or go through one of the three types of investment companies: mutual funds, closed-end funds, or unit investment trusts.

TAX CONSIDERATIONS

Interest income from most municipal bonds avoids taxes at the federal level. Payments would also be tax-free at the state level if the bonds are issued within your state. A large and growing number of single-state muni funds offer local residents double tax-exempt yields.

It is also possible to obtain triple tax-free munis and bond funds in areas that slap on local income taxes. For example, a New York City resident purchasing New York City bonds could obtain income that avoids city, state, and federal levies.

Municipal bonds can protect an investor to some degree against rising taxes. That's because rate increases tend to boost the prices of munis and muni funds due to the greater value of the tax exemption. The opposite would be true if rates fell. *Tax rate risk* reflects the danger of falling municipal-bond prices due to a tax cut.

But the Tax Reform Act of 1986, which lowered rates, didn't hurt the municipal market. Why? Because although tax rates dropped, the number of substitutes for sheltering income was reduced. The net effect was an increased demand for the bonds, which pushed up prices and reduced yields. Investors who had previously bought munis or muni funds did well on a total-return basis.

The Alternative Minimum Tax

Not all municipals can claim to be tax-exempt. In particular, investors must watch out for "private-activity" bonds issued after August 7, 1986. The interest from these might be subject to the federal "alternative minimum tax." The AMT applies to high-income individuals who derive a significant benefit from certain deductions or exemptions called "tax preference" items.

You or your accountant will know if you're wealthy enough to be affected by the AMT. If so, check to see to what extent, if any, a muni fund could produce dividends subject to the AMT. Some portfolios invest significant amounts in these bonds because of their somewhat higher yields. Others hold none. If you aren't subject to the AMT, there is nothing to worry about.

Capital Gains and Losses

Despite their alluring names, even the purest muni funds aren't completely tax-free. Why? Because any capital gains realized on municipal bonds sold by the fund manager at a profit would be taxable to you. Losses, in turn, can be deducted, according to the usual IRS rules. The same is true of any gains or losses you might realize when selling a municipal-bond portfolio.

Keep in mind that a large part of a muni fund's performance may be subject to tax if the portfolio has enjoyed a high total return within a particular year. Assuming you have owned shares during a year when interest rates declined sharply, you will likely have some gain to report.

Taxable-Equivalent Yields

Because of their tax-exempt status, municipals yield less than otherwise-equal taxable bonds. But even with a smaller nominal payout, you may be better off with the muni investment, especially if your bracket is high enough.

Suppose your combined federal and state *marginal tax rate (MTR)* is 38 percent. This means for every additional $1 you make, you keep 62 cents. But if that income comes from municipal securities, you might be able to keep it all. The value of a tax-free dollar depends on your MTR. The approximate relationship can be calculated as:

$$\text{Taxable equivalent yield} = \frac{\text{Tax-free yield}}{1.0 - \text{MTR}}$$

EXAMPLE: With a 38 percent combined federal and state MTR, the taxable-equivalent yield of a muni that pays 6 percent works out to 9.68

percent [0.06/(1.0 - 0.38)]. This assumes the interest from the muni is exempt from income taxes at both the state and the federal levels.

When comparing tax-exempt and taxable bonds (or portfolios), it's important to look at securities of fairly equal credit risk and maturity. Don't, for instance, compare a long-term, high-quality muni fund to a portfolio of intermediate-term junk corporates. Also, since capital gains on municipals are taxable (and losses deductible), it's only relevant to include yields, not total returns, on a taxable-equivalent basis.

If you buy a national muni-bond fund, your federal tax rate is the relevant MTR. For a home-state portfolio, use your *effective combined* federal and state rate (and local rate, if applicable).

You can estimate your combined MTR by simply adding the appropriate federal and state rates. However, this somewhat overstates the benefit of the exemption for investors who deduct state taxes on their federal returns. To be precise, the combined rate should include the impact of this deduction where applicable. The calculation of the combined federal (FTR) and state (STR) rates can be made as follows:

$$\text{Combined MTR} = \text{FTR} + \text{Effective STR}$$
$$= \text{FTR} + [\text{STR} \times (1.0 - \text{FTR})]$$

EXAMPLE: With a 28 percent FTR and a 10 percent STR, the simple combined MTR would equal 38 percent. Giving effect to the deduction of state taxes on the federal return, the effective STR becomes 7.2 percent [$0.10 \times (1.00 - 0.28)$]. The combined MTR equals 35.2 percent (28 percent + 7.2 percent).

Table 10–1 illustrates sample taxable-equivalent yields. The higher your MTR, the greater the advantage of tax-free income. For instance, with a 35.2 percent effective combined MTR, a muni yield of 8 percent would equal a fully taxable 12.35 percent. Thus, if you could find a muni issue yielding 8 percent, it wouldn't make sense to consider taxable bonds paying less than 12.35 percent. It's very likely, however, that a corporate with a 12.35 percent yield would be riskier than the 8 percent muni. This is why it's important to compare debt securities with similar ratings and maturities.

Table 10-1
Sample Taxable Equivalent Table

Tax-exempt Yield	Investors Marginal Tax Bracket				
	15.0%	28.0%	33.0%	35.2%	38.0%
4.0%	4.71	5.56	5.97	6.17	6.45
6.0	7.06	8.33	8.96	9.26	9.68
8.0	9.41	11.11	11.94	12.35	12.90

Due to demand-and-supply conditions, you can normally expect to see lower nominal yields on bonds issued within high-tax states such as California, New York, and New Jersey.

The Tax-Exempt Yield Ratio

An important yield relationship to watch is the one between high-grade tax-exempt and taxable bonds. For example, if high-quality municipals yield 6 percent when comparable corporates are paying 8 percent, the "tax-exempt yield ratio" would be 0.75 (6 percent/8 percent).

The higher this ratio, the lower the tax bracket necessary for municipals to start becoming attractive. Simply subtract the yield ratio from 1.0 to determine the marginal tax rate at which investors would be indifferent between the two types of bonds. This can be thought of as a break-even MTR. For example, if the tax-exempt yield ratio is 0.75, investors in tax brackets above 25 percent (1.00 - 0.75) would prefer munis. But if the ratio were 0.60, the bonds would make sense only for people in a tax bracket above 40 percent.

The tax-exempt yield ratio changes inversely with tax rates. As rates fall, the appeal of municipals diminishes and they must pay more to stay competitive. In the extreme, if there were no income taxes, the yield ratio would be 1.0 since a municipal bond would be paying roughly the same as any other debt security with a similar rating and maturity.

CHARACTERISTICS OF MUNICIPAL BONDS

Munis come in two basic groups: *general obligation* (or GOs) and *revenue bonds*. The former are backed by the full faith, credit, revenue-generating ability and taxing authority of the borrower. This makes them the more secure of the two categories so they therefore yield somewhat less. Virtually all GO bonds mature serially. That is, they have staggered maturities.

Revenue bonds account for most of the total value of munis issued in recent years. These bonds are used to finance specific revenue-generating projects such as bridges, toll roads, and public utilities and hospitals. The money earned by the project pays the interest and principal on the debt. Revenue bonds have a set term to maturity. Most come with lengthy maturities, commonly 30 years. Thus, longer-term muni funds have a larger proportion of their assets invested in these issues. The average maturities of these portfolios typically range from 15 to 25 years.

A special type of revenue debt is secured by the payments of a private user. These are known as "private-activity" bonds. Industrial development bonds fall into this category. Buyers of private-activity securities generally do not have access to the resources of the municipality that issued the debt on the user's behalf. For this reason, the bonds tend to be of lower quality than other munis. Interest from private-activity bonds may be subject to the alternative minimum tax. Not surprisingly, the issuance of private-activity debt has declined sharply since the Tax Reform Act of 1986.

Risks of Municipals

Munis face the same dangers that apply to taxable bonds. They're affected by interest rate, credit, purchasing power, call, and liquidity risk. In addition, munis can be harmed by a tax law change that would adversely impact the prices of outstanding issues.

Still, municipal bonds generally can be considered highly secure investments. Like corporates, the various general obligation and revenue issues are graded for creditworthiness. Standard & Poor's and Moody's are the best known rating agencies. Investment-grade munis range from triple-A down to triple-B. Some bonds are insured by very solid consortiums and thus sport a triple-A rating. But other bonds—the high-yield or so-called "junk" issues—carry gradings of double-B and lower.

In addition to rating individual issues, Moody's and Standard & Poor's also evaluate the general obligation bonds of most states. These ratings can be found in *Moody's Bond Record* and *Standard & Poor's Bond Guide*, both commonly available in libraries. State ratings can and do change. Before you invest in a single-state municipal fund, become familiar with the overall credit quality of its debt. The grade on the state's GO bonds is a good place to begin, although it's not necessarily linked to the ratings of revenue bonds issued within that state.

Because individual munis carry credit and liquidity risk, it's wise to use a mutual fund. Unless you are investing hundreds of thousands of dollars and thus are able to spread your assets over many different issues, you will probably do better with a fund and its diversified, professionally managed approach.

MUNICIPAL-BOND FUNDS

Unmanaged unit investment trusts (or UITs) provided the earliest means for individuals to acquire a diversified portfolio of municipal bonds. The first tax-exempt UIT was introduced in 1961. Then the Tax Reform Act of 1976 allowed open-end funds to pass tax-exempt income through to shareholders.

To be considered federally "tax-exempt" by the SEC, a fund must normally: (1) invest at least 80 percent of its assets in federally tax-exempt securities or (2) derive at least 80 percent of its income from tax-exempt debt.

Muni-bond funds can be divided into two basic types: national and single-state.

NATIONAL FUNDS

These portfolios hold bonds issued in a number of states and thus offer geographic diversification. This is important since some states have riskier bonds than others. When examining a national fund, determine which states have the greatest representation in the portfolio and what their credit reputations are.

Muni-bond interest from any state avoids federal taxes, but the income generally would be subject to tax at the state level. For example, a Californian has money in a national fund that, in turn, has 7 percent of its portfolio in California bonds. That portion of the yield would be tax-exempt for the investor at the state level. National muni funds provide an annual breakdown of the percentage of assets invested in each state.

SINGLE-STATE FUNDS

These funds limit themselves to issues free from taxation in a specific state. Their portfolios thus enjoy a double exemption. Some might even enjoy a triple tax exemption, assuming they hold local bonds in cities or counties that impose personal income taxes.

Single-state funds have proliferated in recent years. By far the largest number cater to residents of California and New York—big states with high tax rates. Massachusetts, Minnesota, Ohio, and Pennsylvania also have substantial numbers of these products.

A drawback with single-state funds is that you don't get the diversification you would with a national portfolio. This can lead to greater risk. Consequently, investors should look for large funds that are as widely diversified as possible within their state.

It may seem puzzling that a number of single-state funds exist for both Florida and Texas, which currently have no income tax. Why? In part, some residents may simply like the idea of having portfolios made up of bonds from their home states. It's also a possibility that Texas may introduce an income tax, in which case a Texas muni fund would likely appreciate as its bonds become more valuable. In Florida's situation, even though there is no income tax, there is a small "intangibles" tax. Florida residents who hold munis of other states have to pay a levy on the income derived from those bonds.

One fund invests primarily in Puerto Rican municipal securities. As well as being tax-exempt at the federal level, these bonds spin off interest that's tax-free in most states.

Two other ways to distinguish among municipal-bond funds is by examining maturity and credit quality.

1. *Maturity.* Most tax-exempt portfolios invest in longer-term munis. However, short- and intermediate-term funds exist, as do tax-free money-market portfolios. What you choose depends on how far out on the yield curve you want to go in terms of risk and return. Longer portfolios face the greatest interest-rate danger.

2. *Credit Quality.* Most funds hold bonds in the top four rating categories. But even here there are differences.

INSURED FUNDS

The highest-quality muni portfolios hold what are known as "insured" bonds, along with other top-grade issues.

Simply put, insured obligations are guaranteed by an outside underwriter as to the timely payment of interest and principal. The reputation of this additional party is obviously crucial. That's why fund managers generally use only those insurers rated triple-A by S&P or Moody's. Five large, reputable firms specialize in guaranteeing muni bonds.

If the issuer defaults on interest or principal payments, the insurance company steps in and meets the obligation. Thus, investors would receive all scheduled payments in full. The insurance covers credit risk only, not interest-rate risk or any other dangers.

Types of Insurance

An insured portfolio can be built in various ways:

1. *Insurance on a newly issued bond,* paid for by the municipality. The idea is to enhance the bond's creditworthiness from the start.
2. *Secondary-market insurance.* In this case, the fund manager pays for the policy to cover eligible bonds.
3. *Insurance for the entire portfolio,* obtained by the fund to cover all of its holdings.

Many fund managers tend to use the first option, purchasing bonds that have been insured since their inception. A fairly high percentage of all munis are covered in this manner.

The kind of insurance used isn't that important to investors. The main point is to know that you have protection—and that you're paying a price for it. Since coverage has a cost, insured funds generally yield less. The difference in return might range from about 20 to 50 basis points (0.2 to 0.5 of a percentage point). Thus, you have to decide if the protection is worth it. In general, a well-diversified portfolio investing in high-grade munis will be sufficiently safe for most people without insurance.

HIGH-YIELD FUNDS

At the other extreme, the so-called "junk" tax-exempt funds invest in lower-grade munis with longer maturities. Their managers hope to generate higher returns by finding bonds where the issuer's credit situation appears to be improving.

As with corporate high-yield funds, these products face greater credit and liquidity risks. The least aggressive portfolios in this group might hold only a few junk munis. Others may invest nearly all their assets in the most speculative areas.

Still, high-yield municipal-bond funds generally don't assume as much credit risk as their corporate counterparts. This is because there simply aren't as many seriously troubled municipalities as there are companies.

Some junk funds may move a large part of their assets into better-grade bonds when the yield spread between the two isn't enough to compensate investors for the added risk. As a general rule, good managers venture into riskier securities only when they expect to receive a sufficient reward for doing so.

LOOKING FOR VALUE

The huge, heterogeneous municipal-bond market offers opportunities for skilled value investors. These opportunities exist because of the large number of tax-exempt issuers relative to the fairly small number of full-time analysts. Nuveen Advisory, a Chicago-based muni-bond investment firm, estimates that about 60,000 entities issue tax-free securities, yet fewer than 1,000 professionals follow them. Conversely, 18,000 analysts track the roughly 7,000 stocks in the United States.

In addition, there's less publicly available information on tax-exempt securities compared to stocks. Scarce information is a key characteristic of less efficient markets.

A large number of muni issues do not carry an agency grading. But just because a bond is "nonrated" does not mean it's speculative. Some municipalities won't obtain a rating for a relatively small issue because the costs of doing so can't be justified. Nonrated bonds can represent excellent values, but it takes a skilled fund manager to find the best ones.

ADVANTAGES OF MUNICIPAL-BOND FUNDS

Tax-exempt portfolios offer many of the same benefits as do other mutual funds. These are the advantages:

1. *Wide diversification for a relatively small required investment.* A fund may hold more than 100 issues in different sectors and regions. The initial cost to purchase shares can be as low as a few hundred dollars.

2. *Continuous professional management.* Though municipal defaults are rare, problems can occur, as happened with the infamous Washington Public Power Supply System ("Whoops") disaster in 1983. Good managers can sense trouble developing and get out early—before the bonds are downgraded by the rating agencies. Managers are also able to locate inefficiencies in the vast muni market.

3. *Excellent liquidity.* Individual municipal bonds can be difficult to sell, especially if you own small positions. Bid-asked spreads may be very wide, resulting in excessively high transaction costs. With bond funds, you can easily buy or sell shares or switch into other types of investments for little or no expense.

4. *Daily pricing information on funds.* By contrast, it can be difficult for individuals to get accurate quotes for many municipal bonds. You won't find prices or yields in the newspaper—you have to go to a broker to obtain quotes. And even then, prices on a given bond can vary widely among dealers.

ALTERNATIVES FOR MUNI INVESTORS

Mutual funds aren't the only way to access tax-free bonds. You can also purchase closed-end funds or unit-investment trusts. There are even "mini-munis," which have become quite popular recently.

Closed-End Municipal-Bond Funds

These were first introduced in 1987. Like their open-end cousins, closed-end municipal portfolios have become very popular in more recent years, thanks to the public's appetite for tax-free income. But unlike open-end funds, the closed-end products don't issue new shares to incoming investors, nor do they redeem shares when you want to sell. Instead, the funds trade like common stocks. Most, in fact, are listed on the New York Stock Exchange.

You can now choose from over 150 closed-end muni funds in different categories: national, insured, high-yield, and single-state. Several companies offer both open- and closed-end products.

Which type is better? That's largely a matter of investor preference. Because closed-end funds trade like stocks, they may appeal to people who prefer to deal in the stock market. In particular, some individuals might like the idea of picking up shares at a discount to NAV. Closed-end muni prices can range from discounts greater then 5 percent to premiums of over 10 percent. Although most generally trade at premiums, discounts tend to appear when the market is depressed. Thus, closed-end funds appeal to people who like to watch for special trading opportunities.

In terms of liquidity, there is a difference between the two types of investments. With an open-end portfolio, you could buy or sell a large number of shares on a given day without affecting the fund's price (which is based on its NAV). But with a closed-end fund, a big trader could easily move its price up or down with a large transaction. However, for most individuals who trade fairly modest dollar amounts, the liquidity difference between the two types of funds would be immaterial.

Open-end portfolios offer an advantage when you wish to make additional investments. All you would need to do is send in a check or arrange for a direct transfer from your bank account. You could also switch your money into another fund in the same family. But with closed-end portfolios, you would need to place an order with a stockbroker each time you wanted to buy or sell. In the process, you would incur transaction costs, as you would with any other stock.

An important advantage of the closed-end structure is that managers do not have to keep a cash cushion to meet daily investor redemptions. Thus, these portfolios can remain more fully invested than regular mutual funds, thereby earning a higher yield and possibly also a higher total return. Open-end muni funds tend to keep at least 5 percent of their assets in cash. A closed-end portfolio might maintain only half as much.

A significant difference between the two types of municipal products is that a large proportion of the closed-ends leverage their holdings. This approach promises to enhance returns but also adds risk to a portfolio.

Unit Investment Trusts

Both open- and closed-end portfolios are managed on an ongoing basis. A unit-investment trust, on the other hand, is not. It's a fixed portfolio with a finite life. UITs hold various bond securities, commonly municipals or Ginnie Maes. Combined, UIT assets exceed $100 billion.

The lives of these trusts range from several months to 25 years or more. In this sense, a UIT is like holding an actual bond. Investors have several choices as to maturity and portfolio type. For example, you can find both insured and uninsured muni-bond UITs, as well as single-state and national portfolios.

A trust normally isn't liquidated until the last of its bonds has matured. Investors receive periodic income: monthly, quarterly, or semi-annually. They can take their interest and principal distributions in cash or they can reinvest the payments in a mutual fund, but not into the UIT. Ongoing fees are generally very low because the trusts are unmanaged. However, front-end loads range up to 5 percent, with breakpoint discounts available for larger investments.

If you want to redeem a UIT before maturity, you can do so daily at that day's price, as with a mutual fund. This is a legal requirement stipulated in the Investment Company Act of 1940.

Shop around carefully and ask a lot of questions before investing in a UIT. For instance, you should know how much call protection you're getting. This should be at least 7 or 8 years with the longer-term portfolios. You also need to consider the quality of the bonds if the UIT is uninsured.

Principal payments from bonds that are called, redeemed, or sold are passed along to investors. This reduces the value of the portfolio and the periodic income it generates. If a lot of investors want out, the sponsor may have to sell bonds to meet redemptions. In fact, a UIT may be liquidated prior to the stated maturity if its asset base declines to a small percentage (usually below 20 percent) of the original value. Sponsors typically can also sell bonds when their creditworthiness deteriorates, but they can never add issues to the portfolio.

The main advantage of UITs compared to bond mutual funds is their lower ongoing fees. But the funds enjoy an edge in that they're managed. This flexibility to adjust to changing market conditions can pay off for shareholders during periods of heavy calls, temporary yield disparities, and the like.

"Mini-Munis"

Many people have been deterred from buying individual muni bonds by the large investment required. With regular munis, you would need at least $25,000 to establish a meaningful position in just a few issues.

The recent advent of so-called "mini-munis" offers an alternative way to invest. These are simply small-denomination bonds, often issued in zero-coupon form. The denomination may be as low as $1,000 or so. One advantage of mini-munis is that, as zeros, they have no reinvestment risk. They can also be used to lock in a given yield for a fixed period. But these bonds should not be purchased unless you intend to hold to maturity. They are illiquid, which means you might have to accept a significant price concession if you had to sell before they come due.

In short, muni-bond funds have three compelling advantages over the mini bonds: diversification, professional management, and liquidity.

FACTORS TO CONSIDER IN SELECTING A MUNI-BOND FUND

Shopping for muni-bond funds can be fairly difficult. In part, this is due to the fact that there are so many choices. The following points are worth heeding:

- In general, most people should probably be looking at the open- and closed-end portfolios rather than at the UITs. It's important to have continuous management, and there is more information available on the funds. UITs aren't listed in the paper like the managed portfolios are.

- Consider a single-state fund if you live in a high-tax state. But remember, these portfolios are riskier than the national funds because of their limited geographic diversification. In addition, they may have lower yields. For these reasons, it may pay to invest at least some of your tax-free money in a national fund.

- The insured funds may help you get a better night's sleep if you need more security. But insurance carries a cost—a lower yield than what's available on an otherwise-equivalent portfolio. In- surance probably makes more sense with a single-state portfolio than with a national one.

- Funds that chase the highest yields are not always the best choices. Those higher rates may reflect some significant problems.

- Examine the fund's composition. Pay particular attention to portfolios with high concentrations in specific sectors, such as hospital or housing bonds. If a fund has 50 percent or more of its assets in one or two sectors, be careful no matter what they are.

- Read the newspapers and keep on top of major national and state trends. This will help you spot threats to the bonds of particular states or sectors. Of course, with any fund, you should rely primarily on the portfolio manager to do the detailed analysis for you.

- If you plan to hold your municipal investment for many years and can accept some fluctuations, consider a long-term, uninsured portfolio for its higher potential return. Just remember that these funds have substantial interest-rate risk. Many unsuspecting muni-fund investors got burned in 1987, when rates spiked upward. Widespread redemptions only exacerbated this problem.

CHAPTER 11

How to Analyze a Bond Fund

Compared to stock mutual funds, bond portfolios are a homogeneous lot. You won't likely see one corporate-bond fund surge 15 percent in a year while another slumps 10 percent. Nearly all bond investments rise or fall more or less according to interest-rate fluctuations or other market trends. Certainly, they move more closely together than equity investments do.

Still, some fixed-income funds perform moderately better than others due to such factors as management, expenses, and the type of securities held. Superior funds in a particular category might best their rivals by two or three percentage points a year—a significant margin over time. Astute investors know what factors to look for to identify the better bond products. This chapter discusses those key ingredients.

MANAGEMENT AND PERFORMANCE

Good management is certainly crucial for stock funds, but some people don't think it's that important for bond portfolios. Over any particular period, total returns generally don't vary as dramatically among bond products within a category as among stock portfolios. This is true for the most part, with the obvious exception being the high-yield arena. Still, good bond managers can produce incrementally superior results and will keep their funds at the top of the pack. Every little bit helps, especially in an arena where returns cluster together.

Thus, it is important to know who the manager is, how long that individual has been at the helm, and what philosophy he or she follows. Talented managers can spot pricing anomalies and inefficiencies, can act promptly and add value. They frequently don't take bond ratings at face value but instead do a lot of digging, always looking for opportunities.

Avoid Big Losers in Down Markets

You also want to see how the portfolio performed during at least the past five to seven years, in different market environments. For example, how did a long-term U.S. government fund do when interest rates were rising in 1987? How did a mortgage-backed securities portfolio fare when rates were falling in the early 1990s? How did a high-yield fund do when the junk market tottered in 1989 and 1990? Even though past returns are not necessarily indicative of future performance, by sticking with proven funds your odds for success are better.

Total return data on bond funds can be obtained from the major sources identified in Chapter 3 and in Appendix 1 for stock portfolios. You want consistent performers that handle risk better than their peers. For example, *Forbes* Annual Mutual Fund Survey assigns separate letter ratings (ranging from A+ down to F) for the "up-market" and "down-market" results of both taxable and tax-exempt portfolios. Be wary of funds that have earned low grades in bearish phases.

Perhaps you'd like one summary number that reflects overall volatility—a number that takes into consideration all risk factors affecting the portfolio. The best single indicator in this regard is standard deviation. Simply put, it's a measure of the fluctuations of past returns around their average value. Funds with higher standard deviations have greater risk.

By studying the past volatility of a portfolio's total returns you can gain a pretty good feel for its likely future course. Standard deviations can be used to make all kinds of comparisons, even among different kinds of investments. For instance, bond funds can be compared with stock funds as well as with other bond portfolios.

Morningstar reports standard deviations for the different bond fund categories it tracks. They range from about 1 percent to 3 percent per month. The service also reports standard deviations for individual funds. These numbers vary from well below 1 percent to over 5 percent.

FUND COSTS

Remember the lessons from Chapter 5 on costs? They are especially important for bond fund investors. That's because fixed-income portfolios generally produce lower long-run returns than stock products, making every little bit more critical. To determine the level of expenses, study the fee table near the front of the prospectus. Compare the fees of several funds you are considering. Give high priority to lower-cost products.

Examine the portfolio's expense ratio over the past several years. When making comparisons, remember that larger funds should generally have lower per-share expenses because of economies of scale. Also, true no-load funds should have lower numbers than portfolios that levy an annual 12b–1 fee. This charge must be calculated as part of the overall expense ratio.

Also, examine the trend in the fund's costs. Watch out for portfolios that have been getting bigger over the years but don't seem to exhibit a decline in the expense ratio. If the fund's asset size isn't listed, you can calculate it by multiplying the NAV price by the total number of shares outstanding at the time.

The hypothetical XYZ Bond Fund in Table 11–1 shows an extreme case of what to avoid. Its expense ratio actually increases as assets grow over the years. The rise in XYZ's assets—from $110 million in 1987 to $700 million in 1992—has been significant. You would like to see at least some modest benefits from economies of scale.

Table 11-1
Comparing XYZ Fund's Assets and Expense Ratios

	1992	1991	1990	1989	1988	1987
Total net assets (in millions)	$700	$500	$325	$200	$145	$110
Expense ratio	1.50%	1.40%	1.25%	1.20%	1.19%	1.20%

PORTFOLIO TURNOVER

As with stock funds, higher turnovers translate into increased transaction costs, which are shouldered by fund investors. In the case of Treasury and high-grade corporate-bond products, transaction expenses will tend to be relatively low, even with an actively traded portfolio. But, if the fund holds positions in lower-quality debt, high turnover can be a problem.

Transaction costs—specifically, the bid-asked spread and transaction "size" effects—are greater for more speculative, less-liquid issues. The same is true for stocks. The lower the quality and liquidity of a security, the higher the trading costs. Spreads widen and price concessions grow larger. So beware of junk corporate and muni-bond funds with high turnovers.

You should expect even lower turnover in years of interest-rate stability. Conversely, more portfolio activity during periods of increased bond market volatility shouldn't be viewed negatively if accompanied by good performance.

Just steer clear of funds with consistently excessive turnovers. And keep in mind that high turnover can create higher taxes for you. Unless you're investing within an IRA or other tax-deferred plan, this would be a disadvantage.

ANOTHER VIEWPOINT

Some fund experts argue that you should focus only on the bottom line. That is, study past total returns and volatility, but ignore expense ratios and turnover.[1]

This argument has some merit. The logic is that all costs— including management fees, administrative expenses, 12b–1 fees, plus turnover-related transaction costs—are automatically netted out when calculating net asset values and thus total returns.

In the example in Table 11–2, ABC Bond Fund clearly would have been the better choice even though it had a higher expense ratio and turnover than XYZ. ABC looks particularly impressive when you consider that it also exhibited lower risk. The total returns, as noted earlier, are net of all expenses and transaction costs.

Table 11-2
Comparing Two Corporate Bond Funds

Bond Fund	Compound Annual Average Total Return	Standard Deviation	Average Expense Ratio	Average Portfolio Turnover
ABC	14%	1.5%	1.2%	140%
XYZ	10	2.5	0.9	50

The problem with looking only at total return is that it is based on the premise that past performance is representative of the future. Our feeling is that expenses and turnovers are more predictable than total returns. Thus, if you start with a fund that has low expenses, low turnover, and good performance, your odds for success are a bit better.

As a footnote, you should recognize that front- and back-end load charges are generally not netted out of published performance numbers the way expenses are. You would need to calculate the impact of the sales charge to get a realistic view of the investment potential.

FUND SIZE

One more argument about expenses is worth heeding. It's the idea that bigger bond funds are better because they benefit from economies of scale and should have lower expense ratios. In addition, their managers may be able to make better deals since they trade in larger blocks of bonds. This analysis makes sense for higher-quality fixed-income portfolios.

But there is also a good argument for smaller or medium- sized funds when investing in less liquid junk-bond securities. The reason? These portfolios may be able to maneuver more easily. They could take meaningful positions in smaller junk issues without having to worry about affecting prices as much. This can be especially helpful when the manager needs to exit the market in a hurry.

PORTFOLIO COMPOSITION

As with a stock fund, make sure your bond portfolio is being run in accordance with its investment policy, as outlined in the prospectus. To do this, examine the fund's holdings as listed in the annual and semiannual reports. You should look at the portfolio composition in general terms, without trying to analyze each issue's investment potential.

If you have a mixed or flexible fund that can invest in different bond-market sectors, find out what is being emphasized at the present. Ideally, you'd want to see how these proportions have changed with the times. With any other kind of fund that has some flexibility, you need to determine what types of securities are being given the most prominent representation.

CREDIT QUALITY

Here are two important questions investors in high-yield funds need answers to:

1. How much credit risk does the fund intend to assume?
2. How much credit risk has the fund actually assumed?

The prospectus should provide a clear answer to the first question, and it might provide insights on the second. That's because the prospectuses of high-yield funds provide a useful summary breakdown of total assets by letter-rating category. You can also find this information in *Morningstar Mutual Funds*.

An illustration for three hypothetical portfolios appears in Table 11–3. Fund A has the lowest credit risk, while Fund C is the most speculative.

For nonrated debt, the prospectus will provide a breakdown of what the fund's adviser feels the S&P-equivalent ratings would be.

AVERAGE MATURITY

This is an important indicator of volatility. Funds with the longest maturities have the greatest interest-rate risk. They will fall the farthest if rates move upward. Target-maturity portfolios are the most sensitive as they hold zero-coupon bonds. You should be especially careful of long maturities during periods of low interest rates. While investigating maturities, you should find out if the manager hedges with futures or options, which can help lessen the fund's exposure to interest-rate risk. You also want to know how much flexibility the manager has to lengthen or shorten maturities in response to anticipated market changes. For answers to these and other questions, consult the prospectus or ask the fund's telephone reps.

Table 11-3
Asset Composition of Three Hypothetical High-Yield Funds

Standard & Poor's Rating	Percentage of Total Assets		
	Fund A	Fund B	Fund C
U.S. Govt.	4%	0%	0%
AAA	1	0	0
AA	2	0	1
A	3	0	1
BBB	33	0	8
BB	39	84	3
B	8	7	59
CCC	4	4	7
Nonrated*	0	0	13
Cash Reserves	6	5	8
Total	100%	100%	100%

*The adviser will provide its own assessment of the nonrated bonds. For hypothetical Fund C, the nonrated securities are judged to be comparable to: B, 9 percent; and CCC, 4 percent.

Remember that U.S. Treasury securities are not safe in all respects. A portfolio made up entirely of long-term Treasuries could drop more than, say, a shorter-term junk-bond fund. Treasuries protect you from credit dangers, not interest-rate risk. In fact, the higher-quality long-term bond portfolios are the most interest-sensitive.

By itself, a long average maturity (or duration) is not necessarily good or bad. A fund with such a characteristic could fit nicely into your overall portfolio, especially if you hope to profit from an anticipated rate decline.

THE AVERAGE COUPON

If you also study a fund's average coupon, along with its average maturity, you can gain better insight into the portfolio's rate sensitivity than would be possible by examining either component by itself. The coupon rate on a bond represents the percentage of its par value paid out in interest each year. A junk bond may have a 16 percent coupon when a Treasury bond has an 8 percent coupon and a Treasury strip, none.

Coupon size can tell you several different things:

- Higher coupons may mean less interest-rate risk. Suppose one fund has a 14 percent average coupon while another has a 7 percent average. The former would be less sensitive to rate changes if their average maturities are the same.

- High coupons teamed up with a short average maturity mean low duration and less interest-rate sensitivity. Conversely, low coupons coupled with a lengthy average maturity point to potentially high volatility.

- Higher coupons indicate that the fund may be vulnerable to call risk during a period of declining rates. Given the opportunity to save money, bond issuers will take back their most expensive bonds and replace them with lower-cost obligations.

- Higher coupons are often associated with lower-quality debt, since a weak issuer's bonds will have to pay more to attract investors. In a fund, higher coupons may indicate that the manager is opting for yield at the expense of total return.

- A high coupon on a fund investing in mortgage-backed securities often indicates vulnerability to prepayment risk. During times of falling rates, homeowners will seek to refinance at lower rates, stripping the fund of some of its holdings.

You can get a feel for the average coupon by simply examining the portfolio's composition in the shareholder reports, or by calling the fund. Another good source is *Morningstar Mutual Funds*, which calculates a weighted average coupon for the fixed-income products it follows.

But like other averages, the average coupon can be misleading. If the fund holds a significant number of zeros, this would pull its average down substantially. For this reason, it pays to look at the distribution of coupons. *Morningstar Mutual Funds* provides this information on individual portfolios.

THE AVERAGE PRICE

The weighted average price of the bonds in the portfolio is another useful statistic, albeit a less readily available one. If the average price of the bonds equaled their par value, this number would be 100 percent. If the number is below 100 percent, say 90 percent, it indicates that the bonds are trading at a discount. If the fund's average is 110 percent, the bonds would be selling at a premium.

You may see bonds trading at a premium because rates have fallen and their prices have risen accordingly. This could indicate a high probability that some obligations will be called from the portfolio. It also means the premiums will eventually erode as the securities near maturity.

Conversely, if the bonds trade at a discount, this could be favorable during a period of falling rates since their prices would have more room to rise. Assuming discount bonds stay out of trouble, you can also look forward to appreciation—to the par values—as the maturity dates approach.

A portfolio's average price can be found in *Morningstar Mutual Funds*.

BOND FUND YIELDS CAN BE SLIPPERY

A fund's yield—or, more precisely, its *net income distribution rate*—is similar to the current yield on a stock or bond. It is based on the interest or dividends paid, expressed as a percent of the net-asset value. Capital gains are not included, since they are far more irregular and unpredictable than income.

Twelve-Month Yield

People use different approaches to calculate yield, and the concept can be rather elusive. One common method calculates total income distributions over the past 12 months, divided by the NAV:

$$\text{12-Month Yield} = \frac{\text{Total income distributions over past year}}{\text{Net asset value}}$$

This can also be thought of as a "12-month distribution rate." Expressed as a percentage, it's similar to the "ratio of net investment income to average net assets" found in the per-share income and capital changes table of the prospectus, discussed in Chapter 3. You can get a good feel for the past range of a fund's yield by looking at several years' worth of information.

Since the yield tells you what kind of income return you can expect, it's most important to people looking for a monthly cash flow. These individuals should remember that a mutual fund's yield fluctuates whenever the NAV moves up and down or the income distributions vary. Thus, a portfolio's yield isn't "locked in" as is the rate on an individual bond, a Treasury bill or a CD.

SEC Annualized 30-Day Yield

In the past, fund companies calculated yields in various ways to paint the most favorable picture for their ads. In particular, companies often manipulated the period over which the yield was compiled, depending on which way interest rates had been heading. For example, if rates had been rising of late, the fund might calculate a 7-day annualized yield to reflect the high recent numbers.

But since July 1988, the SEC has required funds to report uniform, annualized 30-day yields for advertisements and telephone inquiries, including automated phone messages. The SEC standardized yield is a more realistic number and won't be inflated if the fund holds a lot of high-yielding premium bonds. It also won't be distorted upward by option income, assuming the fund writes covered call options on its government bonds.

The SEC supplies an intricate formula for fund companies to use in calculating their 30-day yields. Thus, all funds are using the same equation. It is a complex, theoretical calculation that assumes all bonds in the portfolio are held to maturity, which, of course, they aren't. So in contrast to the usual yield or distribution-rate formula, the SEC's equation considers the amortization of premiums or discounts. In other words, if a fund holds a lot of premium bonds, its SEC yield would be lower than the number obtained from a simple yield calculation.

The SEC's formula might be thought of as a "30-day annualized yield to maturity." To appreciate what it's trying to accomplish, it helps to understand the concept of yield to maturity. The following example illustrates the difference between this measure and the current yield for a single bond.

EXAMPLE: A 14 percent coupon bond is selling for $1,400. The bond matures in 10 years. At maturity, the holder would receive $1,000, or $400 less than the present price. The current yield is 10 percent ($140/$1,400) but the yield to maturity is only about 8 percent. Simply put, the yield to maturity is less than the current yield because it reflects the amortization of the $400 premium.

The SEC's formula is very sophisticated. Individuals can't calculate the standardized yield themselves since they can't get the data needed to do so. Incidentally, the formula also takes any fund sales charges into account.

The standardized 30-day yield, which is recalculated daily, can be obtained by calling the fund company. Money-market portfolios report a 7-day annualized yield compiled in the same way. Funds must also list 1-, 5-, and 10-year annualized return figures along with their standardized yields if they've been around long enough for all these numbers to be available. The reason total returns must accompany yields is that the former can be low or negative even when the latter is high.

In addition to these requirements, funds may also supply investors with other, simpler yields, but they need to preface them by quoting the SEC's yield first. These other formulas simply provide a distribution rate, such as was previously illustrated with the 12-month yield. Annualized-distribution rates can be based upon income paid out over various intervals.

Incidentally, most bond funds accrue dividends daily and pay them monthly. This means that if you redeem your shares on, say, the 18th of the month, you will get 18 days of dividends. You earn dividends up to the day you redeem. Not all portfolios work this way, however. Some may pay dividends quarterly and not accrue them daily. You can determine the approach being used simply by checking the prospectus or calling the fund.

ALWAYS FOCUS ON TOTAL RETURN

Recall that the equation for total return includes capital gains or losses along with net investment income. Never buy a fund on the basis of yield alone. Yield tells only part of the story and can be misleading. Total return is a far more complete measure of performance. A high yield does you little good if you lose a good portion of your investment through an erosion of principal.

In fact, high yields inevitably spell greater risk. That's because there are only three ways managers can boost the yield of a bond portfolio, each of which entails some dangers:

1. Increase interest-rate risk.

2. Increase credit risk.

3. Invest in high-coupon issues.

Interest-rate Risk. The effect that longer maturities have on the prices of individual bonds was illustrated in Table 8–1. Lengthening the average maturity of an entire portfolio to increase yield could have the same negative impact whenever interest rates rise.

Credit Risk. Here the danger is one of falling prices if the issuer's financial condition deteriorates. Investors can suffer even if the bond doesn't go into default.

EXAMPLE: Suppose a 12 percent coupon, double-B bond is selling for $850. Its current yield is 14.12 percent ($120/$850). A fund manager purchases the security, but the issuer's financial problems worsen and a year later the bond price is down to $650. The total return amounts to -9.41 percent, computed by taking the 14.12 percent yield and subtracting the 23.53 percent price decline. High yields can be dangerous for funds or for individual bonds.

The High-Coupon Portfolio. Another yield-enhancing strategy is to purchase high-coupon bonds at premiums to par. You can assume this is happening when you notice that a fund's 30-day SEC annualized yield is below a simpler distribution rate computed for the same period. Premium bonds typically sport relatively high current yields. The bad news comes when they are called or they mature.

EXAMPLE: A 12 percent coupon, triple-A bond trading at $1,200 offers a current yield of 10 percent ($120/$1,200). Similar bonds selling close to par yield 9 percent. There is virtually no credit risk, as the issue is highly rated. But the bond could turn out to be a poor choice if it is called for redemption and the proceeds have to be reinvested at the prevailing lower level of rates. The high-coupon issue could also be a bad investment even if it remains outstanding to maturity, since its premium will evaporate. The bond that cost $1,200 would be redeemed at par, or $1,000, 20 percent below cost.

Thus, high-yield bonds trading at a premium have their pitfalls even though they may have little credit risk.

Avoid Funds that Cannibalize Assets

Finally, some funds go so far as to pay a portion of the dividend out of principal. They "cannibalize" assets to avoid cutting their distribution in times of falling interest rates. But this is a highly undesirable practice that can hurt your investment. Fortunately, this approach seems less common today thanks to performance numbers that focus more on total return and less on yield.

AVOID THE "REAR-VIEW MIRROR"

Too many investors jump on the bandwagon by overemphasizing the recent past. Loading up on the previous quarter's or last year's winners often leads to disappointment. Bond market sectors go in and out of favor and so do the top-performing mutual funds. Select managers who have shown consistently good long-term results.

You might even look for opportunities among fund categories that have done poorly over the past year or so. Different sectors and investing styles go through periods of hot and cold. Sometimes it pays to be a contrarian with a portion of your money.

Note

1. See, for example, Michael D. Hirsch, *The Mutual Fund Wealth Builder*. New York: HarperBusiness, 1991, pp. 103–104.

CHAPTER 12

Dealing with Market Fluctuations

Buy low and sell high. As basic as this advice sounds, a lot of people wind up doing the opposite. Following the crowd, they succumb to the emotions of greed and fear. They lose money in speculative bubbles by paying too much when prices overshoot value. It's easier to make this error with individual stocks than with mutual funds since a stock is far riskier. But still it can happen with funds, especially the more volatile aggressive-growth, sector, and high-yield portfolios.

Enter market timing. Investors who follow this approach don't try to fight the trend or their emotions. They don't try to buy at the absolute low or sell at the very top. Instead, they hope to participate in most of a rally while avoiding most of a decline. Even though market timing is an inexact science and has some serious pitfalls, it is, at least to a modest degree, practiced by most individual investors and portfolio managers.

Timing approaches come in many forms. Some are highly intricate, requiring lots of work. Others are simple and maintenance-free. Dollar-cost averaging, for example, one of the most basic of strategies, is actually an effective timing tool. Why? Because it gets you to buy more shares when prices are low and fewer when they are high. The more active trading strategies involve switching among funds within a family based on signals generated by market indicators. The larger the proportion of assets switched, the more aggressive the approach.

In our view, markets aren't totally efficient. Thus, a little bit of timing makes sense. We are, however, skeptical of highly aggressive systems for three reasons. First, they may keep you out of stocks during a brief but poignant bull market stampede. Second, short-term moves are virtually impossible to predict with consistent accuracy. And third, taxes and even transaction costs could offset a good portion of your gains.

In fact, academic studies on market timing are mixed at best. Many students of investing remain bitterly opposed to the more aggressive forms of timing. Staunch advocates of market efficiency and index funds hold that any timing system is futile.

STOCK MARKET CYCLES

Stock prices gradually work their way upward over the years but fluctuate dramatically around a trend line, moving in cycles. Bull and bear markets vary in length and intensity, but the former usually last longer than the latter. Stock prices rise, on average, about 7 out of every 10 years. A typical stock market cycle is illustrated in Figure 12–1.

The more aggressive timer has to be reasonably successful at identifying troughs and peaks. But buying low and selling high is easier said than done. It's difficult to pinpoint peaks and valleys until after the fact. What looks like a ceiling or floor might merely be a temporary resting spot.

TWO MARKET TIMERS

Kevin and Tim, our two contrasting timers, illustrate how strikingly different good and bad switchers can fare. For simplicity, suppose that at the beginning of each year, Kevin and Tim have two choices: Each can move

**Figure 12-1
A Stock Market Cycle**

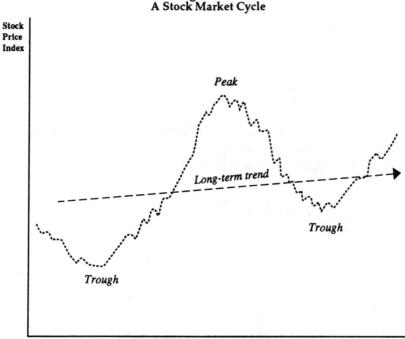

entirely into a money-market fund or 100 percent into a no-load, aggressive-growth portfolio. Table 12–1 lists the total annual returns for each option.

Table 12-1
Total Returns of Investment Options

Year	Fund A	Money Fund
1	25%	5%
2	-5	6
3	10	4
4	-8	6
5	14	6
6	90	5
7	-30	7
8	12	4
Compound annual return	9.3%	5.4%

Kevin, the fortunate timer, makes the right choice at the beginning of
each year. Tim does the opposite. Their yearly results and compound
annual returns appear in Table 12–2.

Table 12-2
Performance Results of Kevin and Tim

Year	Kevin	Tim
1	25%	5%
2	6	-5
3	10	4
4	6	-8
5	14	6
6	90	5
7	7	-30
8	12	4
Compound annual return	19.0%	-3.2%

Kevin realizes a 19 percent compound annual gain, in sharp contrast
to Tim's -3.2 percent return. At the same time, Fund A returned 9.3 percent
on average over the period, and the money fund rose at a 5.4 percent
annualized clip. Among other mistakes, Tim's poor judgment kept him on
the sidelines in year 6, when Fund A surged 90 percent. Thus, he did far
worse than he could have with a simple buy-and-hold strategy.

Most people who try to time the market won't be as lucky as Kevin or as unlucky as Tim. However, you can see that aggressive timing can have a major impact on one's results. An individual who makes the wrong moves could do terribly even though the fund may be a winner.

Suppose now that Kevin messed up in two crucial bull market years—1 and 6—but held the right positions in the remaining periods. By sitting it out in the money fund those two years, his annualized return falls from 19 percent to 8.1 percent. Even though he was right six out of eight years, Kevin fared worse than he would have by simply holding on to Fund A.

To do well as an aggressive timer, you've got to forecast bull and bear markets correctly at least 70 percent of the time, according to Professors Jess H. Chua and Richard H. Woodward, who conducted a rigorous academic study of timing.[1] They concluded that bull-market gains far outweigh bear-market losses for long-term investors. You will never miss a rally if you simply stay put. Aggressive timers risk being in cash when prices move suddenly and sharply higher.

By contrast, a conservative timer might always remain 70 percent to 90 percent invested in equity funds. This person would lighten up when he or she perceives a cyclical peak, and would perhaps switch from more aggressive stock holdings into lower-beta, equity-income portfolios. The investor might subsequently move more into volatile funds at what appears to be the trough, keeping about 90 percent of his or her money there in anticipation of market advances.

Buying at Yearly Highs

Even if you don't try to time the market, you can do well as a long-term investor. This is illustrated by the trend line in Figure 12–1. The stock market fluctuates around the line, but the long-term direction is upward. Some fund companies have done simulations demonstrating that even if you consistently bought shares at the worst time of the year—the market's annual high—you would still make money. The main thing is to keep making regular investments.

For example, T. Rowe Price did a study based on $2,000 yearly investments in the S&P 500 at its annual high, beginning January 11, 1973. By reinvesting your dividends quarterly, you would have earned 11.28 percent compounded annually over the 20-year period ended December 31, 1992. The details appear in Table 12–3.

Table 12-3
Investing $2,000 Annually at Market Highs

Investment Date	S&P 500 Index	Cumulative Investment	Account Value at Years End	Cumulative Gain (Loss)
01/11/73	120.24	$2,000	$1,676	$(324)
01/03/74	99.80	4,000	2,675	(1,325)
07/15/75	95.61	6,000	5,596	(404)
09/21/76	107.83	8,000	8,962	962
01/03/77	107.00	10,000	10,182	182
09/12/78	106.99	12,000	12,690	690
10/05/79	111.27	14,000	17,006	3,006
11/28/80	140.52	16,000	24,478	8,478
01/06/81	138.12	18,000	25,154	7,154
11/09/82	143.02	20,000	32,553	12,553
11/10/83	172.65	22,000	41,795	19,795
11/16/84	170.41	24,000	46,381	22,381
12/16/85	212.02	26,000	63,069	37,069
12/12/86	254.00	28,000	76,733	48,733
08/25/87	336.77	30,000	82,198	52,198
10/21/88	283.66	32,000	97,734	65,734
10/09/89	359.80	34,000	130,588	96,588
07/16/90	368.95	36,000	128,338	92,338
12/31/91	417.09	38,000	169,280	131,280
12/18/92	441.28	40,000	184,147	144,147

Average Annual Total Return: 11.28 percent

Notes: S&P 500 index is high for year. Account value assumes quarterly reinvestment of all dividends.

Source: T. Rowe Price Associates, Inc.

People who consistently invest—even at the worst possible times each year—still have two things going for them.

1. They are diversifying over the years. The annual highs in some years, such as 1974 through 1979, are simply not that high in absolute terms. Besides, with a regular investment plan, you're never committing an overly large sum in any given period. You would still be following a form of dollar-cost averaging.

2. They are using time as an ally, riding the market's multiyear uptrend. Specifically, long-term investors can take advantage of the power of compounding, which can do amazing things over

lengthy periods. This is especially true if you reinvest your fund distributions, another way to average into the market.

GREED AND FEAR

The most successful investors have a good understanding of the many factors that move stock prices. These include not just numerical items such as corporate earnings or economic growth but also crowd psychology and human emotions.

Greed and fear drive prices to extremes of overvaluation and under-valuation. For centuries, the public has overreacted, buying too high and subsequently selling too low. Sentiment swings haven't just been limited to stocks, either. They have also shown up in real estate, gold, fad collector items, even Dutch tulip bulbs–once a hot commodity. When a bull market is in force, more people jump on the bandwagon. They hear stories of profits from friends and acquaintances and want a piece of the action. They believe there is still a chance to make money. Greed becomes the predominant emotion.

Some market timers—though certainly not all—think like *contrarians*. They take profits when others are greedy, rather than hold on for more excitement. "No tree grows to the sky," as the old Wall Street saying goes. Sooner or later, every rally fizzles.

Valuation Barometers

To help spot market tops and bottoms, value-oriented timers focus on several key indicators, the most prominent being the price-earnings (P/E), dividend yield (dividend/price), and price-book value (P/B) ratios.

These measures can be tracked weekly in *Barron's* Market Laboratory, which lists valuation measures for the Dow Jones industrial, transportation and utility averages, as well as for the S&P 500 and industrials. The dividend yield, P/E, and P/B for the Dow industrials appear every day on the general market indicators page in *Investor's Business Daily*.

Of the three yardsticks, the market's P/E and dividend yield are most closely watched by investors. Over the past several decades, the P/Es for the market have ranged from under 8 at bottoms to 20 or more at tops. The dividend yield varies inversely with stock levels. Higher prices mean lower yields and vice versa. The yield range has stretched from below 3 percent to more than 6 percent.

Here are some general benchmarks to keep in mind about valuation ratios and the market's extremes:

- The market is pricey when aggregate P/E ratios are near or above 20, dividend yields are close to or below 3 percent, and stocks trade in excess of 200 percent of book value. The summer of 1987 serves as a good example. The S&P 500's dividend yield reached a low of 2.6 percent and its P/E and P/B stood at 23 and 260 percent, respectively, in late August, prior to the October market crash.

- The market is considered cheap when aggregate P/Es are near or below 10, dividend yields equal or exceed 6 percent, and stocks sell for 125 percent or less of book value. The bull market of the 1980s began from rock bottom valuation levels.

Watch for extremes. It is unwise to move heavily into equities when the market appears pricey. But it may be a good idea when stocks seem cheap. If you want to remain pretty much fully invested at all times, consider switching to more conservative, lower-beta portfolios, such as equity-income funds, after rallies. Or you might increase your international exposure following periods when the U.S. market has outperformed most others. Conversely, when domestic stocks appear to have bottomed out, more volatile funds would be the logical choice for risk-tolerant individuals.

Small-Stock Valuation

Funds that invest in small companies can be excellent long-term performers if you can tolerate their ups and downs. Since these funds fluctuate more than their large-stock cousins, timing is crucial. The best moment to buy is when the stocks' P/E multiples are low relative to those of large caps.

Normally, one would expect to pay more for smaller companies because they offer more excitement and growth potential. In fact, the aggregate P/Es for small stocks historically have ranged from slightly less than 100 percent to over 200 percent of large-company multiples, as represented by the S&P 500. When this yardstick is close to 100 percent, as it was in the late 1980s, small stocks can give outstanding value. They still make good buys in the 115 percent to 120 percent range and even beyond. But when the ratio moves above 175 percent or so, caution is in order.

Several fund companies publish charts showing the historic P/E relationship between the two categories of stocks. For example, the Scudder Development Fund, a small-cap portfolio with a long history, details in its shareholder reports the historic P/E relationship between the companies it owns and the S&P 500. The Scudder chart appears in Figure 12–2. T. Rowe Price also maintains a similar chart for its New Horizons Fund. Small caps can remain cheap or expensive for several years at a stretch.

We like small-cap funds because they offer exceptional long-term potential. Younger investors who can tolerate their volatility are especially encouraged to consider them. As noted, a good way to time your purchases is to compare the P/Es of small-stock funds to the S&P 500.

The majority of small-stock managers emphasize growth, but an increasing number are focusing on value investing. A small-cap value fund would tend to have a lower P/E than a growth portfolio. To determine the P/E of a fund, you can call the company's phone reps. As noted, P/Es for the S&P 500 are listed weekly in *Barron's*. *Morningstar Mutual Funds* provides P/Es and P/Bs for individual funds and compares those to the S&P 500.

DOLLAR-COST AVERAGING

Perhaps you prefer a more passive approach to dealing with market fluctuations. As noted earlier, dollar-cost averaging is a good way to space out your purchases to avoid paying too much. It takes the guesswork out of deciding when to buy. It also helps investors diversify over time. You will be purchasing more shares when prices are low, fewer when they're high. Dollar-cost averaging is a good discipline since it forces you to commit cash at market lows, when others are fearful.

Investing $1,000 quarterly in a volatile fund might work out as illustrated in Table 12–4. Just after the July 1 purchase, you would have 305 shares worth $3,812.50. The average cost per share would be $9.84. Note that the average of the three NAVs works out to $10.17, higher than the figure achieved with dollar-cost averaging. This would be the cost if you bought an equal number of shares each time.

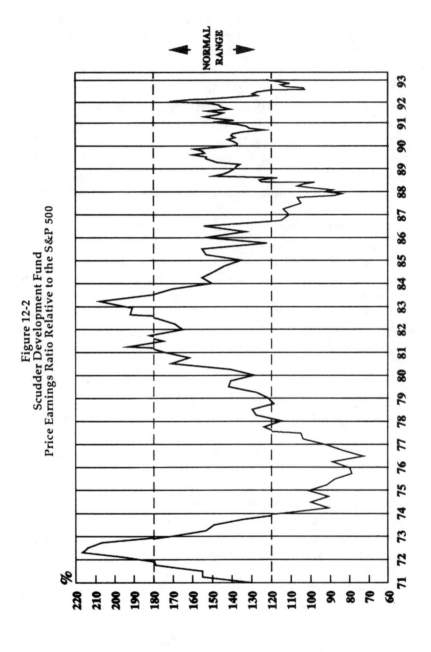

Figure 12-2
Scudder Development Fund
Price Earnings Ratio Relative to the S&P 500

184

Table 12-4
Dollar-Cost Averaging

Date	Amount Invested	NAV	Shares Bought	Total Shares	Account Value
Jan. 1	$1,000.00	$10.00	100	100	$1,000.00
Apr. 1	1,000.00	8.00	125	225	1,800.00
July 1	1,000.00	12.50	80	305	3,812.50

Average cost per share under plan = $9.84 (3,000/305)

Average of net asset values = $10.17 [(10.00 + 8.00 + 12.50)/3]

For dollar-cost averaging to be a success, stock prices and your mutual fund must work higher over time. Fortunately, this describes the long-term trend. One of the problems encountered when applying an averaging strategy to individual stocks is that there's a much greater likelihood that they will fall in price but never recover, especially if the company ends up in bankruptcy. Happily, fund buyers do not have this worry since they own a diversified portfolio. Only a handful of funds have been long-term losers, and they are pretty easy to spot.

When establishing a program, you need to consider the frequency of your investments—monthly, quarterly, semiannually, or whatever. More frequent intervals increase your chances of buying shares when prices are especially low. On the other hand, this can lead to somewhat more complicated record keeping, especially if you must track your transactions for tax purposes.

Many people are already dollar-cost averaging even though they might not realize it. If you invest a fixed amount monthly in a 401(k) plan or annually in an IRA, you are diversifying your purchases. Also, people who reinvest distributions into additional fund shares are following a form of dollar-cost averaging, even though the cash amounts won't be equal.

VALUE AVERAGING

You don't have to follow dollar-cost averaging strictly by the book. For instance, you will likely improve your results by investing more than your fixed amount when prices are depressed and investing less or perhaps even selling some shares when prices are very high. This describes a relatively new approach known as "value averaging."

Developed and popularized by Michael Edleson, a Harvard University professor, value averaging requires that you increase the dollar amount of your holdings by a set figure each period.[2] To do this, you would need to put in more money when prices have dropped to offset losses on your existing shares. After prices have risen, you would buy fewer shares, perhaps do nothing, or even unload some shares. Unlike dollar-cost averaging, this method has built-in sell rules. In addition, the system makes it easier to estimate how much money you will have by a specific future date. For instance, if you want $40,000 in 10 years, your account would need to grow by about $1,000 each quarter.

Value averaging requires more work than dollar-cost averaging and is not as easy to implement because different amounts of cash must be invested each period. It can also complicate your record keeping for tax purposes, although if you practice it in an IRA or similar plan, you need not worry about this.

Taking the illustration in Table 12–4, and assuming you desire your account to grow by $1,000 quarterly, the value-averaging program would work out as detailed in Table 12–5. The columns are ordered differently here since the focus is now on account value. Notice that to determine the total shares needed on each purchase (or sale) date, you must divide the account value by NAV. The shares bought or sold would be the difference between the number previously held and the new number needed. For example, on April 1 the target account value is $2,000. With an NAV of $8, you require a total of 250 shares ($2,000/$8). Since you already hold 100, you must purchase 150 more.

Table 12-5
Value Averaging

Date	Account Value	NAV	Shares Needed	Shares Bought (Sold)	Amount Invested (Sold)
Jan. 1	$1,000.00	$10.00	100	100	$1,000.00
Apr. 1	2,000.00	8.00	250	150	1,200.00
July 1	3,000.00	12.50	240	(10)	(125.00)

Average cost per share:

Value averaging = $8.65 [(1,000 + 1,200 - 125)/240]

Dollar-cost averaging = $9.84 (from Table 12-4)

After the July 1 transaction, your average cost works out to $8.65, well below the $9.84 obtained with dollar-cost averaging. The more volatile the portfolio's NAV, the greater this advantage. Since value averaging generally results in a lower average cost, it would also generate a higher compound annual return.

Both value and dollar-cost averaging can sometimes pose problems for people trying to maintain specific weightings in each of several asset categories. Suppose you want to keep 15 percent in money-market funds, 25 percent in bond portfolios, and 60 percent in equity funds. With an averaging strategy, you will find that your asset proportions have changed after some time, requiring you to rebalance your holdings. This, in turn, may interfere with the results of your averaging program. While this might not be a serious problem, it is something to be aware of.

Investing Large Sums of Money

The whole rationale behind averaging strategies is to avoid taking a big plunge into the stock market. People who receive a large sum of money may feel compelled to put it to work immediately. A better idea is to break a big amount into smaller increments and buy in gradually, especially if you're dealing with a more volatile equity fund. Rather than invest $500,000 all at once, you could park it in a money-market fund or short-term bond portfolio, moving $50,000 or $100,000 into stock investments at equal time intervals, perhaps every six months. Or, you could use value averaging, requiring your account to grow by, say, $100,000 semiannually.

Don't go too slowly, however, because the opportunity cost of a large sum sitting in a money fund can be high. For example, it would be illogical to park $1 million in a money-market fund and then average in at a rate of only $100 each month. Here you face the risk of having too much cash on the sidelines. The danger of sitting out a bull market is too great to ignore.

Notes

1. Jess H. Chua and Richard S. Woodward, *Gains From Stock Market Timing*. New York: Salomon Brothers Center for the Study of Financial Institutions/New York University, Monograph 1986–2.

2. Michael E. Edleson, "Value Averaging: A New Approach to Accumulation," AAII Journal, August 1988, pp. 11–14.

CHAPTER 13

More on Market Timing

Most mutual fund managers use *fundamental analysis*. In short, this means they evaluate individual companies by scrutinizing their financial statements, products, industry, markets, and management.

Conversely, the more aggressive market timers focus heavily on *technical analysis*. They look primarily at stock price movements and trading-volume patterns, as presented on charts. They identify trends and search for evidence that those trends are either continuing or ending. As long as a trend is in progress, timers will stick with their positions. But when they spot a reversal—especially if several indicators are saying so—they will make changes.

Pure technicians ignore fundamental data and work instead with information on prices and trading volume, perhaps complemented with some additional indicators. Some of these tools can also be of use to fundamental investors.

The realm of technical analysis spans a good four or five dozen indicators, although not everyone uses all or even most. The list includes yardsticks such as relative strength, on-balance volume, the short-interest ratio, the put-call ratio, and the like.

So-called "tape watchers," awaiting a big move up or down in the market, check on gauges such as the New York Stock Exchange tick. This counts the number of stocks whose last price change was an increase, an up-tick, then subtracts the total recording a down-tick. A reading of, say, minus 40 indicates that down-ticks exceed up-ticks by 40. This sort of information might be of some value to mutual fund traders trying to select a good day to switch in or out of an aggressive-growth or sector portfolio.

Although it's nearly impossible to predict near-term changes in the market, some of the most basic technical indicators might help investors pinpoint the best times to enter or exit the market.

TECHNICAL INDICATORS

Trading Volume. Daily stock market volume reflects investor participation or lack thereof, often indicating the strength of an underlying trend. Suppose the market has been going up for several weeks, showing heavy volume on up days and light activity on down days. In this example, volume confirms the existence of strong investor demand. Conversely, if the market has been dropping sharply on heavy volume, but on those days when prices rise slightly volume is light, that reflects definite bearish sentiment.

A popular indicator, the "Arms" or short-term trading index, compares the average volume of declining stocks to that of advancing stocks. It tells whether there is greater activity in rising or in declining issues. This indicator can be found in *Barron's.*

Breadth of Market. You can't be confident that an upward trend remains intact just because the market indexes may be hitting new highs. For greater insight, technicians tabulate the direction of price changes of individual stocks. Each day, several newspapers list the number of advancing and declining issues. *Barron's* publishes this information weekly.

What does it mean? Suppose the Dow Jones industrials have repeatedly hit new highs on successively lighter volume. A technician would examine the number of advances minus declines, perhaps on a daily or weekly basis. The results would offer insight into the probable strength and duration of the rally.

Perhaps losers start to outnumber winners, and the pattern persists, as illustrated in Table 13–1. Summing the net-advances figures for the first two days results in a cumulative breadth of -200. This running total, continued for each successive day, could give you a clue that the bull market may be losing steam. This example shows that a relatively small number of issues are responsible for the new highs on the Dow, but that most stocks are starting to head south.

Table 13-1
Breadth-of-Market Analysis

Day	(1) Advancing Issues	(2) Declining Issues	(3) (1) - (2) Net Advances	(4) Cumulative Breadth*
Monday	900	800	100	100
Tuesday	700	1,000	-300	-200
Wednesday	750	1,150	-400	-600
Thursday	550	1,350	-800	-1400
Friday	400	1,300	-900	-2300

*Cumulative breadth is a continuing total of the net advances.

Cumulative breadth analysis can also signal the possible end to a bear market. The major advantage of this technique is that it tells you in which direction most stocks are moving.

New highs and lows. As a companion to market breadth, technicians also consider the number of stocks making new 52-week highs and lows each day. Again, if the market is near a peak but you notice a decrease in the number of new highs, it provides evidence of dwindling support for a continued advance. And at a trough, if the number of new lows each day begins to decline, the worst of the sell-off may be over.

Momentum. Technicians study momentum in the overall market as well as in individual stocks. This refers to the rate of acceleration or deceleration in the percent changes of a stock's price or the NAV of a mutual fund. Incidentally, some fund managers who focus on growth stocks look for companies with accelerating earnings and price momentum.

Suppose we're working with a stock-market index and calculate its percentage changes on a weekly basis. The results for four successive weeks are as follows: +3 percent, +5 percent, +8 percent and +10 percent. This would be bullish to technicians. You could apply a similar analysis to the NAVs of mutual funds, especially the more volatile aggressive-growth and sector portfolios. The momentum approach works best in a strong, extended bull market.

Moving Averages

Market indexes, stock prices, and fund NAVs fluctuate constantly. Anyone trying to follow all these gyrations could wind up switching excessively. A moving average smooths out short-term price fluctuations, allowing you to discern the long-term trend and avoid whipsaws. The longer the period over which prices are averaged, the smoother the trend line. A 200-day average would result in more smoothing than would a 20-day average.

A moving average may help you detect major changes in the direction of a fund's NAV. It can also be used with indices such as the Dow Jones industrials, Standard & Poor's 500, or Value Line composite to determine the market's trend. When computing a moving average, you must decide how frequently to observe a variable (daily or weekly, for example) and how many observations are to be included. These factors determine the "sensitivity" of the average.

To calculate, say, a 39-week moving average, simply add the current week's NAV to the past 38, then divide by 39. Later, the next week's result would be added and the most distant one dropped. As you continue to recalculate in this manner, the average moves across time.

The computations can be both tedious and complex, especially if you must make adjustments for shareholder distributions. For instance, if the NAV is $10 and you receive a capital gain of $1, the NAV would have to fall by that amount. In cases like this, the technician routinely makes such adjustments by adding back the distribution.

Next, you need to plot actual prices against the moving average to detect buy and sell signals. Table 13–2 provides a simple illustration. Compare the NAV numbers with those in the 5-week moving average column. From weeks 5 through 9, the moving average exceeds the corresponding NAVs, reflected by the negative numbers in column (3). But in week 10, the fund's NAV crosses above the moving average line and the differences in column (3) start to become positive. It appears that the fund has changed course from a declining to an increasing trend—the technician's buy signal.

Table 13-2
A 5-Week Moving Average

Week	(1) NAV	(2) Moving Average*	(3) Differences (1) - (2)
1	12.00	-	-
2	12.75	-	-
3	12.25	-	-
4	11.00	-	-
5	10.25	11.65	- 1.40
6	9.50	11.15	- 1.65
7	8.30	10.26	- 1.96
8	8.75	9.56	- 0.81
9	9.10	9.18	- 0.08
10	10.15	9.16	+ 0.99
11	11.50	9.56	+ 1.94
12	12.50	10.40	+ 2.10

*Determined by adding the current week's NAV to the preceding 4 and dividing by 5. For week 5, 12.00, 12.75, 12.25, 11.00, and 10.25 are summed and divided by 5. The pattern is repeated weekly.

Many market timers follow two key trading rules:

1. *Buy Rule:* Buy the fund when the current NAV rises above the moving average line and that line has begun to trend upward, as illustrated in Figure 13–1.

2. *Sell Rule:* Sell or switch out of the fund when the current NAV drops below the moving average line, which has begun to trend downward, also as seen in Figure 13–1.

In our example, five weeks would not realistically be enough to use in computing a moving average. That's because it would generate too many

Figure 13-1
Moving Average Signals

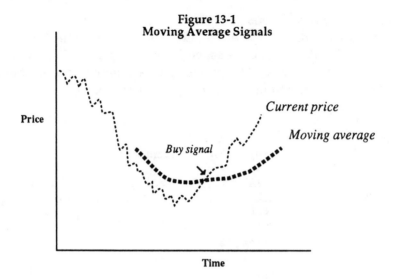

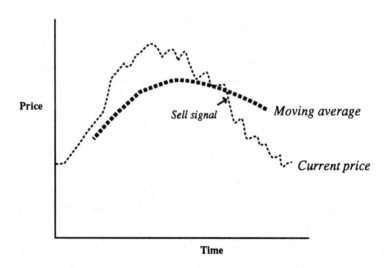

signals, resulting in whipsaws. In other words, the average would give premature signals—putting the investor into stock funds or cash before a trend is clearly established. The more days or weeks you use, the fewer the signals. Conversely, if your moving average encompasses too long a period, each signal might come too late—you could be buying well into an upswing and selling late in a downturn.

Moving averages may cause headaches in flat, trendless markets since they may generate frequent false alarms. Using a short-term average together with a longer-term one can help deal with this problem. You would watch for times when the short-term line crosses above or below the long-term line. The latter would be used to identify trends, while the former would be employed to time switches.

Moving averages can be fine-tuned in other ways. For example, some analysts use exponentially weighted averages, which attach progressively more importance to the most recent prices. Although moving averages can be followed in isolation, it is probably a good idea to use them along with other technical and fundamental indicators to help decide when to make a switch.

A Close Look at Cash

Mutual fund managers always hold some "cash" or money-market securities. They do so for any of the following three reasons:

1. Cash acts as a buffer to meet shareholder redemptions. This way, the manager normally doesn't have to liquidate stocks. Managers who anticipate an increase in redemptions would generally want to build their cash positions, especially if they feel the market is weakening.

2. A portion of the cash balances can represent proceeds from stock sales that have not been reinvested. Perhaps the manager has a pessimistic outlook and does not want to buy more stocks.

3. New shareholder money may be coming in at such a rapid pace that the manager can't keep up with the large inflow. Perhaps the stock market has become pricey, and the manager wants to wait for better buying opportunities.

The Investment Company Institute tabulates a composite *liquid asset ratio* for equity funds. Also known as the *cash ratio*, it shows the percentage of cash holdings by stock funds each month. The ICI began this in 1961, and the ratio has ranged between 3.9 percent and 12.9 percent since then. The annual highs and lows since 1961 are reported in Table 13–3.

Table 13-3
Equity Fund Liquid Asset Ratio

Year	High	Low	Year	High	Low
1961	5.9%	4.4%	1977	8.2%	5.3%
1962	7.1	5.2	1978	10.3	6.5
1963	6.4	4.9	1979	8.9	7.9
1964	5.8	4.4	1980	10.4	8.5
1965	5.8	4.9	1981	11.4	8.1
1966	9.8	5.5	1982	12.2	8.4
1967	7.9	5.2	1983	9.9	7.7
1968	9.4	6.2	1984	10.1	8.0
1969	9.5	7.4	1985	10.7	8.3
1970	10.3	6.6	1986	10.1	8.6
1971	6.3	4.0	1987	11.2	8.8
1972	5.5	3.9	1988	10.8	9.4
1973	8.0	4.6	1989	11.2	8.7
1974	11.8	8.0	1990	12.9	10.7
1975	9.7	6.8	1991	10.7	8.0
1976	6.0	4.5	1992	9.6	7.9

Source: Investment Company Institute

Recent values for the liquid asset ratio can be found in various publications, including *Barron's*, *The Wall Street Journal*, and *Investor's Business Daily*. By tracking the numbers each month, you can tell if managers collectively are making significant changes in their cash positions. An increase generally signifies that managers are building up cash because their outlook is becoming less sanguine; a decrease may reflect optimism.

The liquid asset ratio tells the most at extreme levels. Above, say, 10.5 percent, it indicates mutual funds have plenty of cash should they decide to move heavily into stocks. This pent-up buying power can be considered bullish, especially at a market trough. From September 1981 to August 1982, for example, the ratio averaged 10.8 percent. It peaked at 12.2 percent in June 1982, just before the bull market took off.

At the other extreme, a cash ratio ranging from 6 percent to 4 percent would indicate a fully invested position, with little money available to add further momentum to a rising market.

In fact, the mutual fund cash ratio has been used by some technicians as a *contrarian indicator*. The theory holds that fund managers as a group tend to be heavily invested at peaks and underinvested during troughs. Interpreted this way, the behavior of the cash ratio reflects poor timing ability on their part. This contrarian theory tells investors to do the opposite of what fund managers do at peaks and troughs.

Changes in cash positions do not, however, necessarily lend themselves to straightforward interpretation. The cash level could change for several reasons, as we've explained. Since the ratio is affected by both total assets (the denominator) and cash (the numerator), the state of the market will also exert an important influence. During rallies, the value of the stock holdings rises. During a bear market, the opposite is true.

Thus, the ratio could vary even if cash stays constant. Suppose Fund A has a cash value of $12 and assets of $100. Its liquid asset ratio is 12 percent. Now stocks surge and assets rise to $125 but cash remains at $12. The ratio falls from 12 percent to 9.6 percent.

The ICI also provides other monthly data that can be used along with the cash ratio to determine where money is coming from and going to. These include total sales and redemptions of fund shares and total purchases and sales of common stock by managers. During the advanced stages of a bull market, investors often try to get in on the action by purchasing large amounts of equity fund shares. During market troughs, redemptions can run at high levels.

The January Effect

Stocks exhibit some seasonal anomalies. The most noteworthy is the "January effect." Academic research has documented that stock prices, especially those of smaller, thinly traded companies, have a tendency to rally around the turn of the year. This move may begin at the end of December and persist for a week or so in January. In fact, a big part of the returns on small stocks for the whole year often comes in January. We don't know whether this phenomenon will continue to occur with the same intensity it has in the past since more people have become aware of it.

The January effect has been somewhat of a puzzle. One explanation is that people sell stocks showing paper losses in December for tax purposes. These are often thinly traded companies that become grossly depressed. Then, around the turn of the year when the selling pressure has abated, investors snap them up at bargain prices. In some cases, the buyers are managers of small-cap mutual funds.

How does this seasonal pattern affect you? You may want to invest in your small-cap fund in December rather than in January, especially if the small-stock sector has taken a beating toward the end of the year. The problem is that you have to beware of a potential tax trap, since many funds make a capital gains distribution shortly before year end. But if your fund is in an IRA or you can offset the gain with capital losses, there is no problem. Otherwise, contact the fund to determine when the year-end dividend will be declared. There may be an opportunity for you to buy shares on or shortly after the ex-dividend date, which trails the declaration date by one business day for mutual-funds.

MARKET-TIMING SERVICES

Anyone interested in more aggressive switching may wish to consider subscribing to a mutual fund timing service. Many use technical indicators, commonly moving averages. However, each has a somewhat different focus. The addresses and phone numbers of several leading services are given in Appendix 5.

A good market timer can offer busy investors some guidance. But since this extra help will cost you money, you want one that has demonstrated a successful track record and provides clear signals. Mark Hulbert of *The Hulbert Financial Digest* tracks 140 stock and mutual fund newsletters, including many timing services. Of the letters Hulbert follows, about one-third focus on mutual funds. In most cases, timing services provide a hotline so that subscribers can keep abreast of late-breaking developments.

Factors to consider in evaluating a service include:

1. How long has it been around? The older a service, the greater the odds that it has been reasonably successful.

2. How well has it performed? Does it offer advice that is worth substantially more than its cost?

3. How many subscribers does the service have? Some may be unwilling to provide this information, but those that have lots of followers must be doing something right.

4. What is the background of the person doing the research and making the recommendations?

5. Does the service offer clear, straightforward advice on switching? Does it provide the kind of information you're looking for? If the service just makes you more confused, you don't want it.

You can compare several services by taking out trial subscriptions at reduced prices.

THE RISKS OF MARKET TIMING

Our most important warning to market timers can be summed up in a few sentences:

AVOID EXTREME MOVES. NEVER MOVE TOO FAR OUT OF EQUI-TIES. BULL MARKET STAMPEDES ARE WHAT MAKE STOCK MARKET INVESTING SO ATTRACTIVE, BUT THESE BIG SPIKES ARE INFREQUENT AND OCCUR AT UNPREDICTABLE TIMES. THE RISK OF MISSING A BIG SURGE IS TOO GREAT TO IGNORE.

What do we mean by moving away from stocks? That's difficult to generalize because investors have different risk tolerances, cash needs, and other characteristics that will affect their equity holdings. Some might want 50 percent of their assets in stocks or stock funds, others 25 percent and still others 80 percent.

Professors P. R. Chandy and William Reichenstein advocate modest portfolio adjustments rather than what they call "full-bore market timing."[1] This describes an approach where the timer is either 100 percent in stocks or cash depending on the investment outlook.

Chandy and Reichenstein emphasize that there have been relatively few months in stock market history when the averages have made a substantial jump to higher levels, with the implication that you don't want to miss one of these moves. Investors who are completely on the sidelines when stampedes occur risk doing significantly worse than the market as a whole. For example, Chandy and Reichenstein calculated a 9.4 percent annualized return for the S&P 500 from 1926 through 1987, assuming a buy-and-hold strategy. But investors who missed the strongest 50 months over this extensive period would have logged a return of zero percent.[2] Because it is very difficult to predict the near-term direction of the market, complete switches between cash and stocks are highly risky.

Professors Chandy and Reichenstein advocate a modest form of market timing based on changes in the aggregate dividend yield.[3] In general terms, they say when market yields are high, invest more heavily in stocks, and when they are low, lighten up. (Our guidelines for using the market's dividend yield as a timing tool were given in Chapter 12.) A portfolio that is normally 50 percent in stocks might vary between proportions of 35 percent to 65 percent. This way, you avoid extreme moves and lessen the risk of missing a sharp upward surge.

HOW FUNDS TIME THE MARKET

You may want a fund that always maintains a fully invested position so you can decide for yourself when to be in stocks, cash, or other assets. Or you may want one that does some or all of the timing for you. Some portfolio managers are highly aggressive market timers. In fact, most do more timing than you might realize, even though they consistently maintain a fully invested posture. It's part of their job to keep abreast of changing conditions, rotating their holdings accordingly. Fund managers can time the market in one or more of the following ways:

1. *Altering the cash position.* You can see to what extent a manager times by periodically tracking the cash position. If the proportion of cash equivalents varies from, say, 5 percent to 30 percent or more; it's obvious that the manager doesn't always stay fully invested. Of course, you should be able to learn about the fund's investment philosophy by contacting a shareholder rep or reading the prospectus. Compare the cash positions at a given point in time of different funds you're considering. Also compare your fund to similar types of portfolios.

2. *Value investing.* Value investors look for stocks that are cheap when measured by earnings, cash flow, or book value. A manager might find a company that offers a dollar's worth of assets for 50 cents. This approach might be thought of as a form of indirect market timing since the valuations of individual companies dictate how pricey the overall market is. Value investors tend to be more heavily in stocks at market troughs but hold large cash positions at peaks.

3. *Hedging with futures or options.* Managers who expect a significant decline in stock prices can use futures and options. Usually they don't hedge the full portfolio, just part of it. But futures and options can serve as an effective substitute for increasing the fund's cash position.

4. *Sector rotation.* This means the manager moves in and out of industry or other stock groups based on the economic outlook. For instance, if a downturn looms, he or she may underweight cyclical stocks such as autos in favor of more defensive or recession-resistant groups such as pharmaceuticals or food companies. Managers rotate among sectors based on their perceived growth potential as well as their current valuation.

5. *Country rotation.* Global and international-fund managers often move in and out of specific nations. They overweight countries and regions that offer good value and underweight those that appear expensive.

TIMING GUIDELINES

If you want to follow a timing approach of some type, it might be best to find a fund whose portfolio manager does this for you. At the least, this is the easier, less time-consuming and less costly way to go. But assuming you wish to be actively involved, heed the following tips:

1. Don't expect to be a perfect timer. It's impossible. You simply can't make accurate short-term predictions of the stock and bond markets on a consistent basis.

2. Avoid hyperactive switching. This won't make you rich. It will merely cause confusion, complicate your record keeping, and boost your taxes and transaction costs.

3. Avoid extreme moves in favor of more moderate adjustments. For example, you might normally target 60 percent of your portfolio in equities, moving to as much as 75 percent when you feel the market offers outstanding value and as little as 45 percent when stocks appear overpriced. If you follow this kind of plan, there's less chance for making big mistakes. In the same vein, be skeptical of fund managers who make extreme moves.

4. Consider dollar-cost averaging, an easy-to-use, dependable strategy that is a form of market timing. If you're willing to devote some additional effort, value averaging can lead to even better results. Both programs work best if followed over a long period with good performing funds.

5. Don't spend lots of time trying to track a long list of market indicators. The financial world is highly complex and confusing, even for experts. Stick with several basic indicators such as market P/Es and dividend yields, the levels and trends of market indexes, trading volume and breadth, mutual fund cash positions and the shape and level of the yield curve.

6. Watch for times when greed or fear predominates. These can be periods of opportunity for contrarians. Just keep in mind that extremes in valuation sometimes persist for a long time.

7. Don't overemphasize domestic stocks and stock funds. About 60 percent of the global value of stocks exists beyond our borders. Better deals often can be found in different parts of the world. If the market is richly priced here, that isn't necessarily the case in other regions.

8. Find out how much your fund manager practices market timing. That individual, or team, may be doing more than you think. Some managers rotate to different sectors as industry conditions change, while others go heavily into cash or hedge with stock-index futures or options. The more timing your manager does, the less you need to do.

Notes

1. P. R. Chandy and William Reichenstein, "Timing Strategies and the Risk of Missing Bull Markets," *AAII Journal*, August 1991, pp. 17–19.

2. ———, "Stock Market Timing: A Modest Proposal, *AAII Journal*, April 1992, p. 7.

3. ———, *op. cit.*, p. 9.

CHAPTER 14

Mapping Out Your Retirement Strategy

People are living longer and retiring earlier. That makes proper planning for your later years more important than ever. Mutual funds, with their built-in diversification, flexibility, and efficient services, offer outstanding advantages as savings vehicles. In fact, more than one out of every four individual retirement-account dollars is now held in mutual funds, along with an even greater proportion of self-employed retirement-plan (or Keogh) money.

Most likely, the amount of retirement money invested in mutual-funds will continue to grow in the future.

ABCs OF RETIREMENT PLANNING

Proper planning involves two primary phases: saving or investing during the working years, then carefully managing your assets during retirement. Contrary to what you might believe, the planning and management phase does not end when your employment does.

Individuals generally require 60 percent to 80 percent of their working-years earnings to live comfortably in retirement. It's far better to have more than you're going to need than risk running short later.

Most people build their nest eggs from one or more of the following sources:

1. Employer pension plans

2. Social Security

3. Personal savings and voluntary contributions to various tax-sheltered retirement plans

Your employer should be able to tell you how much monthly income you could expect from your pension program. To obtain an estimate of what you can anticipate from Uncle Sam, phone the Social Security Administration at 1-800-772-1213. Ask for a "Personal Earnings and Benefit Estimate Statement," or Form 7004, which you need to complete and return.

Employer pension plans and social security typically do not provide enough for a comfortable retirement. They have to be supplemented with personal savings and contributions to tax- deferred retirement programs. You should try to estimate this shortfall when devising your investment plan of attack. Figure 14–1 summarizes four common voluntary retirement vehicles.

Figure 14–1
Voluntary Retirement Plans in a Nutshell

Individual Retirement Accounts (or IRA)
Available to all wage earners under age 70½. You may contribute 100 percent of earned income up to a $2,000 annual maximum ($4,000 for a working couple). For those with a nonworking spouse, spousal IRAs may be created with a $2,250 annual limit. Those with adjusted gross income of $25,000 or less ($40,000 for couples) or who are not covered by a pension plan can deduct contributions in full. Earnings are tax-deferred for all IRA holders. Withdrawals start between the ages of 59½ and 70½. A penalty applies for premature withdrawals before 59½ unless you become disabled.

Keogh Plans
These are advantageous for qualified self-employed individuals. Keoghs can be used even if you are covered by a corporate pension plan, provided you have income from self-employment. Contributions can range up to the lesser of $30,000 or 25 percent of your income. Keoghs also can be used along with IRAs.

401(k) Plans
A popular salary-reduction plan available through many employers. The maximum contribution is linked to inflation and was $8,728 in 1992. Employers often contribute money on behalf of their workers.

403(b) Plans
A salary-reduction program available to employees of certain charitable organizations and public-school systems.

First, estimate your total monthly expenditures during the first year of retirement. Then forecast how much annual income you'll be receiving from pension plans and Social Security.

Next, project how much you'll need to have saved by the time you attain retirement age to supplement these sources. Mutual fund companies may be able to help you. For example, T. Rowe Price will provide a comprehensive retirement-planning workbook on request.

The best retirement plans allow you the flexibility of making large, deductible contributions, which reduce your taxable income and tax bill. Your savings then grow tax-deferred until you make withdrawals.

MANAGING YOUR NEST EGG

Obviously, the comfort of your retirement years will depend largely on how much money you have accumulated. This is why you need to follow a wise, profitable investment program. The following guidelines can help you compile a respectable nest egg:

1. Select the appropriate tax-sheltered retirement plan or plans, based on your circumstances.

2.   Get started. Young people should start saving early in life, even if it's just a few hundred dollars a year. Older individuals who have neglected to invest for retirement should begin as soon as possible.

3.   Minimize the tax bite on lump-sum distributions. Lump sums received from company pension and profit-sharing plans may be transferred into an IRA to retain the sheltering benefits. Mutual funds are attractive vehicles for transfers because of their generally low annual fees and exchange privileges.

4.   Watch out for inflation. Invest as much as you can in stock funds, to maintain purchasing power. And try to take advantage of the better long-term performance possible with small-stock and international portfolios.

5.   But avoid high-risk investments. Speculation is the quickest way to lose wealth. Mutual funds generally offer more safety for retirement plans than do a few individual stocks.

TAX-DEFERRED COMPOUNDING

This is the key to long-term wealth accumulation. By keeping Uncle Sam out of your nest egg, your investments build up faster. All of the retirement options identified in Figure 14–1 offer tax-deferred compounding. It makes a lot of sense to have your money grow in this manner whenever possible.

Suppose you can earn 10 percent a year on a stock fund. If you contribute $2,000 to a deductible retirement plan, the full $2,000 goes to work for you. The future values of annual $2,000 investments for various periods appear in Table 14–1.

Conversely, in a nonsheltered or taxable account, you would first pay taxes on your $2,000 of income, leaving a smaller sum for investment. Assuming a 36 percent combined federal and state bracket, your $2,000 would be reduced by $720 in taxes, leaving $1,280 to invest. In addition, your annual return would shrink. With a 36 percent bracket, the after-tax gain amounts to 6.4 percent.

With a nondeductible retirement plan, you pay taxes on the income you contribute, but that money then grows tax-deferred. Table 14–1 shows that even a nondeductible IRA is not that bad a deal.

Table 14-1
Future Values of $2,000 Pre-Tax Anuual Contributions*

Contribution Period (in years)	Deductible Retirement Account	Nondeductible Retirement Account	Taxable Account
5	$13,431	$8,596	$7,739
10	35,062	22,440	18,292
15	69,899	44,736	32,683
25	216,364	138,473	79,069
40	973,704	623,170	233,190

*Contributions are made at the start of each year and earn 10 percent compounded annually before taxes. In the taxable account, both contributions and earnings are taxed at a 36% combined rate. In the nondeductible account, only the contributions are taxed. The after-tax contributions equal $1,280 each year.

Suppose that at retirement in 40 years you withdraw $973,704 from the deductible account and pay taxes at a rate of 36 percent. You would still have $623,171 left over (the same as if you had used a nondeductible IRA), which greatly exceeds the $233,190 balance in the taxable account.

A better strategy from a tax viewpoint would be to take your payout in annual increments—waiting as long as you can after retirement before starting to draw money out. You *must* begin withdrawing from an IRA by the time you reach 70½. But the longer you are able to wait, the longer the money keeps compounding tax-free.

THE ADVANTAGE OF AN EARLY START

Suppose Monica, a 22-year-old college graduate with foresight, anticipates needing at least $1 million at the time of her planned retirement in 40 years. Assuming a 4 percent inflation rate, Monica calculates that in four decades that $1 million will have the purchasing power of a little more than $208,000 in today's dollars. How much will she have to contribute each year—and in total—assuming tax deferral?

The answer depends on two variables—the length of time until she retires and the rate at which her savings will compound. Assuming a 10 percent annual return and various investment horizons ranging from 10 to 40 years, the answers appear in Table 14–2.

Over a 40-year period, Monica needs to invest a total of $82,160 ($2,054 x 40). Subtracting that figure from the $1 million accumulated shows that her earnings amounted to $917,840. In other words, 92 percent of the $1 million came from the earnings. The later Monica begins investing, the smaller this percentage. If she started just 10 years before retirement, she'd have to contribute 57 percent of the $1 million accumulation, with earnings accounting for only 43 percent.

Table 14-2
Contributions Needed to Accumulate $1 Million

Contribution Period (in years)	Annual Amount*	Total Contribution
40	$2,054	$82,160
30	5,527	165,810
25	9,244	231,100
20	15,872	317,440
15	28,613	429,195
10	57,041	570,410

*Assumes contributions are made at the beginning of each year and earn 10% compounded annually.

The power of time is so great that a young person could invest modest amounts in a tax-deferred account for a few years, then stop and simply let the money build up. Given enough time, this approach would still result in a substantial sum. An investor who began later in life would have to contribute more for a longer period to compile an equivalent nest egg.

To illustrate, suppose a 25-year-old socks away $2,000 in a retirement plan at the start of each year for 10 years, then stops but leaves the money alone for another 30 years. The ultimate value would be $611,817, assuming a 10 percent compounding rate. To build the same nest egg, a 45-year-old would need to invest $9,711 for 20 years—nearly 5 times as much for twice as long.

But don't be disturbed by all this if you're older. Although you can't turn back the clock, you still may have a chance to earn a substantial amount on what you contribute. Life expectancies have increased significantly, and good stock funds can offer attractive growth potential prior to and during your retirement years. It's a fallacy to think you'll be withdrawing all your money at age 65 anyway. Chances are, you'll let at least some of it compound for another 5, 10, or 20 years.

INVESTING FOR RETIREMENT

The Investment Company Institute keeps track of what people put into their IRAs. According to a recent breakdown of assets in the ICI's *Mutual Fund Fact Book*, about half of the IRA money in mutual funds was committed to various categories of equity funds, including aggressive-growth, growth, and growth-and-income.

It's good to see equity funds well represented on the ICI's list. Increasingly, people are recognizing that stock portfolios offer the best hope for avoiding the erosion of retirement dollars from inflation. Simply put, it's well documented that stock funds provide far higher total returns over long stretches than fixed-income portfolios do.

Take the case of William, a 30-year-old, self-employed writer who wants to begin saving for retirement. He estimates that a growth stock fund could return 10 percent a year and a conservative bond fund, 6 percent. William, who plans to retire at 65, expects to invest $4,000 annually for the next 35 years in a Keogh plan. How much purchasing power can he accumulate with each investment?

William first needs to distinguish between the nominal and the real rates of return. The *nominal rate* is simply the observed rate, such as 10 percent on the stock fund. The *real rate* is an inflation-adjusted number that measures the *growth of purchasing power*. You can estimate it by subtracting the expected inflation from the nominal number. With inflation projected at 4 percent a year, the real rate works out to 6 percent (10 percent - 4 percent) on the stock fund and 2 percent (6 percent - 4 percent) on the bond portfolio.

Assuming William made his investments at the beginning of each year, the bond and stock funds would compound to the following nominal and real future values:

	Future Values:	
	Nominal	*Real*
Bond portfolio	$ 472,483	$203,977
Stock portfolio	1,192,507	472,483

When you look at results in terms of inflation-adjusted real values, it becomes clearer that you need the higher returns of a stock fund to protect and enhance your dollars over the long haul.

Even though stocks are more volatile than bonds, long-term investors benefit from time diversification, as we've explained earlier. Younger people planning for a retirement decades away need not let the volatility concern them. They should focus instead on the long-term upward trend in stock prices, perhaps using dollar-cost averaging to buy more shares in a fund when its NAV is down and fewer shares when it's high. In this sense, bear markets can actually benefit long-term savers.

Many types of equity funds can supply solid results for younger retirement investors, including small-cap, international, growth, and even growth-and-income portfolios. Index funds are also attractive for retirement purposes because of their modest expenses and very low portfolio turnovers. As explained in Chapter 6, a variety of index vehicles are available today, including large-cap, small-stock, and international funds.

As people grow older, they tend to lighten up on equity funds and focus more on income. But it's generally unwise to move too far away from stocks, even at retirement, because bonds don't mix well with high inflation. A person retiring at 65 could easily live two or three more decades. People who call it quits at a younger age have even more time to worry about inflation. For these individuals, stock funds provide a hedge. One approach might be to redeem shares from a stock fund periodically to meet your income needs rather than to invest heavily in bond funds for their monthly income.

In short, it's difficult to manage with only fixed-income funds. True, you may need to have some bond holdings for income and stability, but you also need equities for growth.

MOVING RETIREMENT ASSETS

You've been reading about the merits of tax-deferred compounding. If you want to protect this tax advantage, you must be careful when taking a lump-sum distribution from a former employer's pension plan.

A lump-sum distribution can occur for several reasons, including retirement, job changes, layoffs, or disability. In some cases, you might wind up with a significant amount of money that you hadn't anticipated receiving. Normally, you can contribute no more than $2,000 a year to an IRA. It takes time to build an account. Conversely, you might be able to move $20,000, $30,000, or even a lot more from an employer's pension into an IRA at once.

Much of the time, people take a lump-sum distribution and simply pay taxes on it. Depending on your circumstances, however, moving the assets into an IRA may be better since you can continue to reap the benefits of tax-deferred compounding. Plus, you will typically enjoy even greater control of the money since it can be invested in whatever fund you want. If you haven't yet decided which portfolio you want within a chosen family, simply park the assets in a money fund while you're deciding.

The IRS requires employers to withhold for federal taxes 20 percent of lump-sum withdrawals from company pensions—including 401(k) and 403(b) plans—unless you initiate a "direct" transfer into an IRA or a new employer's program. By direct, that means you personally can't touch the distribution check. Keep in mind that the 20 percent withholding now applies even to money you temporarily take possession of, intending to roll it into an IRA within the 60-day period allowed by the IRS. This complicates matters. To keep things simple and avoid facing the danger of paying taxes on the 20 percent withheld (as well as a 10 percent premature distribution penalty if you're under 59½), use the direct approach. Transferring assets directly from a qualified pension plan into an IRA is not a taxable distribution.

Suppose you later decide you don't like Fund Family A and want to move your IRA to Fund Family B. In this case you could use either a direct IRA transfer or an IRA rollover (where you receive a distribution check then reinvest it). The 20 percent withholding referred to above does not apply to IRA-to-IRA moves. However, the IRS permits only one 60-day rollover per IRA account in each 12-month period. Conversely, with the IRA transfer you face no 12-month limit on the number of moves you can make. To learn more about IRA rollovers and transfers, ask your tax adviser or fund company.

CONCLUSION

The two biggest enemies of people saving for retirement are taxes and inflation. Tax-deferred accounts and common stocks offer the best ways to fight back. Tax laws will change from time to time, but the principles of good retirement planning will remain the same. The more assets you can keep away from Uncle Sam, the better.

As a final thought, don't succumb to the temptation of socking away too much money in a retirement plan. Despite the tax-sheltering advantages, it's important to maintain sufficient liquidity. You can take money out of an IRA at any time, but you face a 10 percent penalty for premature withdrawals if you are under age 59½, unless you become disabled. The impact of this penalty becomes less, however, if you have been using tax-deferred compounding for a number of years.

CHAPTER 15

Pros and Cons of Variable Annuities

So far, we've examined tax-sheltered investing through traditional retirement plans. There's another choice you should be familiar with: the variable annuity. What's "variable" about it is the investment return—it fluctuates the same as an ordinary mutual fund does.

Variable annuities have surged in popularity since the Tax Reform Act of 1986 eliminated other types of shelters, including limited partnerships. Typical customers include long-term, retirement-oriented investors who have already contributed the maximum to qualified plans, such as IRAs, yet want an alternative to municipal bonds.

Although an annuity investment isn't tax-deductible, the money grows tax-deferred as it would in an IRA or qualified retirement plan. In that sense, it's similar to a nondeductible IRA. As with any long-term savings vehicle, the sooner you get started with a variable annuity, the more compounding will be working for you.

Like ordinary mutual funds, variable annuities offer built-in diversification and professional management. Simply put, they are really just mutual funds with an insurance "wrapper" containing a minimum death benefit. The insurance component allows taxes on income and gains to be deferred. Don't confuse variable annuities with variable life, a type of life-insurance policy.

As you might expect, dozens of mainstream mutual fund families manage variable-annuity portfolios. The list includes Fidelity, Franklin, Massachusetts Financial, Merrill Lynch, Putnam, Scudder, and Vanguard. Typically, investors get a choice of fund types, though the array doesn't compare in number to the lineup of portfolios offered by a medium- or large-sized mutual fund group. You can invest in one or several portfolios and move the money about as you choose, generally at little or no cost.

CONTRACT BASICS

An annuity is a contract between an individual and a life-insurance company to provide future payments. Figure 15–1 identifies the major contract options, and Figure 15–3 at the end of this chapter provides for quick reference a glossary of annuity terms.

Figure 15-1
Annuity Options at a Glance

PREMIUM PAYMENTS	TIME TO PAYOUT
•Single	•Immediate
•Periodic	•Deferred
INVESTMENT RETURNS	PAYOUT CHOICES
•Fixed	•Lump sum
•Variable	•Fixed period
	•Lifetime
	•Lifetime with period certain
	•Joint and last survivor

An annuity can include up to three parties:

1. *Contract owner.* The person in control of all contract terms.

2. *Annuitant.* Often the owner, the individual who receives payments during the payout period.

3. *Beneficiary.* The person entitled to residual benefits from the contract should the annuitant die.

Annuities, in turn, can be divided into two basic types: fixed and variable.

The *fixed annuity* is the older type. With this guaranteed contract, the owner locks in an interest rate for a period of a year or so. At the end of this period, the insurer designates a new rate that's typically above the guaranteed base amount of interest that the company must pay. Like a bond or a bond fund, a fixed annuity may fail to provide a satisfactory inflation hedge, thereby subjecting the investor to purchasing-power risk.

Fixed-annuity assets are invested in the insurance company's *general account.* This means the company's creditors can get their hands on this money in the event of trouble. For this reason, fixed-annuity purchasers need to check the rating of the insurer's financial health. You'd want a company rated at least "A" by sources such as A. M. Best Co. and Standard & Poor's.

With *variable annuities*, there's no such locked-in rate. In fact, you get to choose among several portfolios to find one that suits your risk tolerance. With variable products, the investment risk gets passed from insurer to contract holder, which offers the latter a chance of earning substantially higher returns than he or she would on a fixed account. Also, variable-annuity assets are "walled-off" from insurance-company creditors in a *separate account,* which means you don't have to worry about the firm's credit rating. Variable annuities are sometimes called *self-directed* annuities because you have the ability to move money in and out of different portfolios.

Annuity Stages

There are two phases in the life of an annuity:

1. The accumulation, or asset-building, phase.

2. The payout, distribution, or "annuitization" phase.

The accumulation phase. You can purchase an annuity by paying either a single premium or periodic amounts. You buy "accumulation units" similar to mutual fund shares. The "accumulation unit value" is analogous to a fund's NAV. Unlike a mutual fund, however, a variable annuity pays no income and capital gains distributions to investors so its accumulation unit value builds up over a period of years.

During the accumulation phase the retained income and capital gains grow tax-deferred, as in the example of a nondeductible retirement account in Table 14–1. You can set up an automatic dollar-cost averaging program with a variable annuity. For example, you may start out with your premium allocated to a money market account, then initiate a program to have cash put into an aggressive-growth portfolio on a regular basis.

As noted, the annuity contains a minimum death benefit. This protects your beneficiary against any market losses during the accumulation period. If you as annuitant should die before payments begin, the beneficiary would receive the amount of your total contributions (less any withdrawals) or the current surrender value of the account—whichever is greater.

Some variable annuities offer a "stepped-up" death benefit option, which would increase the base amount payable to the beneficiary, say, once every five years. Once you annuitize, you lose this death benefit, however. By annuitizing, you set up a plan for periodic distributions, as we'll illustrate.

The death benefit really isn't an important reason for purchasing a variable annuity. It provides a modest security blanket for people who worry about low-probability, worst-case scenarios of losing money within the first few years of buying an annuity.

The payout phase. In the contract, the insurance company agrees to make a series of payments consisting of principal and earnings for a defined period to the annuitant or to a named beneficiary. Besides lump sums, the common payout options are as follows:

1. *Fixed period.* This commonly ranges from 5 to 30 years with payments made monthly.
2. *Lifetime.* Payments continue for as long as the annuitant lives.
3. *Lifetime with period certain.* With this option, payments continue for a designated period, even if it exceeds the annuitant's life span. Suppose the period certain is 180 months and the annuitant

dies after 90 months; the present value of the remaining payments would go to the beneficiary.

4. *Joint and last survivor.* Payments continue until the death of the last survivor. This can be a logical choice for a husband and wife.

Unlike regular life-insurance, which protects you against the risk of premature death, the lifetime payout options on variable annuities insure you (and your joint annuitant if you name one) against the danger of outliving your retirement nest egg. It's worth noting that the insurance company may make a rather lengthy estimate of your life expectancy if you take the lifetime option. A longer estimate results in smaller monthly payments, since the company would be paying you money for more years.

Just how does annuitization work? Here's a simple illustration.

EXAMPLE: Suppose Helen, a 65-year-old retiree, has accumulated $500,000. She wants to convert this sum into an annuity that will provide constant monthly payments over the next 15 years. She decides to purchase a contract offering a 6 percent fixed rate of return. How much will she receive each month? She can plan on payments of $4,219.28 each. Helen's $500,000 initial lump sum will provide 180 monthly payments totaling $759,470. Part of each payment is principal, and the remainder is taxable interest.

As with an IRA, there is a 10 percent penalty tax imposed on accumulated earnings if you start taking out money before age 59½. No penalty would apply if you become disabled or die. At or beyond 59½, you can take a lump-sum distribution or annuitize. You can also annuitize at a younger age without penalty if you choose to take income spread over your remaining life expectancy.

When the payments start, you as annuitant must pay taxes on the portion that represents earnings. Alternatively, you can compound your money tax-deferred until age 85 before making your first withdrawals.

With a "deferred" annuity, which is commonly used to save for retirement, the payment stream does not begin until some future date. With an "immediate" annuity, you start receiving money soon after you have paid the premium. Thus, the immediate type of plan has no accumulation period. Someone who has just retired might purchase an immediate annuity. A deferred product can be converted to an immediate annuity, commonly at retirement.

A variable annuity can pay either a fixed or a varying income stream. With the latter option, the amount you receive depends on how well your investments performed.

In particular, the size of your monthly payments would be based on four factors:

1. The total amount of your investment.

2. The length of your accumulation period.

3. Your investment performance, net of expenses.

4. The insurer's estimate of your life expectancy, if you choose a lifetime annuity.

You can also receive a lump-sum distribution with a variable annuity or move into a fixed contract.

SUBACCOUNTS

Technically, the person who invests in a variable annuity does not acquire a *direct* ownership interest in the mutual fund. Rather, that person owns a stake in a variable annuity "subaccount" through the sponsoring insurance company, which is the legal owner of the mutual fund. Without going into more detail, suffice it to say that this arrangement is legally necessary for the investor to get the tax-deferral advantage.

The subaccount is simply a division of a separate (or variable) umbrella account. In other words, the individual portfolios within the separate account are the subaccounts. For example, if Fund Family A has six subaccounts, it would have six mutual funds within the wrapper. Figure 15–2 illustrates this relationship. As measured by total assets, subaccounts are typically much smaller than comparable mutual funds.

The insurance company maintains the subaccounts and keeps them separate from its general account. As stated earlier, if the insurer gets into trouble, creditors can't lay their hands on the money in the subaccounts, an obvious plus for variable-annuity holders.

Figure 15-2
The Subaccount Mutual Fund Connection

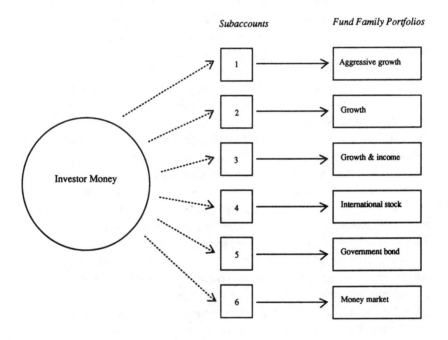

In addition, ordinary mutual funds must be segregated from any subaccounts. Each subaccount is therefore set up as a distinct portfolio, although it may mirror or "clone" an established fund offered by the same company. In fact, the subaccount managers are frequently the same individuals who oversee the family's regular mutual funds.

To make things even more confusing, some variable annuities offer "fixed-rate accounts." They are not the same as a fixed annuity but give the variable investor a similar option.

These fixed options within a variable annuity pay a guaranteed rate of interest. They are part of the insurance company's general account and require you to make a commitment for a specific period, such as one or three years. For instance, you might go into a fixed option when rates are high to lock in a certain level of interest. Or they might appeal to someone who has just retired and wants stability. Since the fixed account is in the insurance company's general account, the insurer bears the investment risk, unlike with a variable account.

To get daily unit price, yield, and performance information on the individual variable portfolios, you can call the fund company on its toll-free 800 number. You can't get daily prices in the newspaper since the subaccounts are not publicly traded. *Barron's* contains a weekly table on variable-annuity unit values based on data from Lipper Analytical Services. Subaccounts are grouped under the name of the underlying insurance company.

Both Lipper and Morningstar track the performances of variable annuities. Ask your broker or financial planner about these reference tools. The Morningstar *Variable Annuity Sourcebook*, published annually, may be available in larger libraries. It contains a wealth of information that can be used to make a detailed analysis and comparison of different portfolios, just as you can with the Morningstar mutual fund service.

Analyzing a variable annuity would be similar to researching a regular fund, but you should do a more thorough job since you're dealing with a far more complex product and making a long-term commitment. Read the prospectus and shareholder reports carefully, along with the Statement of Additional Information if you want further details. As with an ordinary fund, fees and past performance are highly important.

SORTING OUT THE COSTS

Costs associated with a variable annuity can be broken down into at least four categories:

1. *Surrender charge.* A back-end surrender charge, similar to a contingent-deferred sales charge on a regular mutual fund, usually exists—front-end loads are rare. The amount might be 7 percent in the first year, 6 percent in the second, 5 percent in the third, and so on, phasing out completely after seven years. Surrender charges may kick in again, however, under certain conditions—if you make additional investments, for example. On the plus side, variable annuities don't have 12b–1 fees.

2. *Maintenance fee.* The annual contract maintenance fee generally ranges from $25 to $40.

3. *Fund operating expenses.* These costs include the portfolio-management fees and other expenses you would have with an ordinary mutual fund, expressed as a percent of net assets.

4. *Insurance-related charges.* Called the "mortality and expense-risk charge," they can range from 0.5 percent to 1.5 percent a year of average account value. This is the fee for the guaranteed death benefit and covers a longer "lifetime" payout period should the annuitant, or joint annuitant, outlive normal life expectancy. In addition, it covers a guarantee by the insurance company that your expenses will never exceed a specified amount. There is also an administrative fee under this category.

Of course, expenses vary widely, so shop around. In fact, there are even some pure no-load funds with no surrender charges.

An important question to ask about a variable annuity is how long it will take before the tax-deferred growth begins to outweigh your additional expenses, making you better off with the annuity than with a regular fund. The following factors would lead to a shorter break-even time:

1. Lower costs.

2. A higher tax bracket.

3. Higher investment returns.

The most appropriate variable-annuity investments include aggressive-growth, growth, growth-and-income and international-stock portfolios since they should be much better long-run performers than fixed-income funds are. The variable annuity is where the most aggressive part of your portfolio should be, provided you can tolerate a risky component.

You're going to want to stay put for a long time if you face stiff surrender charges. For this reason, you have to be extra cautious before buying. Since you will probably switch among different funds within a family eventually, you want a group that offers an attractive menu where all the investment choices are good performers. We advise going with a large, well-known complex that has a reputation for superior returns and reasonable expenses.

Although annuities are designed for retirement investing, you are not locked into a fund group forever. You can transfer from Family A to Family B using what is known as a "1035 exchange." This is not a taxable transaction, as your money remains under a tax-deferred umbrella, but you do have to move 100 percent of your account balance. You can't transfer into an existing annuity with a 1035—a new contract must be established. Of course, normal surrender charges, if any, apply. In addition, a 1035 can involve a lot of paperwork.

ARE VARIABLE ANNUITIES FOR YOU?

The investments offer several advantages.

1. *Tax-deferred compounding.* This is the most important reason to buy. The higher your combined federal-plus-state bracket, the greater your benefit. Also, the sooner you start, the greater the advantage.

2. *No investment ceiling.* Unlike tax-qualified retirement plans, you face no maximum on what you can invest during the pay-in period. With an IRA, you can set aside only $2,000 a year.

3. *A variety of choices.* Many variable accounts offer a half dozen or more portfolios. The selection may include several specialized products, such as index funds.

4. *Growth potential.* By choosing well-managed stock-oriented funds, you can get long-term growth as you would with regular mutual funds.

5. *Switch privileges.* You can move money among the portfolios within the insurance wrapper. In addition, you can transfer from one fund complex to another with a 1035 exchange. Neither kind

of transaction would be a taxable event. A variable annuity can be an attractive vehicle for market timers who want to switch aggressively. You generally wouldn't face any charges for switching, but you may be limited to a certain number of transactions each year.

6. *Another form of savings plan.* Like voluntary tax-qualified retirement programs, a variable annuity may offer the kind of incentive you need to sacrifice current consumption for greater financial security in later life. They can be especially good for people who might otherwise lack the discipline to save.

Variable annuities also come with several important disadvantages, especially when compared to regular mutual funds.

1. *High fees.* The various costs may offset the advantage of tax-deferral. The insurance-related fees add substantially to the expense ratio. You may not need the modest insurance feature anyway, even if you have dependents.

2. *Illiquidity.* The surrender charges and the 10 percent penalty on distributions before age 59½ make it costly to pull money out of variable annuities prematurely.

3. *Complexity.* Variable annuities are more difficult to analyze than ordinary mutual funds. You're definitely going to have to dig deeper into the prospectus and research all the funds within the wrapper. You might want to use a financial planner.

4. *Tax-status risk.* It is difficult to predict what kinds of changes in federal tax laws will occur in the future and how they might affect annuity owners. If you are considering a large investment in a variable contract, it would probably make sense to seek competent tax advice.

Because of the higher costs associated with annuities, you should first invest as much as you can in regular retirement plans, such as the 401(k), IRA, and Keogh. If you still have money to put away on a tax-sheltered basis, then you can start thinking about a variable annuity. Obviously, you wouldn't want to hold a variable annuity in an IRA account, just as you wouldn't want a tax-exempt bond fund put into an IRA. You would be placing one tax shelter into another, a mistake.

In general, you can expect variable annuities to perform about the same as their mutual fund cousins having similar objectives. Discrepancies could result, however, from various factors such as differences in portfolio sizes, managers and, especially, fees.

Finally, variable annuities offer a brief grace or "examination period" during which you can change your mind if the contract doesn't suit you. If disappointed, you can exit after a few days without any penalty. Keep this provision in mind, as it could come in handy.

Figure 15–3
Glossary of Annuity Terms

Accumulation phase The period of a deferred annuity during which the account value builds up from portfolio earnings and additional investments by the owner.

Accumulation unit Similar to shares in a mutual fund, the units are used to calculate the value of your ownership interest.

Accumulation unit value Similar, but not identical, to the net asset value of a mutual fund.

Annuitant The person(s) entitled to receive payments during the payout period. The annuitant is often the contract owner.

Annuitization A plan for making periodic distributions.

Annuity A series of periodic payments over some stipulated time frame, such as the life of the annuitant.

Beneficiary The person(s) entitled to the contract value in the event of the annuitant's death.

Contract owner The person(s) in control of all contract terms.

Death benefit The amount payable to the beneficiary upon the death of the annuitant should it occur prior to annuitization.

Deferred annuity A contract with an accumulation phase. Variable annuities are usually deferred.

Examination period A brief window after the signing of the contract during which the owner can cancel, penalty free.

Fixed account A part of the insurance company's general account, available as an investment option to variable-annuity owners. The fixed account provides for a locked in, guaranteed return.

Fixed annuity Provides guaranteed, level payments during the payout period. Fixed-annuity assets are part of the insurer's general account.

General account Consists of insurance company assets other than those allocated to separate accounts.

Immediate annuity An annuity with no accumulation phase; annuitization begins shortly after the contract is initiated.

Payout phase The time frame during which the annuitant receives either a lump-sum distribution or periodic benefits according to the selected payout option.

Separate account An asset account distinct from the insurance company's general account. The segregated assets are invested in a particular family of funds. Also called a variable account.

Subaccount Accounts established for investors in specific funds within the variable account. Each subaccount is linked to a particular portfolio.

1035 exchange Used to transfer money directly from one mutual fund group to another, tax free.

Variable annuity A contract with an insurance wrapper that earns a variable rate of return, based on the performance of the underlying mutual fund.

CHAPTER **16**

Dealing with Your Fund Family

You can still find good solo funds, but families are what the mutual fund business is all about these days. The problem is that small operations often have trouble gathering sufficient assets to realize economies of scale for the benefit of shareholders and adequate profits for the management company. In fact, tiny portfolios often don't register their shares for sale in all 50 states because it's costly. We sympathize with these entrepreneurs since small funds with their greater autonomy can serve as ideal incubators for the development of tomorrow's celebrity managers. But the trend is toward larger groups, based on the economic rationale of building assets and thus higher profits.

The ideal fund family would have four attributes: a wide spectrum of portfolios to choose from, consistent top performers in all categories, a broad range of top quality services—including the friendliest, most knowledgeable telephone reps you could imagine—and rock-bottom expenses. If you could find this ideal family, there would be no need to keep any money anywhere else. Needless to say, you probably won't find one superior group that merits an across-the-board five-star rating, although there are certainly several first-class outfits.

Most families have at least one money market fund, one longer-term bond portfolio, and one stock fund. In fact, some groups have two dozen or more portfolio choices. The largest family, Fidelity Investments, has about 200 funds.

In picking your first or primary family, it's best to select a group that has at least one reasonably good choice in each of the following six areas: investment-grade bond, tax-exempt bond, growth stock, growth-and-income stock, small-company equity, and international stock. Often, the best way to begin is to put your dollars in the family's money fund. Then, gradually move cash into riskier portfolios as you become more familiar with them.

Should you stay with one family? Perhaps. It can make life simpler. If the group provides consolidated statements, for example, all your fund holdings will appear on one or two pieces of paper.

Eventually, though, you may want to invest in a few other families, especially as your holdings become larger and more diversified. When you go beyond your first family, you might look at smaller, more specialized groups or even solo funds that have something special to offer. The advantage of going with several management firms is that you can pick and choose the best of what each has to offer.

In addition to good performance, your primary family—and any other groups or funds you use—should also have reasonable expenses and the kinds of services you will use. Performance and expenses have been dealt with earlier. But the following pages provide greater details on the full range of services available.

SHAREHOLDER SERVICES

All the big fund companies are paying more attention to this end of the business. They know people simply won't tolerate incapable telephone reps, poorly written reports, and the like. Figure 16-1 lists the services you need to be familiar with. Some, like periodic shareholder reports, are a legal requirement for all funds so everyone gets them, although quality still varies. Others, such as automatic investment plans, are offered by many but not all complexes.

Figure 16-1
Mutual-Fund Shareholder Services

1. Retirement plans
2. Automatic reinvestment
3. Automatic investment
4. Transactions by phone
5. Telephone exchange
6. Check writing
7. Systematic withdrawals
8. Periodic account and tax information
9. Shareholder reports
10. Information by phone and literature

Obviously, some features will be much more important to you than will others. But when starting out you might not know exactly which ones you will make use of and how often. For this reason, it's a good idea to sign up for all services you might conceivably use. That way, they'll be available should you need them.

To find out what's offered, consult the shareholder-services sections of the prospectus. These sections are generally found near the back. Different groups present the information in various ways, but all the facts you'll need to get started are there. You will learn the procedures for opening a new account, purchasing additional shares, and exchanging and redeeming shares. And depending on the company, you might find out about additional services as diverse as asset-allocation plans that tell you where to put your money, periodic newsletters, a telephone device for the hearing impaired, local investor centers, personalized attention for large accounts (say, $100,000 and above), managed accounts for large investors, and discount brokerage. A few companies may even allow you to exchange any stock certificates you might have for shares in a fund.

The prospectus also spells out other, related information that you will need to deal effectively with your group. For example, the prospectus explains details on dividend and capital gains distributions. You can also learn about limitations on fund switching, any required minimum account balance that you must maintain, and any special conditions placed on especially large redemptions. If you need further clarification after going through the relevant sections of the prospectus, you can always contact a shareholder rep.

Retirement Plans

The prospectus will tell you whether the fund allows investments in IRAs, Keoghs, corporate pension and profit-sharing plans, simplified employee pension (SEP) programs, and nonprofit group retirement plans or 403(b)s. Make sure the plans you want are available from the fund company. The bigger families typically offer the full gamut of retirement vehicles. The small ones often do not.

Be aware of annual custodial fees. Charges for mutual fund IRAs are typically modest, but they can add up quickly if you own several portfolios. One family might charge $10 irrespective of whether you invest in 1 or 10 funds. Another could charge a separate fee for each portfolio held.

It's worth noting that fund companies usually lower their required initial investment for an IRA. For example, the minimum might be $5,000 normally but only $2,000 through an IRA. In this sense, many funds are more accessible through retirement accounts.

Automatic Reinvestment

Virtually all funds allow you to reinvest dividend and capital gains distributions in additional shares. You can typically select one of the following three options:

- Reinvest both dividend and capital gains.
- Receive dividends in cash, reinvest the gains.
- Receive both dividends and gains in cash.

The reinvestment service is an excellent way to build wealth through the magic of compounding. Most funds allow you to reinvest both forms of distribution into additional shares at NAV, without sales charge. Thus, this is an economical, efficient service. Check the current prospectus for information on distributions and their scheduled dates. If you can't determine this from reading the prospectus, call the fund company to find out when dividends will be paid. Some funds allow you to go a step further and reinvest the distributions of one fund into another portfolio within the group. Suppose you are in the ABC Family and have a large investment in the equity-income fund. You might reinvest all distributions from it into ABC's international-stock portfolio. This type of service offers you great flexibility, and it's a relatively painless way to diversify into more speculative products.

Automatic-Investment Plans

Often the simplest strategies are the best and most profitable. A surefire way to make more money with a good fund is simply to get more dollars into the pool working for you. Automatic-investment plans allow you to invest a fixed sum periodically, say $100 monthly, in a designated fund. The amount would typically be debited to your bank account. To establish this program, you complete an authorization form and send it to the fund company along with a blank check marked "void." Some families will also let you have the money withheld from your paycheck, with your employer's consent.

Automatic-investment plans offer an ideal way to dollar-cost average by making saving a simple, ongoing process and encouraging discipline. If you don't see the money before it's invested, you're less apt to miss it. Since they're automatic and ongoing, the plans can also encourage investment in depressed markets when many people don't want to have anything to do with stocks. Of course, you can change or terminate this service at any time.

Transactions by Phone

You can purchase or redeem shares in a fund by calling a shareholder representative, who will have your bank account debited or credited. As with the automatic-investment plan, this service first has to be established with both your bank and the fund company. These transactions are generally subject to minimum dollar amounts. Purchases may also be subject to a maximum.

Keep in mind that whenever you buy shares in a fund for the first time, you are supposed to have the prospectus in hand. If not, the company will mail it with the first transaction confirmation. Even so, it's a good idea to obtain prospectuses for all the portfolios in the family that you could conceivably want to invest in. More groups are combining information on several portfolios into a single document. For example, they might list all the international funds in one prospectus.

The transaction-by-phone service is available through banks that are members of the Automated Clearing House (ACH) network. You generally will be buying at the next day's price, if you place your order before 4 P.M. Eastern Time, unless you prearranged to have money wired from your bank and it reaches your fund account before the market closes. You would be billed by the bank for the cost of the wire.

Your fund may or may not allow transactions using an "unpaid purchase order." This option lets you buy shares by telephone, locking in that day's price if you call your fund company before 4 P.M. Eastern Time. You must then immediately send in your check for the balance due so that the company receives it within five business days. You could also wire your payment. Where available, this service is usually restricted to people who already have an account established at the fund complex. Also, a purchase minimum, such as $5,000 or $10,000, usually applies. There may be a purchase maximum too.

Generally, you don't need to move all that fast when you want to invest in a mutual fund, but suppose you're in a hurry for some reason. Some companies will let you open a new account without having an application on file, provided you submit one promptly. To do so, you need to call the group, provide information about yourself, obtain an account number, and give them your purchase instruction. You then tell your bank to wire the money to your new fund account. The shares are priced at the NAV prevailing the day your bank wire is received. But you should have a prospectus in hand when you do this, and the telephone rep will generally ask if you do. It doesn't make sense to jump into a fund without some familiarity with it.

Some fund complexes have a 24-hour "transaction line," which enables you to determine your account balance, exchange money between portfolios, and, in some cases, make purchases and redemptions through your bank account without speaking to a representative. You use a pin number to access your account with a touch-tone phone.

Telephone Exchange

This privilege allows you to transfer money between funds within a particular family by calling a toll-free 800 number. It's the quickest, most efficient way to sell shares. For example, if you want to redeem $5,000 from a stock portfolio, you can simply switch that balance to the money fund, then draw a $5,000 check on the latter. Switching was used extensively in 1987, a time of extreme volatility. More than 25 percent of fund assets were exchanged that year, according to Investment Company Institute data. Usually, you can switch for free, although some families charge $5 and a few, $10. In addition, there may be a limit on the number of exchanges you can make in a year. Families frown on hyperactive switchers, because when investors shuttle big sums between different portfolios, this poses obvious management problems and can hurt other shareholders. Check with your group about the number of allowable switches.

In any case, the exchange service is a huge bargain if used intelligently. Consider what it would cost in dollars, time, and irritation to do a complete switch of a stock or bond portfolio if you held, say, 50 individual securities—especially if some traded in foreign markets. Remember from Chapter 3 that transaction costs include much more than simply brokerage commissions.

Redeeming fund shares through the mail is time-consuming and requires more effort on your part. The letter must include the pertinent details, and usually you need to have your signature guaranteed. And since a number of days will elapse before your shares are redeemed, you risk a falling NAV during this period.

It's important to recognize that a switch between funds is a taxable event unless the money is held in a retirement account. The reason it's taxable is that you're selling one fund and purchasing another, generating a gain or loss on the investment sold.

Check Writing

Typically, you can write checks against fixed-income funds, but not against stock portfolios. There is usually a minimum of $100 to $500 placed on each check. The service can be an efficient way to redeem part or all of your shares, or to pay large bills. Many families will return canceled checks, an added service that may be important to you.

A caveat: If you write a check on any bond fund (including tax-free portfolios) with a fluctuating net asset value it can complicate your tax preparation, since you have a taxable event. With each check you write you're basically redeeming a portion of your shares. This would not be a concern with money market funds, which have constant NAVs of $1.

Withdrawal Plans

Many groups offer voluntary, systematic programs to take out money. To use them, you need to have a certain minimum amount invested, usually $10,000, and must withdraw a specific minimum, say, $50. Withdrawals can be made monthly, bimonthly, quarterly, semiannually, or annually. You can have the check sent to your home, your bank account, or to another person. You can change the amount of the withdrawal or terminate the plan whenever you wish.

The advantage of setting up a withdrawal plan with an equity fund is that your remaining balance will likely be compounding at a higher average rate, allowing you to make withdrawals over a longer time horizon. But if you expect to take all your money out within just a few years, you are probably better off using a bond fund, to minimize the risk of losing principal. Chapter 17 takes a closer look at withdrawal plans.

Periodic Statements and Tax Information

One advantage of a mutual fund is that it can greatly reduce the amount of paperwork you need to compile. It's certainly a lot easier to keep records for a single fund than it would be for many individual companies. But the paperwork can still be a headache if you're not well organized and misplace or lose statements.

Your fund company will supply you with various documents. Four common ones are:

Confirmation statements. These list details of each of your transactions, including purchases, sales, and exchanges. You should retain all confirmation statements—at least until you receive your year-end account-activity summary—as they contain information needed to figure your taxable gains or losses.

Account-activity statements. These updates are sent out on a monthly, quarterly, or annual cycle, depending on the fund type. You will also receive one after each distribution. So for a bond fund that pays monthly dividends, you would get one every month, reflecting year-to-date activity.

The year-end summaries list purchases, redemptions, distributions, and all other transactions. Fund companies are usually very efficient and accurate, but it can't hurt to check for possible discrepancies between your confirmations and the activity statements.

Form 1099-DIV. This lists the amounts and tax status of income and capital gains distributions paid to you throughout the prior year. Typically, they're mailed in late January or early February. The Form 1099-DIV provides information you need to report on your tax return, even if you reinvested distributions in additional shares. Funds holding foreign stocks or bonds may also report any foreign taxes paid on your 1099-DIV, allowing you to deduct those taxes or claim a credit for them.

Form 1099-B. You receive this form, typically by early February, if you sold shares. It contains a copy of the information reported to the IRS on your sales or exchanges during the prior year. You use this information to determine your taxable gains or losses.

People who have been with a fund for many years may find they've lost some of their records. If this happens to you, don't hesitate to contact the company. You might have to pay something to have the firm dig up this information, but usually the cost is modest.

Shareholder Reports

Fund companies must send you at least an annual and a semiannual report, although many report quarterly. The yearly and six-month documents contain a statement by the management as well as a list of the current portfolio holdings and changes. Quarterly reports typically offer less information. Morningstar assigns a letter grade—ranging from A to F—to each company's reports. The ratings reflect factors such as candor, substance, timeliness, and organization. A high rating may indicate greater concern for shareholders, according to Morningstar.

Information by Phone

You can obtain current price and yield information by telephoning fund companies, most of which provide toll-free numbers. Usually, you must call during East Coast business hours, although more complexes are offering 24-hour phone lines. Fidelity offers different prices each hour on its 36 sector portfolios. Otherwise, mutual funds are priced once a day, at the market's close. Thus, it makes sense to make your purchases, sales, or switches shortly before the market's close. That way, you'll have a better idea whether the fund's NAV is up or down that day. Even if you place your transaction in the morning, you still get the market-closing NAV.

Telephone reps will answer questions about your account, and they can provide information about the funds offered by the complex. You may note some differences in the level of knowledge and communication abilities of reps at different companies. Load-fund representatives may refer you to a broker for answers to your more difficult questions. Incidentally, you may encounter some delays when you call a fund company. This could be a particular problem for a smaller yet successful family that is experiencing rapid growth. Good times to call are generally early in the morning and later in the afternoon. Lunch time on the East Coast is usually the worst time, and you might have trouble during the hour prior to the market's close.

A number of fund groups also provide educational literature to shareholders. This includes pamphlets or guides covering topics such as retirement planning, fixed-income investing, international investing, and variable annuities. Some families also distribute a periodic newsletter.

In dealing with your fund, make sure it has the services you want. Once you sign up for these services, check to make sure they're working as you'd expect. If there's a problem, it's best to get it resolved early on. With telephone switching in particular, you don't want to hit a snag the first time you really need to use it.

CHAPTER 17

A Mutual Fund Action Plan

Now you know what's required to be a successful mutual fund investor. You've learned about the time value of money, risk and return, portfolio categories, fund analysis, market timing, retirement planning, variable annuities, and how to deal with investment companies. At this point, you probably have a good understanding of how mutual funds work. Now it's time to put the pieces together.

PORTFOLIO BUILDING BLOCKS

Different categories of funds can be viewed as building blocks for constructing an overall portfolio. The question is, what kinds of building materials do you need and in what quantities? The answer depends, in part, on the total amount you're investing. The more dollars you're putting to work, the more funds you will likely want.

Your core portfolio might consist of the following: a money-market fund, a good-quality bond fund and a growth-and-income fund. The proportions you invest in each would depend on factors such as your age, risk tolerance, financial sophistication, income, job security, and need for liquidity. If you're in a high tax bracket, you may want a municipal-bond fund. Younger people could invest more heavily in equity portfolios.

In any event, it's wise to keep the familiar investment pyramid in mind (Figure 17–1). With this type of portfolio structure, a significant portion of your assets would be kept in stable, conservative investments such as a money fund, which could meet your needs for liquidity and emergencies. Two levels higher is the "average-risk" sector of the pyramid, where you would find balanced, equity-income, growth-and-income, utility, convertible-security, and option-income portfolios. These categories offer a lot more long-term inflation protection than you'd get from low-risk, fixed-income funds. For younger, more aggressive individuals, the core should also contain more volatile growth, small-company, and international-stock products, and less in the way of bond funds.

With a core established, you are ready to consider more volatile, specialized fund types. These might include sector funds, junk-bond portfolios, and more focused international products such as those investing in geographic regions or even single countries. Wealthier individuals could afford to dabble more in the high-risk portion of the pyramid.

With sufficient core diversification, these more volatile portfolios might not add that much extra risk to your overall holdings. In fact, investments that sometimes bob up and down independently of one another can help smooth out your total volatility. Your Japanese stock fund may drop, say, 20 percent in a year when your health-care portfolio soars 40 percent. The following year, you might see the opposite pattern. This is the idea behind international diversification.

The very top or highest risk level of an investment pyramid mainly contains assets other than mutual funds. Even the most risky sector fund wouldn't be as speculative as many individual small stocks or junk bonds, naked (or uncovered) put-and-call options, and speculative futures positions. All mutual funds are highly regulated, diversified, and professionally managed—factors that reduce their risk. The very tip of the pyramid is a dangerous no-man's land unsuitable for most people.

Figure 17-1
An Investment Pyramid

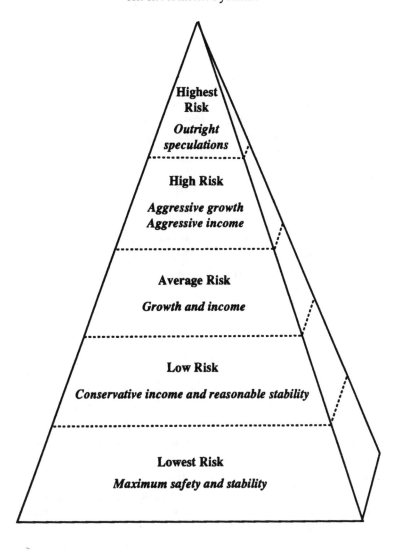

Highest Risk

Outright speculations

High Risk

Aggressive growth
Aggressive income

Average Risk

Growth and income

Low Risk

Conservative income and reasonable stability

Lowest Risk

Maximum safety and stability

Asset Allocation

The idea of spreading money around different funds and investment categories has been growing in popularity. Asset allocators look at the big picture and decide how to divvy up a portfolio into cash, bonds, stocks, and various subcategories. They argue that good long-term performance depends most heavily on being in the right markets or sectors at the right times. Some fund companies even offer personalized allocation programs based on information such as your age, risk tolerance, return expectations, income, and net worth.

In any event, it's wise to have some target percentages in mind for allocating holdings among fund categories. Suppose Manuel, a fairly young, single executive with a $100,000 portfolio, allocated 25 percent each to a money-market, equity-income, aggressive-growth, and international stock-fund a few years ago. When he made his choices, Manuel felt these percentages would be suitable over the next five to ten years. The stock market cooperated with some nice gains during the interim. His portfolio now has the following percentages:

> Money market 10%
> Aggressive growth 33
> International stock 30
> Equity income 27

Whereas Manuel previously had 75 percent invested in the three stock products, he now has 90 percent. To restore the target 25 percent weights, he would simply reduce his holdings in the stock funds and increase his stake in the money fund. He might not feel compelled to alter the amount in the more conservative equity-income fund, since its weight rose only two percentage points, from 25 percent to 27 percent.

It's wise to review your allocations regularly—perhaps annually or at least after a big move up or down in one of your funds. Since many small adjustments complicate record keeping and tax preparation, it's best to defer alterations until the percentages deviate sufficiently from their targets. As an alternative, you might simply channel any new money into portfolios that are down and hold off investing in those that have grown.

Technically, this mechanical strategy is known as a *constant-ratio formula plan*. This approach essentially encourages people to act as *contrarians*, lightening up on funds or markets that have appreciated while adding to those that have dropped. The contrarian's aim is to buy low and sell high by going against the crowd, investing in out-of-favor assets. When the stock market plunges, contrarians move more money into stocks on the premise that they now offer greater value.

Besides being affected by fluctuations in market values, your proportions will change with additional investments, reinvestments and redemptions. Also bear in mind that some stock fund managers radically alter their cash holdings as their outlook changes. A manager who moves from, say, 80 percent to 40 percent in stocks would likely alter your overall holdings by a fair degree.

Constant-ratio plans have their share of criticism, however. First, you might incur a large tax liability when you sell shares from an appreciated portfolio. Second, you might be limiting further growth potential by scaling back on your winners. The allocation weights are best viewed as flexible guidelines. As market conditions change, you may want to alter them to take advantage of special opportunities. But formula plans will at least get you to review your holdings periodically and force you to think about the proportions you should invest in the different categories.

A CASE OF FINANCIAL CLUTTER

Harold and Edna are both in their late fifties. They have owned and operated a popular upscale restaurant in the Chicago area for many years. However, the business has taken so much time and energy that they haven't had a chance to sit down and develop a logical investment plan.

But they have made plenty of investments over the years, often at the suggestion of customers, including brokers and others in the financial community. Harold and Edna always found it hard to say no. As a consequence, they have established accounts at no less then two dozen individual brokerage firms, banks, and mutual funds. They also are in the habit of using the rear-view mirror approach, investing a few thousand dollars in recent top performing funds, including some riskier sector portfolios.

All told, Harold and Edna have nearly $2 million invested, several hundred thousand of which is in 10 different IRA and Keogh accounts. They have almost three dozen mutual funds, including a few variable annuities. They also have a smattering of stocks, bonds, closed-end funds, real estate, and gold bullion.

In short, they suffer from investment overkill, which can be broken down into the following problems:

- The record-keeping and tax-preparation chores are a nightmare with so many different accounts and an annual deluge of IRS 1099 forms.

- They are paying annual custodial fees ranging from about $10 to $50 for each of their 10 different retirement accounts.

- Given their busy schedules and superficial knowledge of investments, it is impossible for them to monitor each individual position.

- It is also hard for them to keep an eye on the big picture. They would be hard-pressed to tell you what percentage of their portfolio is in equities, how much exposure they have to overseas markets, or whether they would be better off with tax-exempt bond funds.

As you might expect, Harold and Edna are holding a fair number of lemons that should have been pruned long ago. In fact, realizing some losses would enable them to offset other income and gains and transfer those dollars into more productive investments.

If they consolidated their holdings into a more manageable number of funds, it would be much easier for them to keep on top of what they own and make changes as the need arose. By combining their investments into as few as a half dozen funds, they could quickly tell the exact percentage of their assets held in various categories.

But before they make any moves, Harold and Edna would be wise to learn as much about investing and mutual funds as they can. Then, if they feel confident, they could make their own decisions and move their assets accordingly. If not, they could stick with just one good financial planner or broker. With their large holdings, they wouldn't be paying much in loads anyway—at least as a percentage of their assets. If they wanted to save on commissions, Harold and Edna might also consider trading through a discount broker, as explained in the next section.

USING A DISCOUNT BROKER

Several hundred funds now can be bought and sold through a few discount brokers, such as Fidelity Investments, Charles Schwab, Waterhouse Securities, and Jack White. For the most part, these are no-load and low-load funds.

The discount approach appeals to individuals who trade frequently, moving in and out of funds within different families. Some of these people are market timers, who place their bets where they feel the action will be in the next few months. More conservative investors with larger accounts may also use a discounter for convenience.

With a single brokerage firm, the record keeping for various funds gets consolidated on one statement, which greatly simplifies the paperwork. You can have just one account for all your funds and other investments. A single account would be especially advantageous for IRA investors, who can avoid the multiple custodial fees that would otherwise result from maintaining investments at different fund complexes. Aggressive investors using taxable accounts (but not IRAs) can buy funds on margin, if they wish.

The fees and other details of trading funds through a discounter differ among brokerages. Basically, the cost increases with the size of the transaction. Another key determinant is whether or not a portfolio has a load. But two discounters have begun to allow individuals to buy and sell certain no-load funds at no commission.

Mutual funds are good vehicles to use in making tax swaps, and trading through a discount broker can facilitate these moves. Suppose you have a tax loss you want to claim on an aggressive-growth fund in Family A. You can sell it and immediately purchase another aggressive-growth portfolio in Family B. Since you are buying a different fund—regardless of how similar it might be— the transaction would not be considered a wash sale by the IRS.

TAX CONSIDERATIONS

Figuring taxes on fund positions can become rather complex, even for those who maintain meticulous records.

As we've explained, mutual funds serve as conduits, passing along virtually all income and net realized gains to shareholders. They can make four types of distributions: ordinary income dividends, tax-exempt interest, net realized capital gains, and return of capital. Income dividends are simply taxable interest and dividend payments, whereas tax-exempt interest would be sheltered at either the federal or state level, or both. You owe taxes on income dividends regardless of whether they're reinvested or taken in cash.

Net realized capital gains represent the profits, if any, on the fund's securities transactions. If losses exceeded gains in any year, the net-realized loss would not be distributed. Rather, it would be carried forward by the fund company, for up to eight years, to offset any future gains. When the fund does realize a gain, this carry-forward can be a boon for shareholders, since they could receive distributions that are partially or wholly tax-exempt.

Return of capital distributions are simply dividends paid out of principal and therefore usually not taxable. They reduce your cost basis, which should be taken into account when you sell shares. The different categories of distributions are itemized on Form 1099-DIV, which will be sent to you by early February for use in preparing your tax return.

Keep the capital gains distribution date in mind when you invest in a fund, unless your shares are held in an IRA or other tax-deferred account. Most stock funds declare capital gains toward the end of the year, then pay them in January. According to the Internal Revenue Code, distributions declared in October, November, or December are considered paid on December 31, even if payment isn't made until January. You can determine the distribution dates by checking the prospectus or contacting the fund.

What if you hold fund shares in a taxable account? You are generally better off waiting until at least one day after the fund goes ex-dividend before making your purchase, rather than buying shares before the ex-distribution date and having to pay taxes on them. The NAV will fall by the amount of the payment on the day the fund goes ex-distribution, so the only thing you gain by getting it is a tax liability.

Selling Shares

Good records are essential when you sell shares. The first point to remember is that any time you reinvest a distribution, you are making an additional purchase in the fund—even though it may be a tiny one—that adds to your cost basis. So when you sell, your cost should include initial and subsequent cash investments plus all reinvested distributions.

EXAMPLE: You acquired 1,000 shares of ABC Fund in March 1991 at $10 each and 1,500 shares in June 1992 at $15. You reinvested two distributions, acquiring 50 shares in December 1991 at $11, and 125 shares in

December 1992 at $14. In January 1993 you sold all 2,675 shares. Your $34,800 cost basis is determined as follows:

March 1991	1,000 shs. @ $10 =	$10,000
December 1991	50 shs. @ 11 =	550
June 1992	1,500 shs. @ 15 =	22,500
December 1992	125 shs. @ 14 =	1,750
Totals	2,675 shs.	$34,800

If you've held a fund for many years, you might have to add dozens of purchases and distributions. But you need to include it all. If you don't, your cost will be understated, resulting in too large a taxable gain or too small a deductible loss.

If you sell some of your shares along the way, the calculations can become more complex. Under the tax laws in effect at this writing, the IRS allows any of three methods—*average cost, first-in, first-out,* or *specific identification*—to determine cost basis. Once you elect a method for a specific fund, you need to continue using it unless you obtain permission from the IRS to change. You need not, however, employ the same method for all of your funds.

In the preceding example, where 2,675 shares were purchased at a total cost of $34,800, the average cost per share works out to $13.01. To determine your basis, simply multiply the number of shares sold by their average cost. Some fund groups now calculate an average cost for each shareholder. This can make record keeping simpler for some individuals. Your average cost obviously changes as additional purchases and reinvestments are made.

The average-cost method often isn't the best choice for minimizing your tax bill. But you may have to go with it if you didn't maintain good records of when, and at what prices, you bought and reinvested.

The first-in, first-out approach is based on the simple assumption that the initial shares purchased were the first to be sold. This will be your best option only if the older shares were acquired at the highest price, which is frequently not the case. In general, specific identification makes the most sense and often results in the lowest tax liability. To put this method into practice, you must notify the fund company of your intentions at the time of sale—a short letter is a good idea, even if you placed your sell order by phone. You identify the shares to be sold by the trade date.

EXAMPLE: In June 1993 you want to sell 1,000 shares of ABC Fund from the previous example. ABC's NAV has recently hovered around $16. Which shares are you selling? Unless you specify otherwise, the IRS assumes you'd be unloading the 1,000 acquired in March 1991 at $10. But it would be better to sell 1,000 of the 1,500 bought in June 1992 at $15, since the higher cost basis would lessen your taxable gain. (Note that this basis is also higher than the $13.01 average cost.) To sell specific shares, you might need to inform the fund company in writing. You should also keep some form of written evidence of the shares sold.

Keep in mind that gains and losses on sales or exchanges of municipal-bond portfolios are taxable events that are treated the same as for taxable funds. The exemption applies only to your income dividends.

An in-depth discussion of tax rules is beyond the scope of this book. And, of course, these rules are subject to change from time to time. For further information, see IRS Publication 564, "Mutual Fund Distributions," or discuss the topic with your tax preparer. You may order Publication 564 and other free IRS guides by calling 1-800-TAX-FORM (1-800-829-3676). Many mutual fund companies also offer tax pamphlets you may find helpful.

Gifts to Minors: A Case

The Uniform Gifts to Minors Act offers a relatively easy way to get a child started in a mutual fund. The account is funded with a gift, typically from a parent who usually serves as custodian.

Here's an illustration. Mike and Joanne are starting to make plans for helping their two sons meet a portion of their college expenses. Their oldest recently turned three and the other is just a few months of age. Mike teaches high school math in Irvine, California, and Joanne is a housewife.

Mike wants to take advantage of current laws that stipulate the first $600 of income and gains for a child under age 14 is tax-free and the next $600 is taxed at the child's rate, which is 15 percent. Above the $1,200 level, income and gains would be taxed at the parents' marginal rate, which may exceed 33 percent. (If high taxes become a problem, the custodian could shift the youngster's investment to a tax-exempt bond fund.) Beginning at age 14, all income and gains would be taxed at the child's rate.

In any case, Mike feels that the tax bite will be small in the early years since the couple's gifts will be rather modest. They intend to supplement their sons' educational costs, which they don't think will be excessive since they plan to send the kids to local public colleges. Mike and Joanne plan to put away $40 a month for each boy through a Uniform Gifts to Minors account. Mike wants to keep the investing simple by using just one fund, most likely a no-load balanced portfolio. At a conservative projected pre-tax growth rate of 8 percent yearly, Mike calculates that a $40 monthly investment would compound to nearly $14,000 in 15 years.

SHOULD YOU PULL UP STAKES?

Generally, mutual funds, especially stock portfolios, should be held as long-term investments. There are, however, times when you need to think about selling some or all of your shares. In making this decision, you need to look at the same factors you considered when buying, only in reverse. The reasons for contemplating a sale can be divided into two groups: fund-specific and general.

Fund-Specific Reasons

In short, you will want to get rid of investments that aren't living up to your expectations. The reasons for being dissatisfied with a mutual fund will likely fall into one of these four categories:

1. *Performance.* If the fund has lagged its peers for perhaps two years, it might be time for a change. You should also check to see how the portfolio has fared relative to an appropriate index. For example, you might compare a utility fund against the Dow Jones Utility average, a growth-and-income fund against the S&P 500 and a small-stock portfolio versus the Russell 2000.

2. *Expenses.* An expense ratio that is climbing noticeably not only costs you money but could be symptomatic of other serious problems. A large expense increase might result from the imposition of new charges, such as a high 12b–1 fee that didn't exist previously.

3. *Management.* A change in management may or may not be a reason to sell. You need to find out the explanation for the move and the background and qualifications of the person taking the helm. Changes are usually of less consequence when a fund is jointly managed by several individuals and only one leaves.

4. *Size.* A fund that has grown so big that its character has changed might also be a candidate for selling, especially if the manager is shifting increasingly from, say, small stocks to medium and large issues. Of course, larger size also results in important economies of scale. What you need to decide is whether management can continue to keep up the good work.

General Reasons

Sometimes, you will want to sell funds that are still looking good. Here are some reasons you might consider such a move:

1. *A need for more liquidity.* For personal reasons such as advancing age, you might want to shift from being a long-term stock fund holder to a more conservative type of investor. Perhaps you're just a few years from retirement and have decided you need more income and liquidity and less volatility. You readjust your portfolio accordingly.

2. *A pricey market.* When valuation yardsticks such as the market's P/E ratio are flashing warning signals, it could be time to start lightening up on stocks, especially if you will need the money sometime within the next few years.

3. *A tax loss.* Suppose you hold a fund that has lost money and you can use this to offset some capital gains on other positions. If so, you might want to sell. You could always buy back the shares at a later date, provided you wait at least 31 days before reestablishing your position to avoid the wash-sale rule.

That having been said, you may be better off not selling in many situations. You never know exactly when the market and your fund might rebound. Besides, selling can give rise to a potentially large tax liability. In addition, you will have to decide what to do with the proceeds. This could lead to two mistakes at once—selling a fund you shouldn't have and buying one that was best left alone.

WITHDRAWAL PLANS

It is useful to think in terms of systematic withdrawals when making long-range financial plans—especially when you consider your needs at retirement. The subject of withdrawal plans is not covered in detail in many mutual fund books or in fund-company literature, yet this topic merits a closer look.

The success or failure of a withdrawal plan will depend on six key factors:

1. The amount of money you need to have invested at the time you start making withdrawals to accomplish your long-term objectives.

2. The annual withdrawal rate as a percent of your account balance. The lower the rate, the longer you'll be able to continue taking out cash.

3. Any periodic increase in the withdrawal amount to reflect inflation. If you plan on pulling out money over an extended period, your payments should be inflation-adjusted.

4. The expected annual total return on the fund. It's best not to overestimate the growth rate. Otherwise, you may discover some unpleasant shortfalls if things don't turn out so well. In fact, you may want to follow an ultra-conservative forecast.

5. The number of years over which you expect to make withdrawals.

6. The final balance, if any, that you want to have invested at the end of your planning period. Most retirees want to maintain at least some money that they can use to meet emergencies or leave to heirs.

How Long Will Amy's Capital Last?

If you plan to withdraw money from a fund at a faster rate than it's growing, you need to ask the same crucial question that confronts Amy.

Amy wants to withdraw 14 percent of her $300,000 original capital—a sum of $42,000 each year—from a fixed-income portfolio that she expects will provide a 7 percent annual return. The withdrawal will be made at the end of each year. So during the first year, the $300,000 will grow to $321,000, after which $42,000 will be taken out, leaving $279,000, as seen in Table 17–1.

This analysis shows that Amy's capital would last 10 years. If she wants to stretch her money, she must either withdraw less, choose a fund with a higher expected return, or both.

Table 17-1
Amy's Withdrawal Plan

Year End	Withdrawal	Account Balance
1993	$42,000	$279,000
1994	42,000	256,530
1995	42,000	232,487
1996	42,000	206,761
1997	42,000	179,234
1998	42,000	149,781
1999	42,000	118,266
2000	42,000	84,544
2001	42,000	48,462
2002	42,000	9,855

For example, suppose that Amy instead invests her $300,000 in an equity fund, which she thinks will return 9 percent a year, and she reduces her annual withdrawals to $30,000. With these modest changes, her money now would last 26 years. And if she could live with a 9 percent withdrawal rate ($27,000 a year) and were able to earn 9 percent each year, her capital would last indefinitely. You need to worry about exhausting a nest egg only if your withdrawal rate exceeds the portfolio's rate of growth.

Amy's case is somewhat simplistic since it assumes annual withdrawals, in which the dollar amount remains constant. If the withdrawals increased each year to keep pace with inflation—a more realistic assumption—the capital would be depleted sooner.

David Crunches Some Numbers

Obviously, you need to consider factors such as inflation very carefully if you're depending on your investment cache to meet living expenses.

David, 65, has just a few months until retirement. He has $400,000 in a conservative value-oriented equity fund. He wants to withdraw 6 percent of his original capital, or $24,000, to supplement his annual pension and Social Security income.

In fact, David wants to take out $24,000 each year starting in 1993 in constant dollars, withdrawing the money in equal monthly increments. Since David expects inflation will average 4 percent a year over the foreseeable future, he would need to boost his withdrawals by 4 percent annually, as seen in his spreadsheet (Table 17–2).

Table 17-2
David's Spreadsheet

Year End	Withdrawal	Account Balance	Year End	Withdrawal	Account Balance
1993	$24,000	$412,000	2005	$38,425	$553,971
1994	24,960	424,120	2006	39,962	563,867
1995	25,958	436,332	2007	41,560	573,054
1996	26,997	448,606	2008	43,223	581,407
1997	28,077	460,903	2009	44,952	588,782
1998	29,200	473,185	2010	46,750	595,022
1999	30,368	485,404	2011	48,620	599,955
2000	31,582	497,508	2012	50,564	603,386
2001	32,846	509,438	2013	52,587	605,104
2002	34,159	521,128	2014	54,690	604,873
2003	35,526	532,504	2015	56,878	602,434
2004	36,947	543,482	2016	59,153	597,499
			2017	61,519	589,755

Total withdrawals over 25 years: $999,502

David projects a constant 9 percent return on his fund. Of course, investment performance can and almost certainly will vary widely from year to year. At the end of 2017, if he should live to 90 and his assumptions prove accurate, he would have an account balance of $589,755—after having made nearly $1 million in withdrawals over the 25 years. Notice that the account balance reaches a projected maximum of $605,104 in 2013. Subsequently, it starts to decline as the withdrawal percentage continues to increase to keep pace with inflation.

Needless to say, David's actual experience could turn out considerably better or worse than this projection, depending on the performance of the stock fund and the actual inflation rate. Thus, it is wise to build a margin of safety into your estimates by planning to have your nest egg outlast your life expectancy, as David has done. Such projections can easily be worked out on a computerized spreadsheet, making it easy to prepare several versions of the analysis based on differing assumptions.

Other Options

Here are some additional methods you can use to set up a withdrawal plan.

Fixed Period. This approach liquidates your entire account within a predetermined number of years. With IRA and Keogh plans, a retired investor must take out the balance over a certain period, based on the individual's or couple's estimated life expectancy. Suppose a person is required to withdraw money from an IRA over a 15-year period. In the first year, 1/15th of the account balance would be taken out, 1/14th in the second, 1/13th in the third, and so on. The account's value at the beginning of each year would be multiplied by the appropriate fraction to determine that year's withdrawal.

Fixed percentage. Yet another option is to withdraw a fixed percentage of your account, say 8 percent, over the course of a year. Your monthly payments would vary somewhat, depending on fluctuations in the fund's NAV and changes in your balance. You would receive larger payments when the NAV is high, smaller ones when it's low.

Fixed Share. Rather than take out a target dollar amount or percentage, you could redeem a fixed number of shares, say 100 monthly. The drawback here is that the amount would fluctuate each month, yet this is really a superior approach since it is a variant of the dollar-cost averaging principal explained in Chapter 12. That is, you receive more money when the NAV is high and less when it's low. Conversely, by withdrawing a fixed dollar amount, you sell more shares when prices are low and fewer when they're high.

Since most people want to receive a constant amount each month, fixed-share plans are rarely used despite their conceptual advantage. Further, this option might not be available from your mutual fund company. But you could implement it yourself, with a little extra work. All you would need to do is call the fund group, instruct the representative to sell the appropriate amount of shares, and have the proceeds transferred to your money fund.

You should keep in mind that the calculations you make for any withdrawal plan are not carved in stone. Retirement planning requires a periodic reevaluation of your situation, at least on an annual basis. You need to make a revised estimate of how long your capital might last, using an analysis similar to David's in Table 17–2. If possible, keep your withdrawals on the conservative side, to allow your remaining balance to grow as much as possible.

Withdrawal approaches are probably most commonly used by retirees and widows. But they can also make sense in various other cases.

For example, a plan could provide regular payments for a son or daughter in college. In general, it's best to stick with more conservative, income-oriented equity funds in a withdrawal plan. More volatile portfolios could lead to bouts of insomnia.

One final note on withdrawal plans: You've got to keep good records for tax purposes, so you can determine the gain or loss on each redemption. You need to decide on a logical method for matching up your sales with purchases; the average-cost approach is typically used. More frequent withdrawals will obviously entail more paperwork.

Alternatives to Withdrawal Plans

If you have a large amount invested in a mutual fund, you may be able to generate a sufficient cash flow simply by taking your income dividends in cash. Receiving cash distributions is easier than using a withdrawal plan, as it greatly simplifies your accounting for tax purposes. Your annual Form 1099-DIV will list the taxable distributions. You don't need to be concerned about matching purchases of shares with sales as you would under a withdrawal plan.

As another alternative, you could always redeem shares at opportune times. You can try to time your redemptions, selling shares when the NAV is relatively high and transferring the proceeds into a money fund to spend as needed. This approach may work better if you're meeting at least some of your cash needs through monthly dividends.

FIFTEEN STEPS TO SUCCESSFUL INVESTING

Mutual-funds generally don't make people wealthy in a short time. But if you're patient, they're the best, most convenient way we know of for building up assets over the years. In that regard, here are some suggestions to keep in mind.

Step 1: Let time work for you. The longer money is invested, the more opportunity it has to grow through compounding. One hundred dollars invested monthly at 10 percent for 10 years compounds to $20,655; in 20 years it amounts to $76,570; in 40 years it swells to an eye-popping $637,678.

Step 2: Save all you can. The simplest, surest way to build wealth is to invest more. Regardless of when you start, the more you sock away, the better your results will be. Putting aside $200 instead of $100 each month in the preceding example leads to $41,310 in 10 years, $153,139 in 20 years, and $1,275,356 in 40 years.

Step 3: Invest as much in stock funds as you can.   Stocks provide the best long-term protection against inflation or purchasing-power risk. Since retirees are living longer, equity investments deserve a place in their portfolios, too. The key is to choose funds that suit your temperament for volatility.

Step 4: Don't forget the base of the investment pyramid.   A large chunk of your assets should be kept in stable, liquid instruments such as money-market funds and short-term bond portfolios. You can meet unexpected needs by drawing a check on a money-market fund rather than being forced to redeem a portion of your stock holdings at what could be a bad time. You can also use cash to go bargain hunting when especially good values appear.

Step 5: Avoid the most volatile investments.   High-risk speculations in options, futures, and individual small stocks aren't worth the potential losses. Money surrendered on highly risky gambles is gone forever. It can never go to work for you where it belonged in the first place—in high-quality mutual funds.

Step 6: Take maximum advantage of tax-deferred compounding.   The main reason most people invest is to provide for a comfortable, secure retirement. You can build more assets if you postpone paying taxes on the gains.

Step 7: Don't buy high and sell low.   This is easier said than done. The key is to know how and when to take profits in bull markets and go shopping in bearish environments. Above all, avoid committing a large amount of cash to a fund when the market may be near a peak. If domestic stocks appear expensive, consider other global markets that may offer greater value. And try to move your money in slowly, bit by bit, perhaps through some type of dollar-cost averaging plan.

Step 8: Think twice before making extreme moves.   The biggest risk of market timing is missing a bullish surge. The opportunity cost of staying in cash can be enormous.

Step 9: Think globally.   The world is becoming smaller but your investment universe is expanding. About 60 percent of the market value of all publicly traded companies exists beyond our borders. Adding an international component to your portfolio can pay off in terms of better long-run performance and reduced volatility.

Step 10: Remember the advantages of indexing. Passively managed index funds can offer a very low-cost way of staying invested. Better yet, you can rest assured of not seriously lagging behind the popular market averages.

Step 11: Don't jump in blindly. Even though time is important, there's no big rush to put money into a mutual fund. Because of their built-in diversification, most funds move up and down more slowly than individual stocks do. Take time to familiarize yourself with the prospectus and learn about the investment—so as not to be unpleasantly surprised later on. With more than 4,000 mutual funds now available, you've got plenty of choices and no need to worry about a high-flyer slipping away.

Step 12: Don't scatter your money too widely. Too much clutter will only make you confused, complicate your record keeping, and lead to mediocre results. Stick with a few good families to meet your needs. Look for good performance in the kinds of portfolios you want, at reasonable cost.

Step 13: Keep your assets in balance. Based on your objectives, determine what percentages you want invested in the different fund categories. Review these weightings at least annually to make sure your percentages haven't drifted too far out of line.

Step 14: Take maximum advantage of fund services. Learn about and use available fund services to your advantage. Automatic investment plans, for example, are a great way to build wealth through a dollar-cost averaging strategy. Withdrawal plans can be helpful for retirees. If you have questions about your fund or its services, call the company. The telephone reps are generally glad to be of assistance. Even if they don'tknow the answer, they can often find out quickly from someone who does.

Step 15: Keep good records. This is an essential by-product of investing, especially when it comes to preparing your taxreturns. You should have complete records on your transactions going back many years.

CHAPTER 18

Mutual Fund Q & A

You've got to ask the right questions to get the real story.

Here are 68 questions and answers, organized into the following topic groups:

- Square one
- Getting the facts
- Sizing up a fund
- Dealing with the market
- Stock funds
- International-stock funds

- Bond funds
- Behind the scenes
- Other alternatives

SQUARE ONE

I am a college student with just a few hundred dollars to spare and mutual funds are new to me. What would you recommend?

This answer partly depends on your risk tolerance and need for liquidity. Balanced funds are a sensible choice for small, first-time investors since they hold both bonds and stocks and thus provide broad diversification. A conservative equity fund might also make a good choice, provided you won't need to liquidate your investment for some time. If you have earned income and are investing for the very long term, you might consider opening an IRA.

Can I select funds on my own, or do I need advice from a broker or financial planner?

Many people can research and choose their own funds, relying on sources such as this book for guidance. Publications such as *Morningstar Mutual Funds* or *The Individual Investor's Guide to No-Load Mutual Funds* offer analysis on specific portfolios. You'll also find useful information in newspapers and financial magazines. The telephone reps at fund families can also be helpful but they won't give advice. Brokers and planners, by contrast, may be the way to go if you don't have the confidence, desire, or time to select and monitor your holdings.

I've invested my money in a load family and am not pleased with the fund I own. Should I move to a no-load?

Not necessarily. If you've paid a front-end commission, you should at least see if there are other portfolios within the group that you might find attractive and could switch into—often at no cost. You've already paid the entrance fee, so you may as well find out if there is something that suits you. And if the portfolio you're in now has a good long-term record, perhaps you should give it a little more time.

On the other hand, if you paid no front-end load but face a high ongoing 12b–1 fee—and you're getting mediocre performance—you might consider moving on. This decision, in turn, would hinge on the amount of contingent deferred sales charge you'd have to pay, if any.

Here's another point to keep in mind. It's occasionally possible to move money from one front-end load family to another without paying a sales charge on the switch—provided you offer proof of a recent redemption from the original fund. This is termed an "NAV transfer," since your money comes in at NAV. It's an asset-gathering tactic used by a handful of firms to attract new customers who are not satisfied with a competitor's product. Check with your broker or financial planner to see what's available. Most fund companies offering NAV transfers charge at least modest 12b–1 fees, so you need to evaluate the move carefully.

How can I learn more about investing in general?

You can discover a lot simply by keeping up with the financial world on a daily basis. Read the business section of a major newspaper regularly, or a financial paper such as *The Wall Street Journal* or *Investor's Business Daily*. Publications such as *Barron's*, *Forbes*, and *Money* contain useful articles.

You may even want to join the American Association of Individual Investors, or AAII. This organization offers educational seminars at chapters throughout the United States and publishes the *AAII Journal* and *The Individual Investor's Guide to No-Load Mutual Funds*.

A good book to help you become better acquainted with the behavior of the stock market is *A Random Walk Down Wall Street* by Burton Malkiel.

How can I get the highest returns with the least risk?

There's no magical answer to this question. Usually, you need to accept more volatility to get above-average long-run results. But the risk-reward tradeoff is not perfectly linear. For example, a gold fund could be highly volatile while not providing superior performance. In general, however, diversification helps to reduce risk without slashing returns to the same degree. Each mutual-fund provides diversification benefits compared to holding individual stocks or bonds, and you should also think in terms of spreading your assets around different types of asset categories.

What are some common mistakes mutual fund investors make?

Here are five of the biggest:

1. Failing to have a good understanding of the objectives, policies, and risks of the funds you buy. This can lead to unsuitable investments and unexpected losses.

2. Investing in the wrong funds, even though they may be in the right categories. Losers will tend to exhibit either high costs, excessive sales charges, or poor management.

3. Using the rear-view mirror approach of buying volatile funds that were top performers over the most recent year or quarter. Funds that beat their peers over the short run usually had to take big risks to get there.

4. Failing to follow a consistent long-term program of buy-and-hold investing.

5. Failing to start planning early enough for retirement, without letting time work for you to the greatest extent possible.

So what's the recipe for success?

Be a patient long-term investor, putting as much as you can comfortably afford in stock funds. Modest monthly contributions into a good portfolio can lead to eye-popping results years later, without causing much sacrifice along the way. And with a systematic approach, you benefit from dollar-cost averaging, buying more shares when prices are low and fewer when they're high. Such a plan also helps you avoid another common mistake—selling too soon.

How much do I need to know about the time value of money?

A basic understanding is essential. By making assumptions about how much you will invest periodically, your expected annual return, and your time horizon, you can estimate the growth of your nest egg in the future. This will help you determine how much to set aside regularly and the kind of funds you will need.

Here's an example of erroneous thinking regarding the time value of money. Say Joe invested $10,000 in a mutual-fund 20 years ago, reinvested all distributions and neither added nor withdrew money. With his account now worth $20,000, it would be wrong for Joe to boast that he earned a 100 percent return simply because his investment doubled. That would be correct if the fund were held just one year, not 20. Joe's compound annual return turns out to be a paltry 3.5 percent.

Can I accurately measure my overall portfolio performance?

That depends. First, you need meticulous records. Your calculations must reflect the amount and timing of all contributions and withdrawals for each fund and the proportionate investment and holding period for each. Returns should be expressed on a time-weighted, after-tax basis. Given these formidable complications, it's safe to say that few people measure their performance precisely.

You can at least keep track of how much you invest in each fund, when you buy, withdraw, and make switches. Then look at the total current value of your portfolio and each position monthly or quarterly. Keep a running tally of the gains and losses on each fund and overall. With this information, you should be able to approximate your compound annual rate of return. A computerized spreadsheet can be very helpful.

Knowing that your after-tax, time-weighted return for, say, the past 10.25 years was exactly 9.581 percent is not that important. The main thing to know is that, on average, you're beating inflation by at least a few percentage points per year after taxes.

GETTING THE FACTS

Is it a good idea for individuals to be allowed to invest in funds without seeing and examining a prospectus first?

SEC regulators in 1993 were leaning toward giving investors the option of purchasing fund shares directly from advertisements containing summary prospectuses, rather than having to first request a more detailed pamphlet prospectus. These "off-the-page" condensed prospectuses would be required to contain key information on each fund. An investor would buy shares by filling out an application included with the ad and submitting a check with the completed form. The pamphlet prospectus would be sent with the trade confirmation. The idea was to expedite sales and cut costs for direct-marketed funds.

We see no harm with this approach. Individuals could still request a more detailed prospectus and read it before investing. More to the point, the ads would still have to summarize the key disclosure information. Whether in legalese longhand or advertising shorthand, fund companies still would be required to set the facts straight and are legally bound by their statements.

ال

What are the essential things to look for in a prospectus?

The portfolio's objectives, policies, risks, sales charges, expenses, turnover, performance, and shareholder services. Also check out the minimum investment amounts and procedures for redeeming shares.

The most important tables in the prospectus list the per- share financial data and the fees.

What information does the Statement of Additional Information have that the prospectus does not?

The statement goes into more detail on topics like the fund's policies, risk factors, investment restrictions, and total return. For example, a fund that can use options and futures may devote a number of pages to a detailed discussion of derivative securities, including the risks of different strategies.

The SAI also provides the names of the fund's directors and officers and brief background information on them. Another section identifies investors who own 5 percent or more of the shares. If you really want to learn all you can about a fund, you need the SAI, which is available on request.

What should I look for in the fund's annual report?

Read management's letter to shareholders to get a broad overview of how things have been going. Look at the fund's portfolio to make sure management is following its stated plan. A fund's name doesn't necessarily describe the type of investments held.

If you intend to stay with a fund for a long time, you might want to save the annual reports to see how the portfolio evolves over the years.

What kinds of mutual fund advisory services are available? Should I subscribe?

There are dozens. Some focus on market timing and switching, others have a more general orientation and simply help you select good funds. A few services focus on just one fund family, namely Fidelity or Vanguard.

An advisory service costs money, so you have to determine whether it's worth the expense. You may also find that some newsletters promote switching more frequently than you might like. As we've said before, you can learn a lot about investments just by reading standard business publications. *Barron's* quarterly mutual funds survey and *Forbes'* annual fund edition both are good sources of performance data and commentary. Appendix 1 lists other worthwhile guides.

What kinds of current events should I keep up on?

As a mutual fund investor, you don't need to do the kind of detailed research that people purchasing individual stocks and bonds must. Nevertheless, it's a good idea to keep abreast of current trends in the financial markets. Focus on the big picture. What have interest rates been doing? What is the outlook for corporate earnings? Is the stock market overpriced, or does it offer value? International investors should have a general knowledge of what's happening with the world's major economies, stock markets, and currencies. This is especially important for anyone investing in single-country or regional portfolios.

I want to keep as current as possible on the performance of the funds I own as well as their peers. Where can I find the most timely information?

Each day *The Wall Street Journal* publishes year-to-date total returns for the funds it lists. In addition, the newspaper updates results on specific days for each of the following periods: 4, 13, 26, and 39 weeks as well as 1, 3, 4, and 5 years. For example, each Tuesday the *Journal* runs 4-week and 1-year performance, each Wednesday it carries the 13-week and 3-year results, and so on.

If a fund has been around as long as the longest stretch listed that day—say 5 years—its performance is ranked in one of five categories, relative to comparable portfolios. The most volatile funds could see their rankings change from week to week. The data are supplied by Lipper Analytical Services and cover some 2,700 portfolios.

I want a benchmark against which I can measure the daily percent changes of my fund's NAV. I know stock market indexes are available, but are there any daily mutual fund price indexes?

Yes. Lipper Analytical Services publishes daily indexes for different fund categories including capital appreciation, growth, small-company growth, growth and income, equity income, science and technology, international, gold, and balanced. They appear in Part C of *The Wall Street Journal*.

What is the Investment Company Institute and what are its functions?

Since it began in 1940 in New York, the Investment Company Institute, or ICI, now based in Washington, D.C., has served as the national association of mutual funds. A clearinghouse of facts and data, its members include more than 4,000 mutual funds that account for over 95 percent of the industry's assets. Often working with the Securities and Exchange Commission or state regulators, the ICI serves as the industry's main lobbyist.

Useful ICI publications include the *Directory of Mutual Funds* and the *Mutual Fund Fact Book*. Both are published annually. *An Investor's Guide to Reading the Mutual Fund Prospectus* is also helpful. The ICI's address and phone number can be found in Appendix 1.

SIZING UP A FUND

How does a fund's NAV differ from a stock's price?

Since a fund is diversified, its NAV will normally be more stable than a stock's price. That's because some of the fund's stock holdings will zig while others zag, producing an overall smoother ride.

Another difference is that each fund is required by law to distribute virtually all realized capital gains to shareholders. Thus, the NAV usually does not grow over the years as much as a stock's price does.

How does a distribution affect the NAV of my fund?

Suppose Fund A has an NAV of $10 on Wednesday, the day before it goes ex-distribution. The capital gains distribution is $1. When it goes ex-distribution on Thursday, the NAV would fall by $1 to $9 (other things being constant), since people who buy on or after the ex-distribution day are not entitled to the dividend.

Now suppose the portfolio value declines on Thursday because the market's down. Thursday's NAV would be less than $9. The entry in the mutual funds table of your newspaper might appear as follows:

	NAV	Offer Price	NAV Change
Fund A	e8.80	N.L.	-1.20

The "e" preceding the $8.80 NAV indicates Fund A is ex-distribution. The $1.20 decline in NAV reflects the $1 dividend and a $0.20 per-share drop in portfolio value. If the market rises instead, the NAV would be greater than $9. If you want to know the amount of the distribution, you can call the fund.

I noticed the symbol "s" in the newspaper beside a fund's name. What does it mean?

When a fund has had a stock split or stock dividend, you will find an "s" beside its name. However, this happens far less commonly with mutual funds than with individual stocks.

Stock splits or dividends are merely bookkeeping adjustments made to alter the fund's NAV for cosmetic purposes—they don't increase your wealth. Say Fund A has an NAV of $100. If it declares a 10-for-1 split, its new NAV would be $10. If you previously held 100 shares, you would now own 1,000. A fund with a very low NAV might have a reverse split to raise its value.

As opposed to the far more common cash dividends, stock dividends do not represent a distribution of portfolio income and thus are not taxable.

Can a new fund be a good investment?

Yes, but there are several reasons not to buy one. New funds commonly debut in the advanced stages of bull markets, when investor interest is at its peak. Portfolios are often trotted out in areas that have been hot, such as global health care. (It's especially wise to avoid new closed-end funds, which often go public at a premium then slip to a discount within a few months.)

Also, new funds have no track record. If they stay small, they won't enjoy the same economies of scale and thus will have relatively high expense ratios. And since there are always many good, proven portfolios to choose from, why select a newcomer?

Perhaps the biggest argument in favor of new funds is that small portfolios are more nimble. This is especially important for funds that invest in smaller stocks. If the cash-flow theory discussed in Chapter 3 is correct, a small fund could do very well if it experiences large cash inflows over several years.

So if you want to invest in a new fund, pick one that's already registering steady asset growth. It's generally safer to buy a portfolio that's a member of a well-regarded family. A new fund can be a good investment if it has been set up to clone a successful portfolio that's grown too large.

What are the pros and cons of investing in tiny funds?

We define "tiny" as assets of $10 million or less. These funds are especially well suited to investing in small, illiquid stocks. Here's why: Suppose a $10 million fund puts $200,000 into a promising small company.

That stock would make up 2 percent of its portfolio, a meaningful stake that would give the fund a nice pop if the company does well. That same $200,000 investment would make a much smaller impact on a $1 billion fund. As such, the larger portfolio would get much less of a boost from truly small-growth companies.

The main disadvantage of a tiny fund is that it would have a high expense ratio. And if it's managed by a small organization lacking much marketing clout, it might never grow large enough to be cost-effective.

Not all mutual funds appear in the daily newspaper listings. Why not?

Requirements to be listed in newspapers are set by the National Association of Securities Dealers, a self-regulating industry group. Initially, a fund must have either 1,000 shareholders or $25 million in assets. To maintain its listing, 750 shareholders or $15 million is needed. More funds may be left out of newspaper listings in the future due to the shortage of space resulting from the significant growth in the number of portfolios. If you feel your fund should appear in your local newspaper but it doesn't, call and ask the newspaper if they could include it.

In plain English, what is the standard deviation, and why is it important to me?

Simply put, it's a yardstick of risk. It measures the fluctuations of a fund's monthly returns around their average. The higher the number, the greater the volatility.

If the monthly returns were always the same, the standard deviation would be zero. This never happens.

When the returns bounce up and down like a yo-yo, the standard deviation would be relatively high. You might see this with an aggressive growth or gold portfolio.

The standard deviation is the best measure of volatility and can be used to make comparisons among all types of funds—stock, bond, gold, and so on. We much prefer it to beta, which has been the subject of increased criticism. Standard deviations are not that easy to find, unfortunately. But when you see this information, keep in mind that higher numbers reflect more risk.

Is it important for me to know whether my manager hedges with futures and options?

Yes. Hedging is done to reduce a portfolio's volatility. Options and futures can be used to lessen market risk, interest-rate risk, and currency risk. Many funds today can hedge. The question is to what extent does the manager actually do so?

Hedging should be viewed as insurance. Too much can prove costly and might reduce returns. That's why we prefer funds that don't do much hedging. Long-term investors need not be concerned about a portfolio's near-term ups and downs.

Is it important for managers to own shares in their funds?

That depends. If the fund is large and the manager has a good track record, it makes little or no difference. But if the fund is small or the manager is not that well known, it shows that the manager is confident enough to put his or her own money into the portfolio. You won't necessarily have an easy time learning about the manager's personal investment habits, however.

How can I tell if an expense ratio is too high?

Compare a fund's expense ratio with that of its peers. Remember that smaller funds tend to have higher ratios, as do international and global portfolios because of the greater costs of investing overseas. Expense ratios are especially important for bond funds, which earn lower total returns than stock portfolios and thus need every little bit of economizing.

Of the major expense components, look at the management fee. This outlay should be declining in percentage terms as total assets increase. So-called 12b–1 fees also constitute part of the expense ratio, making it important to avoid funds with high 12b–1 charges.

How can I size up a fund family?

Let the following questions guide you:

1. Is the family generally known for good long-term performance?

2. Does it charge relatively low expenses? The expenses don't have to be the lowest, but they should be reasonable.

3. Does the family offer a wide range of services?

4. What is the range of investment choices in different funds?

5. Which of the fund categories have built the best performance records? A family might be known for expertise in a certain area, such as international-stock, small-stock, or bond portfolios.

6. Does the family offer clear, informative, and timely literature? This may not be important to you but it's generally an added plus and can help you keep on top of things.

DEALING WITH THE MARKET

What are the main things to remember about market timing?

The basic idea is to be in stocks or stock funds when the market is rising and out when it's declining.

A big risk is that you'll miss a rally by sitting on the sidelines. Thus, it's often unwise to move too much of your money out of the stock market, even when the outlook is bleak. A better strategy might be to lighten up a bit on equities when the market looks pricey or to shift into more conservative, higher-yielding stock funds. The problem with market timing is that it's not easy to predict when a big rally might come.

How can I tell if the stock-market is cheap or dicey?

No single indicator works all the time, but some fairly simple benchmarks are pretty reliable at market extremes. For example, if the price-earnings ratios of the Standard & Poor's 500 or Dow Jones industrial average exceed 20 and their dividend yields drop near or below 3 percent, you can be fairly sure the market is pricey. Conversely, P/Es around 10 or yields near 6 percent point to bargain-basement values. *Barron's* publishes both indicators on a weekly basis.

What is the difference between growth and value investing, and what do I need to know about these strategies?

These are the two primary investment styles. Growth managers seek companies promising dramatic revenue or earning increases, which typically are smaller to medium-sized firms. For the most part, they don't mind paying high prices to get the right stocks.

Conversely, value investors search for firms that can be bought cheaply. These outfits may sell at low ratios of price to earnings or book value, or they may have high dividend yields or "hidden" assets. As contrarians, value managers are more patient, longer-term buyers than growth investors. It often takes time for the market to recognize the value in a particular situation. Thus, a value portfolio would tend to have lower turnover and assume less risk than a growth fund would.

Many managers stick to their investment style at all times. But some more flexible funds might modify their orientation with changing market conditions. As in the clothing business, one approach could be hot for several years while another runs cold. Value managers tend to do best coming out of an economic slump as their teetering companies begin to recover. Growth seekers fare better during the advanced stages of a bull market, when investors often turn more aggressive.

You can easily find out what style your fund managers follow. You can't predict the future, but you can smooth out the ups and downs by diversifying among the growth and value camps. They tend to do well at different times.

What are the best and worst times to invest in a small-stock fund?

Obviously, you would want to buy when the funds offer the best values. This would be when the average P/E for small stocks is roughly equal to that for big stocks (usually defined as the S&P 500). Literature for both the T. Rowe Price New Horizons Fund and Scudder Development Fund includes historic charts of their average P/Es relative to the market. Graphs such as these put things into perspective. Small stocks are expensive when they sell at multiples greater than about 1.8 times that of the S&P 500.

What is meant by the term "efficient market?" What are its implications?

An efficient market is simply one where stocks sell for what they are truly worth. You can't realize above-average performance since there are no significant mispricings to take advantage of. If you are a firm believer in efficient markets, you would want to invest in index funds, which hold a representative group of stocks while trying to minimize costs and taxable gains. The efficient market theory, however, remains a controversial one.

I've heard that the level of discounts or premiums on closed-end funds can be used as a market-timing indicator. How does it work?

This is not a common indicator but one that might be of interest to mutual-fund investors. The size of discounts or premiums on closed-end shares reflects investor sentiment. When pessimism prevails during a market trough, closed-end portfolios usually trade at relatively deep discounts to their NAVs because people are selling. Conversely, discounts narrow or may turn to premiums near market peaks.

Discounts and premiums appear in the "Publicly Traded Funds" box in *Barron's* and *The Wall Street Journal* on Mondays. Watch for changes on the domestic equity funds as an indicator of investor sentiment.

STOCK FUNDS

What is so special about stock funds?

Stock funds deliver much better long-term performance than bond portfolios do. Over many decades, equities have returned approximately 10 percent a year. It is doubtful that bond funds will offer adequate protection against inflation in the coming decades, especially if you consider the impact of taxes. Stock portfolios provide the best hedge against purchasing-power risk.

How exactly do index funds work? What are their advantages and disadvantages?

These portfolios track a particular market index such as the S&P 500, Russell 2000, Wilshire 5000, or Morgan Stanley Capital International Pacific Index. The idea is to match the index's performance, not beat it. The funds hold stocks in proportion to their weight in a particular index. Usually, shares are simply bought and held, to minimize transaction costs and portfolio management fees.

Index funds appeal to people who believe in market efficiency and want to follow a low-cost, long-term, buy-and-hold strategy. This approach assures that you won't significantly underperform the market—not a trivial concern since a large proportion of equity funds end up doing worse than the popular averages.

One complaint investors have about index funds is that they are boring. But what's boring about making money? More exciting portfolios could succumb to bigger losses.

Is there any way fund managers can beat the market?

Yes. Some managers undoubtedly possess rare stock-picking talent. Also, studies have shown that you can realize superior long-term performance by investing in certain groups of stocks. These include companies that sell at low price-earnings ratios and low price-book value ratios. Selected small stocks also promise above-average potential.

What are the pros and cons of trading mutual funds through a discount broker?

This approach may make sense for larger, active investors who want to move quickly between funds in different families. Discount brokers can simplify your record keeping and can offer an economical alternative with a self-directed IRA or Keogh, since all your funds can be consolidated in one account. Naturally, you may have transaction costs with a broker that you wouldn't face with a pure no-load fund.

INTERNATIONAL-STOCK FUNDS

Why is it important to have exposure to international stocks?

About 60 percent of the world's total stock market value exists outside the United States. Many of these markets have outperformed ours over the past two decades. By investing internationally, you're exposed to greater growth opportunities.

In addition, international diversification can reduce volatility, since stock markets in different countries generally don't move in lockstep. True, individual nations often have greater economic, political, and stock market risks, but these dangers are reduced through diversification.

Isn't it unpatriotic to invest internationally?

Only in a myopic sense. The narrow view is that you are providing capital for foreign corporations to grow and prosper instead of putting the money to work at home.

But it's old-fashioned to think that way today. The world is getting smaller and more interconnected. International investing is not a one-way street, since foreigners put money to work in this country just as we invest in theirs. Besides, buying foreign securities creates greater demand for foreign currencies. This can lead to a lower value for the U.S. dollar that, in turn, makes our goods more attractive. And as other nations become more prosperous, this enables them to buy more of our products.

Besides, many foreign corporations employ U.S. workers in some capacity, while many American firms have moved their factories overseas. It's becoming increasingly difficult to distinguish pure foreign companies from pure American ones.

I want to give international investing a try. What's a good way to get started?

The first thing to remember is that the more countries represented in a portfolio, the greater the diversification. A fund consisting only of Japanese stocks would be riskier than another that invests in perhaps a dozen or more markets. Also, big blue-chip foreign companies would be less volatile than smaller overseas stocks, especially those in emerging economies. So the riskiest type of international fund would be a closed-end, single-country portfolio that owns the small stocks of an emerging market.

Most beginners should stick with an established global or international fund investing in good-quality companies in a variety of countries. Global funds differ from international portfolios in that they hold both U.S. and foreign stocks. A global-fund manager may have a big or little U.S. stake at any particular moment.

What are regional portfolios and how are they used?

These are more specialized international funds that focus on one of the three major overseas regions: Europe, Asia and the Pacific Basin, or Latin America. They invest in a group of countries within their target region—anywhere from three or four to a dozen different markets.

Regional funds are a result of the growth and increasing accessibility of foreign stock markets. They appeal to moderately aggressive investors who want more focused holdings. For example, you might want all your international exposure in Europe if you feel it offers the best value. Since regional funds are less diversified than their global or international counterparts, they generally carry more risk.

Why do currency exchange rates fluctuate? How do these fluctuations affect investors in foreign stock funds?

Currency exchange rates move up and down like the prices of bananas, oil, or any other commodity. Rates vary because of shifts in demand and supply. An increase in demand, holding supply constant, will lead to a higher price. The supply and demand for a country's currency are closely related to its balance of trade (the difference between its exports and imports), net foreign investment, and other factors. Major banks, multinational corporations, money managers, speculators, and tourists buy and sell currencies on a daily basis.

Suppose Country A has a healthy balance of trade surplus (exporting more than it imports) and offers relatively high interest rates, thereby attracting foreign investment. Country A's currency would be in strong demand since foreigners would need it to pay for their purchases and investments. The nation's currency might also be bid higher by speculators, if they think it will continue to appreciate.

Long-term investors in international funds shouldn't worry much about currency fluctuations. Gains and losses tend to balance out. Besides, changes in exchange rates are difficult to predict, so we don't recommend buying a foreign stock or bond fund as a short-term currency speculation.

BOND FUNDS

What is the difference between yield and total return?

Yield measures the income from an investment, expressed as a percent of its price. Total return considers the price change along with yield.

Suppose a bond's price is $100 at the beginning of the year and falls to $80 12 months later. It pays interest of $10 for the year. Its yield is 10 percent ($10/$100), but since the price declines by 20 percent, the total return is -10 percent.

Total return is the most important measure of performance, since it tells the whole story.

What is the SEC's 30-day annualized yield?

It's a standardized rate of return that can be used to make meaningful comparisons among bond funds. It is computed with a complex formula prescribed by the SEC and has been in use since 1988. Before that time, funds could calculate their yields in different ways to make their portfolios look more enticing to unwary investors.

The SEC's yield is more complicated than traditional measures because it makes special adjustments. Simply put, it is based on a yield average on the fund's securities for the past 30 days. It provides an estimated yield to maturity assuming all securities are held until their due date.

What are the most serious risks faced by bond-fund investors?

1. *Interest-rate risk.* When rates rise, prices of existing bonds fall. Long-term U.S. government and muni funds have the greatest

interest-rate risk. This danger becomes more serious when rates are at low levels and have the potential to increase substantially.

2. *Credit risk.* Also known as default risk, this reflects the danger an issuer won't make interest or principal payments on time or in entirety. It is a significant problem with high-yield bond funds, especially during times of deteriorating economic conditions.

3. *Purchasing-power or inflation risk.* All bond-fund investors need to consider this peril, since inflation erodes the purchasing power of fixed returns. For this reason, long-term investors—even those who are retired—need some stock market exposure.

My bond fund just cut its monthly distribution. Does this mean trouble?

Probably not. This happens during periods of declining interest rates. Suppose you own a long-term, high-grade corporate fund and rates are falling. Two things may be happening:

1. New cash could be moving into the portfolio, assuming bank and money-fund yields are low. Unless the manager wants to invest the new proceeds in riskier debt, he or she will have to buy bonds paying lower yields, which reduces the fund's yield also.

2. Some bonds in the portfolio will likely be called, allowing the issuers to replace these securities with lower-coupon debt. Again, the manager will have to reinvest the proceeds in bonds with smaller yields.

Under these scenarios, the manager's best alternative is to reduce the dividend. Otherwise, he or she would have to pay dividends out of principal, which destroys the portfolio's long-term earnings potential.

On the plus side, falling interest rates lead to rising bond prices, so even though the fund's yield drops, its total return may increase greatly. But if you rely on the distribution to meet living expenses, you might have to redeem some shares.

How can I keep current on the yield curve?

Both *Investor's Business Daily* and Part C of *The Wall Street Journal* provide this information. The yield curve tells the general level of interest rates, according to different maturities of Treasury securities. By eyeing the relationship between yields on bills, notes, and bonds, you get an idea of the approximate slope of the curve. For example, if bills on average yield 4 percent, notes 6 percent and bonds 8 percent, you can tell that the curve is upward sloping. When interest rates are relatively low and the curve is upward sloping, it tells you the market expects rates will rise.

What does the Federal Reserve do? Why is it important to keep up with its policies?

As the nation's central bank, the Federal Reserve or Fed regulates the money supply, which in turn affects the economic system. An increasing money supply tends to stimulate the economy, a decrease does the opposite.

The Fed uses three tools—"open-market operations," changes in the discount rate, and changes in bank reserve requirements—to control the cost and availability of money. Open-market operations, which involve the daily buying and selling of government securities from the Fed's huge inventory, is the most important.

When the Fed buys Treasury securities, it increases the money supply because its purchases essentially put more cash into the system. Net selling by the Fed would have the opposite result.

The Fed exerts the most immediate impact on short-term rates, which are more volatile than long-term rates and thus respond more quickly to changes in monetary policy. In addition, the Fed can directly change a key short-term rate—the discount rate—which is the amount member banks pay to borrow from the system. If the Fed persists with an easy-money policy, long-term rates will eventually fall, which hopefully will stimulate capital investment by businesses.

By keeping up with monetary policy, you get a feel for whether the Fed is loosening or tightening. Falling rates lead to rising bond prices and usually reverberate into higher stock values. Rising rates tend to do the opposite. Thus, it's important to see in which direction the Fed appears to be leaning.

How do bond funds price their securities?

With few exceptions, mutual funds price all of their securities once a day at the market's close. This enables them to calculate a current NAV, as explained in Chapter 1.

Bonds tend to be more difficult to price accurately than stocks are, since they are not traded in an organized market. No centralized system exists for the dissemination of bond quotes. Different firms making a market in the same issue may have significantly different quotes. A lot of bonds don't trade much, and smaller, obscure issues are especially difficult to value.

To price a bond, the fund's managers may simply call dealers to get quotes at the end of the day. Since a fund may need to price dozens of bonds, it might employ a pricing service, most of which use special computerized systems. On rare occasions, the services can give incorrect prices. For this reason, experienced portfolio managers will often do some spot checking to avoid embarrassment.

BEHIND THE SCENES

How much training and knowledge do mutual fund telephone reps have?

The qualifications of shareholder-service personnel vary, but generally speaking a person must have a college degree. Many applicants were business majors, often specializing in finance, accounting, or economics. Most reps are young.

New employees go through an extensive training program at the fund company, where they learn about the different products and services the firm offers as well as about investing concepts and securities laws. At the end of the program, they take the Series 6 and Series 63 tests, comprehensive examinations prepared by the National Association of Securities Dealers (NASD). These exams include material on mutual funds, variable annuities, and sales practices.

The training is an ongoing process, and shareholder-service reps are required to keep up with new developments. Some may concentrate on particular areas, such as retirement planning or variable annuities. This specialization provides for more in-depth answers to your questions.

Incidentally, when you telephone a fund company, you will likely be told that your call is being recorded. This is done for record-keeping accuracy. In case you dispute a particular transaction at a later date, the recorded conversation can be checked.

What is the background of the typical fund manager?

There are no formal requirements, but many managers have an MBA or related degree from a leading business school. Typically they work their way up in the organization, often beginning as analysts. As you might expect, most are smart and hard working. They have to do well or they won't last.

Is it important for me to know who manages my fund? How can I find out about a manager's background?

You want a portfolio that will do better than the market; otherwise, you might as well invest in a low-cost index fund. You pay a fee for professional management, so you want to get the most for your money.

Well-known, successful managers are written up in the financial press, profiled in books, and interviewed on television programs such as "Wall Street Week." Lesser-known managers might still draw media attention, but not nearly so extensively. It can be difficult to learn much about a particular person. Morningstar's *Mutual Funds Sourcebook* provides a basic biography on the managers of many of the portfolios it covers. You can also call the fund company to find out more. For instance, the firm may be able to tell you if the manager has been written up or has received other special recognition.

Do mutual fund managers have a team of analysts working for them?

Generally, yes. There simply are not enough hours in the day for managers to do everything themselves. They need others to crunch numbers, dig up facts, and so on. But even with some help from analysts, the managers usually have the final say about the portfolio. As explained in Chapter 3, some funds have two or more managers working as a team.

Who are the directors of a fund and what are their functions?

Directors or trustees tend to be experienced, prominent individuals in fields of business, government, or academia. Some are household names. The same group of perhaps 5 to 11 individuals typically oversees all the funds in a family. Some directors are employees of the fund's adviser, but at least 40 percent must be independent. Shareholders vote for the directors on their proxy cards, with each share entitling the holder to one vote.

Directors play an important role in monitoring the fund's operations and policing potential conflicts of interest, particularly in the area of fees. Directors concern themselves with the big picture, not the day-to-day operations. They are responsible for hiring the fund's adviser and renewing the firm's contract.

Some critics have questioned how effective most directors really are, however. They point to the fact that fund expenses have generally crept up over the years, even though you might expect more economies of scale as mutual funds grew in size.

What regulations govern mutual funds and their advisers?

As the nation's third-largest financial industry after banks and insurance companies, mutual funds are heavily regulated. At the federal level, the Securities and Exchange Commission oversees each fund's compliance with the following four laws:

1. The *Securities Act of 1933* requires fund shares to be SEC-registered before they can be offered to the public. The company must provide you with an accurate, up-to-date prospectus meeting SEC guidelines. This statute also controls what is said in fund advertisements.

2. The *Securities Exchange Act of 1934* governs the purchase and sale of fund shares, as well as all other types of securities.

3. The *Investment Advisers Act of 1940* regulates certain activities of fund advisers.

4. The highly detailed *Investment Company Act of 1940* contains provisions to prevent self-dealing and other conflicts of interest. Its purpose is to eliminate widespread abuses within the industry. It provides for the safekeeping of portfolio assets with independent custodians, prohibits the charging of excessive fees, and ensures adequate diversification.

In addition, nearly every state has its own set of mutual fund regulations.

What are options, and how do mutual fund managers use them?

An option contract gives its holder the *right* to buy or sell a certain amount of an asset at a specific price within a limited time frame. The option buyer pays a premium to the seller (or writer) for granting this right.

Fund managers often use options to buy or sell individual stocks, stock indexes, and Treasury securities. Generally speaking, these contracts help the manager hedge the portfolio to reduce risk. Some managers also sell options against their stock or bond positions to generate premium income.

What are futures, and how do mutual fund managers use them?

Futures are similar to options, except that they are *obligations* to buy or sell an underlying stock index, Treasury security, foreign currency, or other instrument at a given price and by a certain date.

Futures, like options, can be used to reduce risk. Suppose the manager of a blue-chip equity fund feels the market will soon head south. Instead of selling lots of stocks to raise cash, he could use stock-index futures as a hedge. If the market goes into a tailspin, the gain on the futures would offset some or all of the loss in portfolio value.

The danger is that, if the market advances, the futures contract will cut off some or all of the fund's gains. Like options, futures can be useful. But neither vehicle is a panacea.

Why are some mutual funds not registered in my state?

Funds have to satisfy state securities laws in addition to federal regulations. The big, well-known families generally have their portfolios registered in all 50 states. But smaller, newer, more obscure funds often do not offer their products for sale everywhere, since it costs more money to do so. The annual fees in some states range up to $2,000 or more per fund. Investors living in certain small states with more stringent or costly regulations face a narrower choice. But for all practical purposes, this isn't a major problem since most funds are registered for sale across the United States.

Why do funds and fund companies merge?

Asset building is the name of the game today. A fund company with $40 billion under management is generally better off than one with $2 billion. That's because more assets means greater economies of scale, a wider range of portfolios and services, better managers, and more marketing muscle. Thus, mergers and consolidations often make economic sense.

The recent mega-purchase of the Templeton family by the huge Franklin group was the largest mutual fund deal ever. Franklin's forte is in fixed-income funds, whereas Templeton is well-known for global stock investing. Thus, the combined organization has strong exposure in several key areas. A bad track record can also bring about a merger. Funds with poor past performances are frequently merged into those with better histories, thereby erasing their unsuccessful pasts.

I've read that the SEC has proposed a new breed of portfolio called the "hybrid fund." What is it?

Because they always face the danger of a wave of redemptions, mutual funds must keep at least 85 percent of their assets in liquid, readily marketable securities. Closed-end portfolios, by contrast, don't have this problem since they do not redeem shares. They are better able to invest in thinly traded small businesses and foreign stocks in small, illiquid markets because they don't have to worry about having to dump them at depressed prices to meet redemptions. But as explained in Chapter 1, closed-end funds tend to sell at discounts to NAV. Widening discounts pose problems for managements as well as for investors.

Enter the hybrid fund. A compromise, it would allow redemptions to be made on a limited, controlled basis, thereby making less liquid, longer-term investments possible. In fact, some of the stocks hybrids could invest in might not yet be publicly traded. In turn, the ability of shareholders to redeem at NAV should alleviate the discount problem.

I remember hearing the term "hub-and-spoke" funds. What are they?

As the name implies, you have two components. The hub is the actual portfolio of stocks or bonds. It works like an ordinary mutual fund except that its only investors are other mutual funds, known as spokes. The spokes sell shares to the public, typically through a bank.

The hub-and-spoke concept was developed by Signature Financial Group for Citicorp and other banks. The hub and all spokes have identical investment objectives. The spokes serve simply as different marketing vehicles for attracting money to the hub.

This versatile arrangement has grown rapidly, even though it's been in use only since 1990. It's an important development for the industry since it offers flexibility—different spokes are sold to various investor groups and can have varying fee arrangements and levels of service. For example, one might have a front-end load whereas another has a 12b–1 plan coupled with a contingent deferred sales charge.

Hub-and-spoke funds will be used more widely outside the banking area in the future. The format can also facilitate the marketing of U.S. portfolios to foreign investors. The arrangement appears to offer an economy-of-scale advantage since the spokes gather money independently.

The mutual fund business appears healthy and profitable. Can I buy stock in any management companies?

Yes, in more than a dozen publicly traded management companies. These include Alliance, Colonial, Dreyfus, Franklin, Eaton Vance, Nuveen, Pioneer and T. Rowe Price. Naturally, buying the shares of a mutual-fund company is different from investing in a fund. You need to research it as you would any other stock.

OTHER ALTERNATIVES

What is a "wrap" account? How does it differ from a mutual fund?

A wrap (or wrap fee) account is a tailor-made, professionally managed stock or bond portfolio providing more personal attention than what's available through mutual funds. The accounts are set up through a stockbroker, who helps you find and monitor a compatible money manager with a good track record. The annual fee, which averages about 3 percent, covers portfolio management as well as re-lated commissions on trades. Wrap accounts appeal to wealthier inves-tors seeking some personalized service. The minimum account size is generally around $100,000.

Conceptually, a wrap account is like a mutual fund, but funds enjoy certain advantages. For example, their managers really operate in the public eye, with performance carefully tracked by independent services and priced in the newspaper each day. Wrap managers, by contrast, might not be that visible. Besides, a $100,000 account might not get you as much personalized attention as you think—chances are, you're get-ting the same stocks as the wrap manager's other small clients. In fact, you might have the same holdings as a mutual fund, if the same person runs one (which is often the case). Most important, a 3 percent annual fee is a stiff yearly expense that would put many mutual funds to shame. A wrap account also would typically face higher dealer spreads on transactions—a less-visible factor that wouldn't show up in the 3 percent flat fee.

Our feeling is that most people won't lose anything by sticking with mutual funds. You will enjoy plenty of investment choices, and you will have access to the most brilliant money managers in the country. Inciden-tally, a new breed of wrap account consisting of mutual funds, rather than individual stocks or bonds, has become quite popular. If you're interested, be sure to look carefully at the fees and make comparisons. Don't overpay.

Should I own some closed-end funds in addition to my open-end portfolios? If so, when is the best time to buy them?

Closed-end funds require greater sophistication. You also need to have an account with a stockbroker and know how to place orders so as to minimize transaction costs.

The best time to buy closed-end funds is when they're selling at big discounts to their NAVs, which typically occurs during bear markets and at year-end, for reasons attributable to tax-related selling. A well-managed stock fund may be a genuine bargain if you can buy it at a discount of 15 percent or more. That's like purchasing a dollar's worth of assets for 85 cents or less.

I like the challenge and excitement of buying stocks directly. Is there anything wrong with owning individual stocks along with mutual funds?

Not at all, assuming you can spend time analyzing and monitoring companies and have been successful at this pursuit in the past.

If you have made money picking your own stocks and enjoy it, by all means continue. But our feeling is that most people will fare better by investing exclusively in mutual funds.

What are the crucial differences between bond funds and unit investment trusts?

The most important distinction is that bond funds are actively managed, while unit trusts aren't. It's also far easier to obtain information on mutual funds and analyze them, partly because their prices are listed on a daily basis in the newspaper. All unit trusts carry load charges, but you can find many good no-load funds. For these reasons, bond mutual funds are generally the best bet, management fees notwithstanding.

Sources of Information for Mutual Fund Investors

This appendix contains popular sources that will help you find funds in different categories and get the data you need to make an evaluation. The more expensive publications might be available in some libraries or through your broker or financial planner. You may also find other guides you like—it's virtually impossible to provide a bibliography of all sources on this subject.

In addition to using the following guides, you can keep up with recent developments and performance numbers by reading the mutual funds sections of the following publications: *Barron's, Business Week, Financial World, Forbes, Investor's Business Daily, Kiplinger's Personal Finance Magazine,*

Money, The Wall Street Journal and the business sections of major
metropolitan newspapers.

The following publications are listed in alphabetical order. Unless
otherwise noted, the cost is quoted as an annual rate. Of course, rates and
other information are subject to change.

1. *CDA/Wiesenberger Investment Companies Service* (annual, $395 including
monthly *Mutual Funds Update* and *Mutual Funds Panorama*; $295 book only)

Published by:
CDA Investment Technologies Inc.
1355 Piccard Drive
Rockville, MD 20850
800-232-2285, 301-975-9600

This familiar encyclopedia has been published for more than 50 years.
The service covers more than 2,800 portfolios including open- and closed-
end funds, variable annuities, unit investment trusts and money-market
funds. The annual book contains returns for various periods, portfolio
volatility statistics, and fund profiles. Full-page profiles are provided for
1,500 larger open- and closed-end funds; smaller portfolios get a shorter
presentation. You'll also find chapters that give basic information about
investing in mutual-funds.

The comprehensive *Mutual Funds Update* contains data on performance
and portfolio characteristics, including alpha, beta, R-squared, and standard
deviation. It also provides commentary and interviews with fund managers.

2. *Directory of Mutual Funds* (annual, $5)

Published by:
Investment Company Institute
1600 M Street, N.W.
Suite 600
Washington, DC 20036
202-293-7700

This is the most complete low-cost mutual fund directory. The ICI's
guide provides names, addresses, and phone numbers of more than 3,700

funds separated into 22 categories. You will also find the year each fund began, the investment adviser, assets, minimum initial and subsequent investments, fees, and where to buy shares. The book includes a discussion of mutual fund basics.

The ICI also publishes other useful materials. For those interested in industry data, the *Mutual Fund Fact Book* (annual, $15) offers a wealth of statistics and other information.

3. *The Individual Investor's Guide to No-Load Mutual Funds* (annual, AAII members $19; nonmembers $24.95); *Quarterly No-Load Mutual Fund Update* (quarterly, AAII members $24; nonmembers $30).

Published by:
American Association of Individual Investors
625 North Michigan Avenue
Suite 1900
Chicago, IL 60611
312-280-0170

These comprehensive publications cover more than 600 no-load and low-load funds. The annual guide contains fund profiles, per-share data, performance and risk statistics, and a variety of other useful information. The quarterly publication reports recent return and risk information, as well as fund developments. Both sources list top-performing funds and show how relevant indexes have fared.

The American Association of Individual Investors also publishes the *AAII Journal* (10 times a year, included in $49 annual AAII membership dues). It contains articles and columns on investing, including mutual fund topics. The AAII, an independent not-for-profit corporation formed in 1978, has more than 130,000 members.

4. *Investor's Guide to Low-Cost Mutual Funds* (January and July, $5 per issue)

Published by:
Mutual Fund Education Alliance
1900 Erie Street, Suite 120
Kansas City, MO 64116
816-471-1454

Appendix 1

This contains descriptions of 32 mutual fund families and data on their more than 650 no-load and low-load portfolios, grouped into 11 investment categories. Each profile lists a statement of the fund's objectives and several statistics, including performance numbers. The low-cost book also includes a discussion of the basics of mutual fund investing.

5. *Morningstar Mutual Funds* (every other week, $395); *Mutual-funds Sourcebook* (annual, $225)

Published by:
Morningstar Inc.
53 West Jackson Blvd.
Chicago, IL 60604
800-876-5005, 312-427-1985

Morningstar Mutual Funds is published in two sections—a summary report and a collection of fund profiles. The service provides comprehensive reports on more than 1,200 load and no-load portfolios. Each profile is updated every 20 weeks. An analyst's review focuses on performance, risk, portfolio holdings, and recent developments. Funds are rated on both return and risk. Profiles contain modern portfolio statistics—alpha, beta, R-squared, and standard deviation. The reports include quarterly as well as annual total returns. Year-to-date returns on all funds are updated regularly.

The *Mutual Funds Sourcebook* consists of two volumes—one for equity funds, the other for fixed-income portfolios. More than 2,200 funds are profiled, in a manner very similar to what's provided in *Morningstar Mutual Funds*, except they don't include analyst opinions. The *Sourcebook* offers background information on fund managers, along with many tables of useful data covering performance, portfolio turnover, expense ratios, and more. Information in the *Sourcebook* can be used to make a detailed comparison of different funds, as you can do with *Morningstar Mutual Funds*.

Morningstar has several other useful publications. *Morningstar Closed-End Funds* (every other week in two sections, $195) is a comprehensive resource that tracks more than 250 closed-end portfolios; *Variable Annuity Sourcebook* (annual, $195) covers more than 1,000 variable annuity and variable-life subaccounts; *The 5-Star Investor* (monthly, $65) is a newsletter designed to help individuals build a mutual fund portfolio.

6. Standard & Poor's *Security Owner's Stock Guide* (monthly, $118)

Published by:
Standard & Poor's Corp.
25 Broadway
New York, NY 10004
800-221-7940

This widely available guide contains a compact "Mutual Fund Summary" providing one line of data on more than 700 funds. Portfolios are grouped alphabetically by family. Given the limited space, there is a surprising amount of information on each fund, including the objective, total assets, cash holdings, performance numbers, and distributions. Footnotes provide information on stock splits, dividends, and the like. The S&P guide also contains a summary section on variable annuities.

7. *Standard & Poor's/Lipper Mutual Fund Profiles* (quarterly, $132)

Published by:
Standard & Poor's Corp.
25 Broadway
New York, NY 10004
800-221-7940

This periodical covers more than 750 stock and bond portfolios, with emphasis given to larger funds. Each presentation includes total return numbers, risk statistics, and per-share data. You will also find lists of top and bottom performers, leaders and laggards grouped by investment objective, and other useful information.

Total Return with Reinvestment

To calculate returns in situations involving reinvested dividends, you need to know the amount of each distribution and the NAV at that time. Essentially, the investor is purchasing more shares at the reinvestment price.

To illustrate, assume a small-company growth fund starts the year at an NAV of $20 and finishes at a price of $22. Assume further that the fund's distributions come to $4 a share and, for simplicity, that all reinvestments were made at an NAV of $21.

The investor held one share at the start of the year and accumulated 0.19 share (the distribution of 4 divided by the 21 reinvestment price) during the year. Thus, our investor held 1.19 shares at year end.

The following steps are used to calculate total returns with reinvestment:

Step 1. Determine the investor's total account value at the end of the period:
(End of period NAV) × (Shares held at end) = 22 × 1.19 = 26.18

Step 2. Determine total value at the start of the period:
(Beginning of period NAV) × (Shares held at beginning) = 20 × 1 = 20

Step 3. Subtract the value obtained in *Step 2* from the one in *Step 1*:
= 26.18 - 20 = 6.18

Step 4. Divide the result in *Step 3* by the result in *Step 2*:
= 6.18/20 = 30.9 percent

The 30.9 percent return with reinvestment contrasts with a 30 percent number without [(4 + 22 - 20)/20].

How to Find the Geometric Average Total Return

The geometric average annual return and the compound annual return are the same thing. Basically, we're taking results for individual periods and averaging them using a special formula. Suppose a fund had total returns of 15 percent, -20 percent, and 40 percent over three consecutive years. The geometric average can easily be found with a finance calculator.

The steps are as follows:

Step 1. Express each return as a decimal. Converting the preceding percentage values to decimals, we have 0.15, -0.20, and 0.40.

Step 2. Add 1.0 to each decimal value. Adding 1.0 to the numbers found in *Step 1* gives us 1.15, 0.80, and 1.40.

Step 3. Multiply together the values found in *Step 2*:
1.15 × 0.80 x 1.40 = 1.288.

Step 4. Raise the value found in Step 3 to the $1/x$ power, where x equals the number of items being averaged. Since we are dealing with three periods, we have $1.288^{1/3} = 1.088$.

Step 5. Subtract 1.0 from the result in *Step 4* and express as a percent.
1.088 - 1.000 = .088, or 8.8 percent.

Thus, our hypothetical fund produced an 8.8 percent geometric average annual return.

(If Step 4 seems confusing, you can often find the average result by trial and error. For example, multiplying 1.09 × 1.09 × 1.09 gives a number that's pretty close to 1.288. With further effort and patience, you can come up with the exact return in question. This procedure may be necessary if you don't have a finance calculator handy.)

Total Returns Can Be Shown in Three Different Ways

There are three standard methods of portraying performance over periods longer than one year: cumulative total return, compound sum of a specific initial investment (typically $10,000), and compound annual return. The following numbers illustrate the differences between the three over a 15-year period.

With a finance calculator you can convert the larger percentage or dollar values to more meaningful compound average annual returns, if they're not also reported. Suppose you know a fund has produced a cumulative total return of 1,500 percent over 15 years. What does that equal on an annual basis?

Cumulative Total Return	Result of $10,000 Initial Investment	Compound Annual Total Return
1,500%	$160,000	20.30%
1,000	110,000	17.34
800	90,000	15.78
500	60,000	12.69
300	40,000	9.68

Step 1. Take your percentage cumulative total return and express it as an ordinary number by moving the decimal point two places to the left, that is, 1,500 percent becomes 15.00.

Step 2. Add 1.0 to your result in Step 1. In the example, 15.0 + 1.0 = 16.0.

Step 3. Determine how many years (x) are involved. Then, using a finance calculator, raise the number obtained in Step 2 to the 1/x power.

In the example, 16 raised to the 1/15 power equals 1.2030. (Note, this is the same as taking the 15th root of 16.)

Step 4. Subtract 1.0 from your result in Step 3 and express it as a percentage.

Concluding the example, 1.2030 - 1.0 = 0.2030, or 20.30 percent.

It's even easier to convert an accumulated sum of money based on an initial investment into a compound annual return. Suppose an initial $10,000 resulted in $160,000 after 15 years. Different calculators require different keystrokes, but in general the $10,000 is the initial (or present) value, $160,000 is the final (or future) value, and 15 is the number of periods. Given these three inputs a finance calculator would generate a 20.30 percent compound annual return.

Mutual Fund Timing Newsletters

Here are 10 mutual fund newsletters that offer market-timing advice. The editor or publisher's name is included.

Bob Brinker's Marketimer
Robert J. Brinker
P.O. Box 7005
Princeton, NJ 08543
908-359-8838

The Chartist Mutual Fund Timer
Dan Sullivan
P.O. Box 758

Seal Beach, CA 90740
310-596-2385

Fund Exchange
Paul A. Merriman
1200 Westlake Avenue N.
Suite 700
Seattle, WA 98109
800-423-4893

Fund Profit Alert
Investment Research Institute Inc.
Bernard Schaeffer
Box 46709
Cincinnati, OH 45246
800-327-8833
513-589-3800

InvesTech Mutual Fund Advisor
James B. Stack
2472 Birch Glen
Whitefish, MT 59937
800-955-8500
406-862-7777

Mutual Fund Forecaster
Norman Fosback
The Institute for Econometric Research
3471 North Federal Highway
Ft. Lauderdale, FL 33306
800-442-9000
305-563-9000

The Mutual Fund Strategist
Charlie Hooper
P.O. Box 446
Burlington, VT 05402
802-658-3513

Switch Fund Timing
David G. Davis
P.O. Box 25430
Rochester, NY 14625
716-385-3122

Telephone Switch Newsletter
Douglas Fabian
P.O. Box 2538
Huntington Beach, CA 92647
800-950-8765
714-536-1931

Weber's Fund Advisor
Ken Weber
P.O. Box 3490
New Hyde Park, NY 11040
516-466-1252

For published performance ratings on these and other newsletters, contact:

The Hulbert Financial Digest
316 Commerce Street
Alexandria, VA 22314
703-683-5905

Glossary

Account	The formal accounting record that tracks a person's financial dealings with a mutual fund. The shareholder receives periodic account statements as well as transaction confirmations. Fund companies may require investors to maintain a certain minimum account balance, such as $1,000.
Adviser	The firm or individual that serves as money manager for a mutual fund. The adviser is compensated by a fee based on a percent of assets under management.
Agency securities	Bonds issued by U.S. government agencies and organizations, such as the Government National Mortgage Association and the Tennessee Valley Authority. Mortgage-backed

301

bonds are a popular type of agency security. *See* Mortgage-backed securities.

Aggressive -   These volatile stock portfolios seek maximum capital ap-
growth fund   preciation. They may employ speculative strategies in an
effort to enhance returns.

Alpha   The amount by which a portfolio's actual return exceeds or
falls short of its expected return. High positive alphas reflect
extraordinary performance; negative numbers show under-performance.

Annuiti-   A plan for taking a periodic distribution of money during
zation   an annuity contract's payout period.

Annuity   A series of periodic payments for a stipulated time frame. *See*
Fixed annuity and Variable annuity.

ARM fund   A special type of fixed income fund focusing on adjustable-rate mortgages, or ARMs.

Asked price   The price at which a security is offered for sale by a dealer. For
a mutual fund, the asked or offering price equals net asset value
plus any front-end load. *See* Bid price and Dealer spread.

Asset   The apportionment of your portfolio to different asset classes
allocation   such as money-market instruments, and bonds and stocks,
including appropriate subcategories.

Asset -   A portfolio holding several asset categories such as domestic
allocation   and foreign stocks, bonds, money-market instruments, gold,
fund   and real estate stocks. The proportions invested in each may
be fixed or varied as the manager's outlook changes.

Asset-based   An ongoing charge against net assets used by a fund com-
sales charge   pany to pay for marketing expenses. This cost, disclosed in
the fund's prospectus, cannot exceed 0.75 percent annually.
It is part of the expense ratio. *See* Service fee and 12b–1 fee.

Automatic -   A service enabling you to have a designated sum of money
investment   transferred on a regular basis to your fund account from your
plan   bank account or paycheck.

Automatic   A service available from virtually all funds, whereby your
reinvestment   dividend and capital gains distributions can be reinvested
into full and fractional shares at the prevailing NAV. A rein-

vestment program might offer several options. For example, you may choose to reinvest only capital gains distributions and take income dividends in cash, or you may reinvest distributions from one fund into another within the same family.

Back-end load — A sales charge paid when selling a fund. *See* Contingent-deferred sales charge and Redemption charge.

Balanced fund — A hybrid portfolio of bonds and stocks.

Balance of payments — A summary number that tracks all money flowing into and out of a country over a specific period. It includes the country's trade balance (the difference between imports and exports) as well as foreign borrowing and lending flows. A nation's currency fluctuations are related to changes in its balance of payments.

Barbell — A bond portfolio that concentrates in short-term debt, commonly T-bills, and long-term bonds, avoiding intermediate-term issues.

Bear market — A prolonged period of falling prices.

Beta — A measure of the volatility of a portfolio relative to an underlying index, such as the S&P 500. Beta values above 1.0 indicate a volatile or aggressive portfolio, those below 1.0 a more stable, or defensive, fund. For example, a portfolio with a beta of 1.25 would be expected to be 25 percent more volatile than the index.

Bid price — The current price a dealer is willing to pay for a security. For a mutual fund the bid is usually called the redemption price and equals the NAV less any redemption charge. *See* Asked price and Dealer spread.

Blue-chip stock — The stock of a large, well-established high quality firm.

Blue-sky laws — State securities laws, which mutual funds are subject to in addition to federal regulations.

Board of directors — Elected by the shareholders, board members are responsible for overseeing fund operations. The board is charged with looking out for shareholder interests. Among other duties, board members are expected to make sure fund fees are not unreasonable and that the adviser is doing a good job.

Bond
A debt instrument promising to pay its holder periodic interest (or coupon) payments and a fixed amount of principal at maturity. *See* Zero-coupon bond.

Bottom-up analysis
A technique used by many fund managers for picking securities. The primary emphasis is on selecting individual companies, with less attention given to industry and economic factors. *See* top-down analysis.

Breadth of market
A cumulative analysis of the number of advancing versus declining issues. Used by technicians to gain a feel for the market's direction.

Breakpoint
Investment thresholds at which the front-end load drops in steps. Eventually, the load levels out at a low percentage or is phased out entirely. Breakpoint amounts are listed in a table in the prospectus. *See* letter of intent.

Bull market
A prolonged period of rising prices.

Call option
A contract granting its buyer the right to *buy* a specific asset, such as a stock, at a fixed price during a limited time. *See* Put option.

Call risk
The danger that a bond carrying a relatively high coupon will be redeemed by the issuer prior to the maturity date. Calls hurt bondholders during times of falling interest rates since the redemption proceeds must be reinvested at lower rates.

Capital gains distributions
The paying out of net realized capital gains to fund shareholders. Gains are typically declared annually in December and payable in January.

Capitalization
The total market value of a firm, used as a measure of size. It is determined by multiplying the current price by the number of shares outstanding. A firm with 15 million shares trading at $10 each would have a $150 million market cap and thus be considered a small company.

Cash flow
Net, new shareholder money going into a fund. Some observers feel that portfolios enjoying consistent cash inflows have a performance edge.

Check-writing privilege	A service enabling investors to write checks against their mutual fund account balances. Checks usually must be for a certain minimum, commonly $100 or $500, and the service is restricted to money-market and bond funds.
Class A and B shares	*See* Flexible pricing.
Clone fund	A portfolio established to mirror another, which may have been closed to new money because of size.
Closed-end fund	A type of portfolio featuring a relatively stable amount of shares outstanding. Unlike open-end mutual funds, they generally do not issue new shares to investors, nor do they redeem shares from sellers. Rather, the shares trade on a stock exchange or over-the-counter like any other stock, so you buy and sell them through a broker. Many closed-ends trade at discounts to NAV. Others change hands at premiums. This introduces an additional dimension of risk—and return—for the investor.
Closed fund	A mutual fund that has shut its doors to new investors. This commonly happens when a portfolio has grown so large that it can't effectively achieve its objectives. Sometimes the management company starts up a clone with similar goals.
Company risk	The danger that some misfortune—such as a lawsuit, poor earnings, or the loss of a key market—will befall a firm. Mutual Fund investors don't have to worry about this danger since it is largely eliminated by diversification. Also known as diversifiable risk or random risk.
Compound interest	See Interest on interest.
Constant-ratio formula plan	The use of preestablished investment percentages to ensure a desired balance among different fund categories. An individual might maintain, say, 20 percent each in a money-market, investment-grade bond, equity-income, small-company, and international-stock fund. The investor would periodically monitor the values of the individual portfolios and rebalance the holdings if the actual percentages deviate too widely from their targets.

Contingent deferred sales charge (or CDSC)	A back-end load accompanying a 12b–1 plan on a broker-sold fund. The CDSC is highest if shares are redeemed in the first year. It might start out at, say, 5 percent and decline by one percentage point annually, usually phasing out after five or six years.
Contrarian	An investor who thinks independently and often goes against the crowd—buying when others are selling and selling when the crowd is buying.
Conversion privilege	*See* Telephone exchange privilege.
Convertible-bond fund	A hybrid portfolio that primarily holds convertible bonds and preferred stock. Convertibles have characteristics of both debt and stock—they often rise along with the regular shares when the firm is enjoying good fortune, but trade more like bonds when things sour.
Corporate-bond fund	A portfolio that holds investment-grade corporate debt, or that rated triple-B or higher. The high-quality corporate funds generally restrict their holdings to issues rated single-A or better. Those in both groups may also own Treasury securities.
Country risk	The danger that a nation will face severe economic or political problems, or even a natural disaster. This peril is greatest with a single-country closed-end fund that invests in a smaller emerging economy.
Credit risk	The danger that the issuer of a corporate or municipal bond will experience financial difficulties causing a deterioration in creditworthiness, perhaps even a default. Treasury securities are considered free of credit risk.
Currency risk	The risk, faced by investors in foreign bond and stock funds, that the dollar will appreciate relative to the currencies in which the securities are denominated. When that happens, the fund will realize a currency loss.
Custodian	The independent organization, usually a bank, that is responsible for the handling and safekeeping of a fund's cash and securities.

Cyclical stock	A company whose earnings fluctuate more or less in sync with the general health of the economy. An example would be an auto manufacturer.
Dealer spread	The difference between the bid and asked price on a security. For example, a stock quoted at 40 bid to 40 1/4 asked has a 1/4-point dealer spread. Highly active stocks have narrower spreads than inactive ones do. In addition to the broker commission, the dealer spread is a part of the transaction costs.
Defensive stock	A company that experiences relatively stable demand for its product or service. Because earnings hold up better than average in a recession, the stock tends to be less volatile. Examples include food, pharmaceutical, and utility companies.
Deferred annuity	A contract with a tax-deferred accumulation or growth period. Variable annuities are typically deferred. *See* Immediate annuity.
Discount	1. Refers to a closed-end fund trading in the market at a price below the NAV of its portfolio. 2. Refers to a bond priced below its par (or face) value.
Distributor	The organization that supplies mutual fund shares to brokerages and investors. Also known as the underwriter, the distributor may sell shares to securities dealers, who then sell them to investors, or it might deal directly with the public.
Diversified fund	A portfolio with many stock or bond holdings. For a fund to be considered "diversified," the Investment Company Act of 1940 requires that it invest at least 75 percent of its assets in accordance with the following rules: no more that 5 percent can be placed in any one company, and not more than 10 percent of any firm's outstanding shares can be purchased. The vast majority of mutual funds meet this definition. *See* Nondiversified fund.
Dividend-payout ratio	The fraction of a company's earnings paid out in cash dividends. Payouts range from zero to 80 percent or more.
Dividend yield	The indicated annual dividend divided by the current price of an investment.

Dollar-cost averaging	The investment of a fixed dollar amount at regular intervals, such as $200 monthly, regardless of whether the market is up or down. More shares are purchased at lower prices and fewer at higher prices.
Dual pricing	The simplest form of flexible pricing where a fund offers investors two classes of shares, Class A and Class B. This gives investors two fee-payment options. *See* Flexible pricing.
Duration	A measure of the interest-rate sensitivity of a bond (or fixed-income portfolio) incorporating time to maturity and coupon size. The bigger the duration number, the greater the interest-rate risk. *See* Interest-rate risk.
EAFE index	A popular index of foreign-stock prices tabulated by Morgan Stanley Capital International. The EAFE or Europe, Australia, and Far East index includes more than 1,000 major companies.
Efficient market	A market where assets sell for what they're worth. Since mispriced securities do not exist, you can't expect professional money managers or anyone else to beat the market indexes. The efficient-market idea remains a controversial one, but academic studies indicating market efficiency resulted in a proliferation of passive portfolios or index funds.
Equity-income fund	A portfolio whose focus is on stocks with high-dividend yields. Similar to growth-and-income portfolios except that these funds usually place more emphasis on dividend yield.
Event risk	A danger faced by corporate bondholders that the issuer may experience a major recapitalization or leveraged buyout, which significantly increases its debt burden, thereby reducing the value of its existing bonds. Event risk is probably less of a danger today than it was in the 1980s, when restructuring mania gripped the financial world.
Ex-distribution	Funds go ex-distribution one business day following the declaration of realized capital gains to shareholders. Investors purchasing shares on or after the "ex" date are no longer entitled to the payout; the NAV falls by the

amount of the distribution. Newspaper tables place an "e" in front of the fund's NAV on its ex-distribution date. The terms ex-distribution and ex-dividend are often used synonymously.

Ex-dividend   Funds go ex-dividend one business day following a dividend declaration from net investment income. Investors purchasing shares on or after the "ex" date are no longer entitled to the payout; the NAV falls by the amount of the dividend. Newspaper tables place an "x" in front of the fund's NAV on its ex-dividend date. The terms ex-dividend and ex-distribution are often used synonymously.

Expense ratio   The annual expenses of a fund, including the management fee, administrative costs, and any 12b–1 charge, divided by net assets. Past ratios can be found in the per-share table of the prospectus.

Family   A group of funds under one umbrella. The most basic family would include a stock, bond, and money-market portfolio, although many outfits are much larger and are growing bigger.

Fee table   A table near the front of the prospectus that explains in detail the various kinds of fees charged to the shareholder and the impact of these charges over time.

Fixed annuity   A contract that provides guaranteed, level payments during its payout period.

Flexible-bond fund   A fund that can invest in a variety of bonds and alter the mix. The manager does not face restrictions on quality or maturity. Also known as "mixed" portfolios.

Flexible fund   A type of hybrid fund that can move its assets around. At the extreme, a flexible portfolio might be 100 percent in stocks, 100 percent in bonds or 100 percent in short-term debt.

Flexible pricing   An arrangement used with some broker-sold funds giving investors a choice as to how they pay their fees. For instance, Class A shares might have a front-end load and 0.25 percent annual 12b–1 charges, whereas Class B shares have no front-end load but carry 0.75 percent yearly 12b–1 fees and a contingent deferred sales charge. Some funds may also have other classes of shares.

Flight to   Tendency for people to get nervous during uncertain times
quality   and consequently shift money to higher-quality securities.
                 You would see, for example, a widening of the spread be-
                 tween junk and Treasury bond yields as the economy slips
                 deeper into a recession.

401(k) plan   A popular salary-reduction program available through
                 many employers. Within these tax-qualified plans, par-
                 ticipants often can choose mutual funds as one or more of
                 the investment choices.

403(b) plan   A salary-reduction plan available to employees of certain
                 charitable organizations and public school systems. Mutual
                 funds are often an investment choice here.

Front-end   A sales fee charged at the time of purchase. The maximum
load   legal front-end load is 8.5 percent, if a fund has no other sales
                 charges. Most funds today charge 5 percent or less.

Fundamental   A stock-research technique that evaluates data pertaining to
analysis   a company, its industry, and the overall economy. Most fund
                 managers conduct some kind of fundamental analysis.

Futures   An exchange-traded contract calling for settlement on a
(or futures   specific asset (such as the S&P 500) at a predetermined price
contract)   and time. Fund managers may hedge with futures.

Geometric-   A compound average rate of return. The geometric-mean
mean return   return for a mutual fund is usually an average of total annual
                 returns over several years.

Global-bond   A portfolio that invests in government and corporate debt
fund   denominated in foreign currencies, perhaps with some U.S.
                 securities included.

Global-stock   A fund that invests in companies headquartered or traded in
fund   a variety of countries, including the United States.

Growth-and-   A fund holding large, established companies offering the
income fund   potential for both appreciation and dividend income.

Growth-and-   A stock that has both price appreciation and dividend-
income stock   paying potential.

Growth fund   A fund holding firms with good or improving profit
                 prospects. The primary emphasis is on appreciation.

Growth investing	A popular investment style whereby the security analyst searches for firms showing promise of above-average earnings. Growth investors are often willing to pay high multiples of earnings or book value for companies with exciting potential.
Growth stock	The stock of a company whose earnings are expected to grow at an above-average rate. Growth stocks are held primarily for price appreciation as opposed to dividend income. *Emerging growth stocks* are those of smaller, embryonic firms.
Hedging	A general term used to describe any of several risk-reduction strategies. A fund manager might partially hedge against a market decline simply by moving a larger fraction of the portfolio into cash. Alternatively, the manager could sell stock-index futures contracts, thereby initiating a "short hedge." If the market falls, the gains on the shorted futures would more or less offset the decline in the portfolio's value.
High-yield bond	*See* Junk bond.
Hub-and-spoke fund	An arrangement, developed by Signature Financial Group, that is used by banks for gathering assets and marketing funds. The hub, which holds the securities portfolio, is the nucleus of the structure. The spokes sell shares to investors and invest that money in the hub. Different spokes can have different fee structures.
Hybrid fund	1. A category of funds that hold both stocks and bonds. Examples are asset allocation and balanced and convertible portfolios. 2. A new type of investment company proposed by the SEC that bears a resemblance to both closed- and open-end funds. Like a closed-end fund, it could invest substantial assets in less-liquid securities, but unlike the typical closed-end portfolio it would allow investors to redeem shares at NAV on a predetermined, controlled basis.
Immediate annuity	An annuity with no accumulation period; annuitization starts shortly after the contract is entered into. *See* Deferred annuity.

Income dividends	In contrast to capital gains distributions, these are paid from the dividends and interest earned on the securities held by the fund, net of expenses. Bond funds often pay income dividends on a monthly basis. Stock funds distribute income less frequently.
Income ratio	The ratio of a fund's net investment income to total net assets. As a kind of yield, it measures the extent to which a portfolio generates income. This number, which can be found in the per-share table of the prospectus, should be examined in light of the fund's objectives.
Income stock	The stock of a company that pays a relatively high dividend. Utilities are an example.
Index fund	A portfolio made up of the same or similar stocks as would be found in a particular market index such as the Standard & Poor's 500. With low-cost, passively managed index funds, you're assured of doing about as well as the target index.
Individual retirement account (or IRA)	A tax-sheltered retirement plan available to all wage earners under age 70 1/2. Contributions may or may not be tax-deductible, but earnings on IRA assets grow tax-deferred. Mutual-funds are a common investment choice for IRAs.
Individual retirement account rollover	A means of moving assets from one tax-sheltered retirement plan to another. Individuals may rollover (1) a distribution from a qualified pension plan into an IRA account or (2) funds from one IRA into another, subject to certain IRS regulations. However, investors moving money from a qualified pension plan to an IRA might want to use a *transfer* instead of a rollover to retain certain tax benefits. With a rollover, the investor receives a redemption check then reinvests the money within a 60-day period. A transfer, by contrast, is a direct movement of money between financial institutions.
Inefficient market	A market where mispriced securities can be found. Fund managers seek inefficiencies so as to boost shareholder returns. An example of an inefficiency could be a small, neglected firm not researched by Wall Street analysts. Another example might be a small, nonrated junk bond.

Interest on interest	The interest income earned on reinvested interest payments such as the periodic coupons received from bonds.
Interest-rate risk	The danger that the price of a bond will fall as interest rates rise. Portfolio managers gauge a fund's interest-rate risk by calculating its duration. *See* Duration.
International stock fund	A portfolio that invests in the stocks of foreign companies. Unlike global funds, international portfolios generally do not have U.S. holdings.
Investment adviser	*See* Adviser.
Investment company	A highly regulated organization that pools the money of many individuals into a portfolio structured in accordance with its objectives. An investment company can be established as a corporation, trust, or partnership. Open-end funds, closed-end funds, and unit investment trusts are all investment companies, but the open-end structure is the most popular.
Investment Company Act of 1940	Detailed federal legislation governing the activities of investment companies. It requires all funds to register with the SEC and to provide a prospectus to potential investors. Among other things, the prospectus must clearly indicate the fund's investment policies and risk factors. The Act also requires that a minimum number of outsiders be on the board of every fund.
Investment Company Institute (or ICI)	The national trade association of the mutual fund industry. The ICI serves its many member companies as well as government agencies, the news media, and the investing public.
Investment-grade bonds	Corporate and municipal bonds given one of the top four ratings by independent agencies. Issues rated triple-B or better are considered investment grade.
January effect	The tendency for the stock market—especially smaller companies—to rally strongly during early January. Some argue that this turn-of-the-year phenomenon could be the result of depressed prices in December resulting from tax-loss selling.
Junk bond	Issues rated below investment grade—that is, below triple-B—by the major rating agencies. Although they often

promise high income, junk bonds carry high credit risk and might be near or in default. Also known as high-yield bonds, junk securities are particularly sensitive to changes in economic conditions.

Keogh plan   A tax-qualified retirement plan available to self-employed individuals such as sole proprietors, business partners, and consultants. Mutual-funds are a common investment choice with Keogh plans.

Ladder   A fixed-income portfolio with bonds coming due at widely different times. The objective is to diversify across a spectrum of maturities. A mutual fund holder might approximate a laddered portfolio by investing equal amounts of money in, say, short-, intermediate-, and long-term government funds.

Letter of   Used by buyers of load funds to indicate their intention to
intent   invest a certain amount of money over a specified period—usually limited to 13 months. By doing so, they can meet the minimum requirement for the fund's commission breakpoint. *See* Breakpoint.

Leverage   The use of borrowed money to try to enhance portfolio returns. Leverage is a double-edged sword, however, because it also compounds a portfolio's volatility.

Liquid asset   The percentage of total equity-fund assets represented by
ratio   cash (short-term marketable securities). The Investment Company Institute computes this ratio monthly.

Liquidity   The ease with which an investment can be sold. A person should be able to sell a liquid asset quickly with virtually no adverse price impact.

Liquidity risk A danger faced by holders of thinly traded or illiquid securities who are forced to sell a relatively large lot in a short period. When the selling pressure is too great, dealers quickly lower their bid prices. Junk bonds, small stocks, and stocks traded in thin foreign markets carry this risk.

Management   Typically the firm that organized the fund, the management
company   company handles the daily administration of the fund's activities and usually also serves as investment adviser.

Management fee	The percentage charge for portfolio management. This expense, which is stated in the fund's prospectus, may decline proportionately as the fund's asset base increases.
Market capitalization	*See* Capitalization.
Market risk	1. The danger that the overall stock market could fall. Fund managers may try to deal with this threat by moving a larger percent of their portfolios into cash or by hedging with futures and options. However, market risk is not a one-way street; it's also the peril of being on the sidelines when stock prices surge. 2. The danger that bond prices might fall as interest rates rise, more commonly known as "interest-rate risk."
Market timing	The shifting of assets between stocks and a money fund in an effort to avoid or minimize losses when prices are expected to fall. At any moment timers might be as much as 100 percent in stocks or 100 percent in a money fund. When they're out of the market, they risk missing a big bull move. Thus, timers frequently underperform during uptrends.
Momentum	The rate of acceleration or deceleration in a stock price, fund NAV, or other asset. Some aggressive fund managers pick stocks on the basis of their momentum.
Morningstar risk measure	A yardstick, published by Morningstar Inc. of Chicago, that focuses only on a fund's potential for losses. The more frequently a fund's monthly returns fall short of the T-bill return, and the greater the underperformance, the higher its risk, according to this statistic.
Mortgage-backed securities	Bonds, such as Ginnie Maes, collateralized by a pool of insured home mortgages. Often referred to as "pass-through" securities. The principal is paid back gradually, along with interest, rather than at maturity, as with an ordinary bond.
Mortgage-backed securities fund	A portfolio that invests primarily in various mortgage-backed bonds such as Ginnie Maes.

Moving average	An averaging of past prices or fund NAVs designed to smooth out short-term fluctuations, allowing you to see the more important longer-term trend. When the daily price is plotted against, say, a 200-day moving average, you may find it easier to identify major changes in the price trend.
Municipal bond fund	A fund that invests at least 80 percent of its assets in federally tax-exempt bonds. *National funds* invest in bonds from a number of different states, perhaps with a focus by type of issuer, quality, or maturity. *Single-state funds* hold the bonds of one state so as to provide its residents with income exempt from both state and federal taxes. *Insured funds* hold bonds guaranteed by an independent insurance consortium. Insured portfolios are available in both national and single-state varieties. *High-yield funds* hold munis of lower grades.
Mutual Fund	By far the most popular type of investment company. A managed portfolio, the mutual (or open-end) fund stands ready to issue shares to incoming investors at net asset value plus any applicable sales charge, and it redeems shares at NAV, less any redemption fee.
NASDAQ	National Association of Securities Dealers Automated Quotation system. A sophisticated pricing system covering a large part of the over-the-counter market.
NASD	National Association of Securities Dealers. A self-regulating organization for the securities industry, which oversees the broker-dealers that distribute mutual funds. Among other responsibilities, the NASD regulates the fees for selling fund shares to investors.
NAV transfer	A load waiver offered by some commission-oriented fund families to individuals who want to invest money they have recently withdrawn from another load fund. Also known as "free-loading," an NAV transfer is typically initiated by brokers or financial planners on behalf of new customers who complain about funds they had purchased from another salesperson.
Net asset value (NAV)	The price or value of one share of a fund. It is calculated by summing the quoted values of all securities held by the fund, adding in cash and any accrued income, then subtracting

liabilities and dividing the result by the number of shares outstanding. Fund companies compute the NAV once a day based on closing market prices.

Net assets   The total value of a fund's cash and securities less its liabilities or obligations.

Nikkei index   The most widely reported stock market index in Japan. The Nikkei tracks 225 large, popular stocks traded on the Tokyo Stock Exchange. Like the Dow Jones industrial average, it is a price-weighted number. It's also known as the "Nikkei Dow."

No-load fund   A fund with no front-end or contingent deferred sales charge. In addition, combined ongoing asset-based sales and service charges, if any, must not exceed 0.25 percent per year. If the portfolio has no sales and service fees, it is often referred to as a "pure" no-load.

Nominal return   The stated, contractual rate of interest on a fixed-income security.

Nondiver-sified fund   One of a small number of funds that have elected not to meet the "diversification" definition of the Investment Company Act of 1940. To satisfy IRS requirements, however, nondiversified portfolios must invest at least 50 percent of their assets in accordance with the same guidelines diversified funds must adhere to for 75 percent of their assets. *See* Diversified fund.

Offering price   *See* Asked price.

Open-end fund   The more formal term for mutual fund. *See* Mutual fund and Closed-end fund.

Per-share table   A table, contained in the prospectus, that presents a concise financial analysis of a fund over the past 10 years or its life, whichever is shorter. Among other information, the table lists investment income, realized and unrealized gains and losses, distributions, and key ratios such as the expense ratio and portfolio turnover.

Portfolio   A group of securities held together. The term is often used as a synonym for mutual fund in this book.

Portfolio turnover *See* Turnover.

Premium 1. Refers to a closed-end fund trading at a price above the NAV of its portfolio. 2. Refers to a bond priced above its par (or face) value.

Prepayment risk A danger faced by holders of mortgage-backed securities that the issuer will pay back principal early during a period of declining interest rates. This results from an increase in the number of homeowners refinancing their mortgages at lower rates.

Price-earnings ratio (or P/E) The price of a stock divided by its earnings per share. P/Es are also computed for individual funds as well as for market indexes like the S&P 500.

Prospectus Like an owner's manual, the prospectus provides essential information about a mutual fund. It discusses the fund's investment policies, objectives, risks, and services, and provides information on fees and important financial data including past performance.

Publicly traded fund *See* Closed-end fund.

Purchasing-power risk The danger that the returns from one's investments will fail to keep pace with inflation. This is a major problem with secure investments such as Treasury bills. Common stock portfolios offer the best long-term inflation protection.

Put option A contract granting its buyer the right to *sell* a specific asset, such as a stock, at a fixed price during a limited time. *See* Call option.

Random walk A theory asserting the difficulty of predicting stock movements over short periods. Academic research has indicated that fluctuations in stock prices—especially shorter-term moves such as hourly, daily, and weekly changes—tend to be unpredictable. The random-walk theory does not, however, deny the generally positive long-term trend in stock prices over many years.

Real return The amount by which a security's nominal return exceeds inflation. If inflation turns out to be much higher than investors had predicted, the real return can be negative. Obviously, the higher your real return, the better.

Redemption fee	A charge paid when selling a fund. Unlike the contingent deferred sales charge, a redemption fee is usually fixed at a low number such as 1 percent and may be ongoing. This kind of fee is relatively uncommon.
Redemption price	The price you receive when you sell your fund shares. It equals NAV less any redemption fee.
Regional fund	A type of foreign portfolio that invests within a defined geographic region, especially Europe, Asia and the Pacific Rim, or Latin America.
Reinvestment privilege	*See* Automatic reinvestment.
Reinvestment risk	A danger, faced by bond and bond-fund investors, that coupon payments must be reinvested at successively lower rates. Zero-coupon bonds and target-maturity funds avoid this risk, which is most prevalent when interest rates are declining.
Rollover risk	A danger faced by holders of short-term debt including money-market funds. If interest rates are falling, these investors must roll over any maturing obligations into successively lower-yielding instruments.
R-squared	A statistical measure used by fund analysts to determine how well diversified a given portfolio is. R-squared values close to 1.0 indicate a high degree of diversification, while numbers near 0.0 indicate the opposite. A high R-squared also tells you that you can have more confidence in a portfolio's beta coefficient.
SEC annualized 30-day yield	A standardized yield reported by all fund companies on their fixed-income portfolios. It is computed daily according to a complex formula provided by the SEC. The objective is to make yields on different bond funds comparable.
Sector fund	Any of various portfolios that invest exclusively in a specific industry or stock group. Often categorized as a "specialty" fund.
Sector risk	The danger that a market sector such as biotechnology will plunge.

Sector rotation	Moving money from one industry or stock group to another based on a change in the portfolio manager's outlook.
Securities & Exchange Commission (SEC)	A federal agency created by the Securities Exchange Act of 1934 that governs the securities industry, including mutual funds and other investment companies.
Service fee	An ongoing charge against net assets used to compensate the registered representative or other salesperson for personal investment advice. It is designed to encourage those selling mutual funds to keep in touch with clients and continue servicing their accounts. This cost, disclosed by the fund's prospectus, cannot exceed 0.25 percent annually. It is part of the expense ratio. *See* Asset-based sales charge and 12b–1 fee.
Sharpe ratio	A measure of risk-adjusted performance calculated by dividing the excess return of a portfolio above the risk-free rate by its standard deviation.
Short hedge	A position taken to offset a risk such as an anticipated stock market plunge. The manager sells (or "shorts") the relevant futures contracts. If the market should fall, the futures position would produce a profit.
Short sale	The sale of a borrowed security in anticipation of repurchasing it later at a lower price, thereby closing out the position with a gain. Short selling is a risky strategy since rising prices would result in losses.
Single-country fund	A fund that targets the securities in a particular stock market. Typically, these funds are much riskier than more broadly based portfolios. Most single-country funds are closed-end, although some—including those investing in Canada or Japan—are organized as mutual funds.
Small-company fund	A portfolio that invests in corporations with relatively low market worth or capitalization. May have either a growth or a value orientation.
Specialty fund	These have a specific, narrow and sometimes unusual investment orientation. Examples include funds that avoid certain objectionable types of companies or industries (such as tobacco), option-income funds, and portfolios investing

in certain regions of the United States. Sector products are a subset of the specialty-portfolio universe. *See* Sector fund.

Speculative stock
A particularly risky equity investment, perhaps involving a small, unseasoned firm or maybe a larger corporation that has gotten into serious trouble. The stock of a financially sound blue-chip company can also be speculative if it becomes grossly overpriced.

Spread
See Dealer spread and Yield spread.

Standard & Poor's 500
A value-weighted price index comprised of 500 big-capitalization U.S. stocks.

Standard deviation
A statistical measure of the month-to-month ups and downs of a fund's returns. Money-market funds, which have stable asset values, have standard deviations of zero. Volatile, aggressive-growth portfolios can have standard deviations of 6 percent or more.

Statement of Additional Information (or SAI)
A more comprehensive mutual fund disclosure statement, also called Part B of the prospectus. The SAI goes into considerable detail on a fund's investment policies, risks, and other matters. In addition, it lists the names of officers and directors and identifies major shareholders. Unlike the prospectus, the SAI is not required to be sent to investors, but fund companies will provide it on request, without charge.

Strips
Separate Trading of Registered Interest and Principal of Securities. These are zero-coupon Treasury bonds that have been formed by separating regular Treasuries into interest and principal components.

Switching privilege
See Telephone-exchange privilege.

Target-maturity fund
A fund that invests mainly in zero-coupon bonds, especially "strips," which mature in a specific year. Like bonds, these funds promise to pay a predetermined value at a specific future date.

Tax-law risk
The danger that changes in personal income-tax laws can affect the prices and yields on tax-exempt municipal bonds and bond funds. If tax rates are cut, munis have less to offer,

so their prices fall and yields increase to match up with the new tax structure.

Technical analysis A type of research frequently used by market timers. "Technicians" make predictions based on the recent trend in prices and trading activity, using tools such as moving averages and momentum.

Telephone-exchange privilege A service that enables investors in a fund family to move money from one portfolio to another by calling a toll-free 800 number and giving their instruction. There is usually little or no cost for exchanges, although some families limit the number of switches an investor can make.

Time diversi-fication The concept of reducing risk by adding more years to a person's investment horizon. Time diversification is most important for stock investors, since the market has a strong tendency to rise over lengthier periods.

Top-down analysis A broad-brush investment approach that focuses on the economy, industry sectors, and market. After the outlook for the big picture has been determined, investors select promising individual securities based on that forecast. *See* Bottom-up analysis.

Total return The most complete measure of performance, total return considers the price increase or decrease of an asset, along with its income or yield.

Transaction by phone A service allowing you to purchase or redeem fund shares over the telephone. The fund company debits or credits your bank account according to your instructions.

Transfer agent The organization, usually a bank or trust company, that handles sales and redemptions of fund shares, maintains shareholder records, computes the fund's NAV each day, and pays dividend and capital-gains distributions. Some fund families perform the transfer-agent functions for themselves.

Treasury securities Debt obligations of the U.S. government. The Treasury issues bills (maturities of one year or less), notes (1 to 10-year maturities) and bonds (maturities of 10 to 30 years). They are all considered to be free of default risk.

Treynor ratio	A gauge of risk-adjusted performance calculated by dividing the excess return of a portfolio above the risk-free rate by its beta coefficient.
Turnover	A measure of the amount of buying and selling activity at a fund. Turnover is defined as the lesser of securities sold or purchased during a year divided by the average of monthly net assets. A turnover of 100 percent, for example, implies positions are held on average for about a year. Past annual turnover ratios can be found in the per-share table of the prospectus.
12b–1 fee	A fee, authorized by the SEC in 1980, that lets funds charge shareholders for various distribution costs, including marketing expenses and service fees to salespersons. The rationale is that the fee will help a portfolio increase its assets and thereby benefit from economies of scale. The fees are part of the expense ratio. More than half of all funds today have 12b–1s. *See* Asset-based sales charge and Service fee.
Underwriter	*See* Distributor.
Uniform Gifts to Minors Act (UGMA)	Legislation containing rules for the administration of an investment account established in a minor's name, often with a mutual fund. A gift, typically from a parent who usually serves as custodian, is used to establish the account. The gift is irrevocable. Upon reaching the age of majority (18 or 21, depending on state law), the child acquires control of the account and its assets. In some states, this legislation is known as the Uniform Transfers to Minors Act. Although the program is easy to use, you may wish to consult your tax adviser for details.
Unit investment trust (or UIT)	An unmanaged portfolio with a fixed maturity. Most hold fixed-income securities, especially municipal bonds and Ginnie Maes.
U.S. government bond fund	These invest primarily in U.S. Treasury and agency securities. May emphasize short-, intermediate-, or long-term issues.
Value averaging	A long-term plan for purchasing fund shares that's more sophisticated than dollar-cost averaging. Value averaging requires that you coordinate your transactions so that your

account grows by a fixed periodic amount, such as $200 monthly. You buy more shares of a mutual fund when its price is down and fewer shares when it's up. You might even sell some when the NAV is particularly high.

Value investing
A popular style of analysis that focuses on finding under-priced securities. In contrast to growth investors, value investors try to buy stocks selling for low multiples of earnings, book value, or other yardsticks.

Variable annuity
A hybrid consisting of a mutual fund within an insurance wrapper. Variable annuities offer tax-deferred growth through a number of portfolio choices with different investment objectives.

Wilshire 5000
A broad index that includes companies traded on the New York and American stock exchanges and in the NASDAQ section of the over-the-counter market. All told, it tracks more than 6,000 stocks.

Wire transfer
The movement of money electronically between a bank account and a mutual fund account. The method is generally used by individuals who want to transfer a large sum of money in a hurry—for example, to pay for the purchase of shares at today's closing NAV. Wires are usually inexpensive. Contact your bank to determine the cost.

Withdrawal plan
A service offered by many mutual fund companies that allows you to receive automatically a periodic check from your mutual fund account.

Yield
The income received from an investment—generally over the past 12 months—expressed as a percentage of its current price. *See* Dividend yield and SEC annualized 30-day yield.

Yield curve
The relationship at a given point in time between yields on a group of fixed-income securities with varying maturities—commonly, Treasury bills, notes, and bonds. The curve typically slopes upward since longer maturities normally have higher yields, although it can be flat or even inverted.

Yield spread
The difference in yields between two fixed-income groups such as high-grade corporate bonds and junk issues. Astute

fund managers often take advantage of unusually large spreads when they materialize.

Yield to maturity The compound annual total return expected on a bond investment if it is held to maturity and the issuer makes all promised payments on time and in full. To realize this return, you must be able to reinvest each interest payment at a rate equal to the yield to maturity.

Zero-coupon bond A bond that makes no periodic interest payments. The final maturity payment includes accrued interest as well as principal. Zero-coupon bonds are sold at a discount to their maturity values.

Index

A

AAII Journal, 19, 261
Account–activity statements, 236–237
Adviser, mutual fund, 8–9
  see also Management company
Advisory services, mutual fund, 198–199,
    264–265
  evaluating timing services, 198–199
  guides and periodicals (*App. 1*), 285–289
  timing newsletters (*App. 5*), 297–299
Agency securities, 132
Aggressive–growth funds, 23, 25
Alliance, 283
Alpha, portfolio, 67
Alternative minimum tax (AMT), 146–147
American Association of Individual Inves-
    tors (AAII), 19, 261
American Funds Group, 8, 48, 70
American Stock Exchange, 25
Analytic Optioned Equity Fund, 30
Annual report, 20, 237, 264
Annual returns:
  analyzing, 57
  computation, 37–38
  may hide volatility, 57–58
Annuitant, 217
Annuities, fixed, 217
Annuities, variable, see Variable annuities
Anomalies, stock market, 89
The Arizona Republic, 42
Asset allocation, 29, 242–243
Asset–allocation funds, 29–30
Asset–based sales charges, 70, 73
Assets, net, computation (*figure*), 7
Automated Clearing House (ACH), 234
Average cost method, for cost basis, 247, 255

B

Babson Shadow Stock, 26
Back–end load, 70, 74
Balanced funds, 28
Banz, Rolf, 25
Barbell, 141–143
  credit–quality, 142
  homemade, 142–143
Barron's, 19, 42, 183, 196, 264
  quarterly mutual fund report, 42
  market valuation measures in, 181, 183
Benham, 91, 133
Beta, 63–64

  see also R–squared
Bid and asked (or offered) prices:
  of fund, 72
  of stock, 41
Black Monday (Oct. 19, 1987), 56, 59
Bond duration, 118–119
Bond funds:
  vs. bonds, 126–128
  categories (*figure*), 130–131
  cut in distributions, significance, 276
  investment strategies for individuals,
      142–143
  option writing, 132
  pricing securities of, 277–278
  risks, 275–276
  see also Bond funds, analysis; Municipal–
      bond funds
Bond funds, analysis:
  average coupon, 167–168
  average maturity, 166–167
  average price, 169
  credit quality, 166
  expenses, 163, 164–165
  performance, 162
  portfolio composition, 165–166
  portfolio turnover, 164
  size, 165
  total return, 171–173
  yields can be slippery, 169–173
Bonds:
  characteristics, 111–113
  duration, 118–119
  investment strategies used by managers,
      140–142
  market for, 109–110
  ratings, 120–121
  risks, kinds of, 116–117
  types, *see specific types*
  volatility vs. maturity (*table*), 118
  see also Fixed–income securities;
      Mortgage–backed securities;
      Municipal bonds; Zero–coupon
      bonds
Breadth of market, as indicator, 190–191
  illustration (*table*), 191
Breakpoints, on load, 72, 81
Brokers, need for, 260
Bull & Bear, 91
Bull and bear markets, 176
Business Week, 19, 42
Buy–and–hold strategy, 83